T0135743

Bibliografische Information der Deutschen Nationalbibliothek

Die Deutsche Nationalbibliothek verzeichnet diese Publikation in der
Deutschen Nationalbibliografie; detaillierte bibliografische Daten sind
im Internet über http://dnb.d-nb.de abrufbar.

ISBN 978-3-8325-1778-6

Logos Verlag Berlin GmbH
Comeniushof, Gubener Str. 47,
10243 Berlin
Tel.: +49 030 42 85 10 90
Fax: +49 030 42 85 10 92
INTERNET: http://www.logos-verlag.de

Cooperative Multi-Robot Soccer in a Highly Dynamic Environment

Dissertation

submitted to the University of Tübingen
for the degree of Doctor of Natural Science
in the Faculty of Information and Cognition Science

by

Dipl.-Technoinform. Patrick Heinemann

from Koblenz

Tübingen
2007

Tag der mündlichen Qualifikation:	07.11.2007
Dekan:	Prof. Dr. Michael Diehl
1. Berichterstatter:	Prof. Dr. Andreas Zell
2. Berichterstatter:	Prof. Dr. Martin Riedmiller

Abstract

The number of robots applied to different jobs in our society has steadily increased over the past years. While industrial robots welding and varnishing our cars are quite common these days, the future generation of robots will enter our everyday life. In contrast to industrial robots working in special evacuated areas for security reasons, these mobile service robots will have to move among and interact with humans, imposing new challenges on the software of the robots. Only the application of sensors to observe the environment and the subsequent use of intelligent data processing algorithms will enable the robots to avoid collisions with moving obstacles, to get information on their current locations, to perform goal oriented tasks and to cooperate with humans as well as other robots.

This thesis addresses these new challenges by describing the development of a team of robots that is able to exhibit intelligent behavior, competitive as well as cooperative, while moving in a highly dynamic environment, as a first step towards a new kind of mobile robots. To evaluate and compare the results of the development, robotic soccer (Robo-Cup) was chosen as testbed for the robot team. Many of the challenges imposed by the RoboCup environment are similar to those found in real-life applications. Robots in RoboCup have to localize themselves, gather information on their environment, including the position and also the velocity of potential obstacles, deal with varying lighting scenarios, as well as competing and cooperating with other robots.

Firstly, the thesis presents the decisions made concerning the co-design of the robot hardware and software. Here, the selection of an omni-directional drive mechanism and a vision sensor with a high frame rate, the software framework designed to be flexible and expandable, as well as the development of a common and simple control interface are the key points in the system design. The main part of the thesis, however, presents the efficient algorithms implemented for image processing, environment modeling, and high-level control. As the only sensor of the robots is an omni-directional vision system that is able to map the complete surrounding of the robot, the performance of the robot system depends on the image processing algorithms and requires a high accuracy and a low processing time. The presented image processing algorithms fulfill both requirements proven by extensive experimental results. Besides landmark and object extraction these algorithms also include new techniques for automatic camera calibration. The environment modeling contains a new combined Monte-Carlo localization and tracking algorithm

i

that is competitive with the best performing algorithms concerning the accuracy and the computation time at the same time, again proven by extensive experimental results. Finally, the high-level robot control component exhibits efficient movement through highly dynamic environments and successful competitive and cooperative behavior. The thesis concludes with an analysis of the team's RoboCup competition results as a final verification of the good performance of the developed system.

Acknowledgments

I would like to thank Prof. Dr. Andreas Zell for financing the Attempto Tübingen Robot Soccer Team and for giving me the possibility to do my research work on a team of up to ten mobile robots. However, these robots would have been useless without my team of students, that accompanied my work with their programming and pushed the team with their ideas. Thank you, Jürgen Haase, Frank Sehnke, Thomas Rückstieß, Michael Drüing, Andreas Masselli, Hannes Becker, Deniz Bahadir, and Sebastian Scherer, you were the real heart of the team! I will never forget the on-site late-night programming sessions with mostly useless but sometimes very important outcome.

At the same time, I would like to thank all members of the Department for Astronomy of the Institute of Astronomy and Astrophysics, University of Tübingen, especially Dr. Eckhard Kendziorra for his cooperative support, Dr. Jürgen Barnstedt for his development of the kicking system and general support, Klaus Lehmann for the design and development of the new robot system, Siegbert Renner and all his apprentices for building the robots, and Wolfgang Gäbele for his support at the RoboCup in Lisbon 2004.

Furthermore, I thank my colleagues, with special thanks going to Michael Plagge for the software he left me and the support during my first months as team leader, to my roommate Achim Lilienthal for the cordial working atmosphere, the interesting discussions, his assistance with the teaching, and the introduction to the Ammerjäger soccer team, to André Treptow for interesting discussions and for his support in Padova, and last but not least to Christian Spieth and Felix Streichert for their never-ending wealth of ideas, physical and mental support previous to the tournaments, and their poignant sarcasm.

I also have to thank the RoboCup community, especially the Mostly Harmless team for the great time we had at the Graz Open 2005, the Brainstormer Tribots team for giving hints on the design of good omni-directional robots, the ISePorto RoboCup team, the COPS Stuttgart, the Ulm Sparrows, the AllemaniACs, and the Philips RoboCup team for the cooperative atmosphere during several tournaments. For keeping my work interesting till the last tournament, by constantly introducing new challenges into the RoboCup rules preferably a few weeks prior to the tournament, special thanks go to the RoboCup MSL technical committee. Thank you, you did a great job!

Finally, I thank my family who supported me throughout the years. Tina, for your assistance and patience, even while working on your own thesis, I love you more than ever!

Contents

Chapter 1

Introduction

The idea of playing soccer with mobile robots was first published by Mackworth [130] in 1993 as a challenge to overcome the problems of the classical approaches to artificial intelligence (AI) and robotics. Robotic systems, at that time, were usually based on a set of implicit assumptions, which Mackworth called the *Omniscient Fortune Teller Assumptions*, that simplified the world. According to these assumptions a robot could rely on a static and deterministic world with itself being the only robot in this world, on a complete and definite knowledge of the world, and finally on all actions as being discrete and sequential. In contrast, robot soccer focuses on the challenges of a realistic environment, with multiple robots, cooperating as well as competing ones, the environment being extremely dynamic and non-deterministic, and the robot's knowledge of its world being incomplete. Thus, robot soccer is an ideal research field for commercial robots of the emerging field of *service robotics*, which is expected to have an enormous growth in the next years [171], and which face a natural and dynamically changing world, as they are designated as couriers at hospitals crowded with people [54] or even to guide elderly people through their environment [160].

Many other researchers adopted robot soccer for their own research. Kitano *et al.* [114] established robot soccer as a new challenge problem for AI and Noda *et al.* [152] used robot soccer for their work on multi-agent cooperation. Seizing the suggestion of Mackworth, Kitano and his coworkers recognized robot soccer as a *standard problem* that could replace computer chess as a benchmark for the progress in AI research. The computer chess standard problem was not only close to its finale with Deep Blue beating a human grand master, it also suffered from fulfilling nearly all Omniscient Fortune Teller Assumptions. Thus, although being an advance in several scientific disciplines, the impact of playing computer chess at the highest level on intelligent agent research is questionable. Comparing the domain characteristics of computer chess and robot soccer, it becomes clear that robot soccer is suited far better as a standard problem of AI (cf. Table 1.1). Furthermore, through the embodiment in a real world, robot soccer as a benchmark is not only restricted to research in AI but also brings forward robotics research.

	Computer Chess	Robot Soccer
Environment	Static	Dynamic
State Change	Turn Taking	Real Time
Information Accessibility	Complete	Incomplete
Sensor Readings	Symbolic	Non-Symbolic
Control	Central	Distributed

Table 1.1: A comparison of the domain characteristics of computer chess and robot soccer. [114]

Yet, besides the challenge to cope with incomplete sensor information about a dynamic environment changing in real time, there is still another aspect of robot soccer as standard problem. Noda *et al.* identified robot soccer as ideal testbed for their research on multi-agent systems. While playing soccer, a robot has to interact with robots that try to achieve the same objective, requiring some form of coordination or even cooperation and competitive robots trying to prevent the robot from scoring a goal. Multi-robot systems are of special interest for tasks that cannot be solved by a single robot, for tasks that can be solved better or faster in a team of robots, or for tasks that have to be reliably solved exploiting the redundancy of a team of robots, if a single robot fails [36, 47]. The domains that possibly benefit from the research on multi-robot systems include traffic control and coordination, foraging, including the cleaning of large areas from (toxic) waste or mines, harvesting, and search and rescue, and mapping of unknown (planetary) terrain [36, 101].

In 1995 Kitano, Noda and their colleagues founded the *Robot World Cup Initiative (Robo-Cup)* [113, 10, 166] and announced the first Robot World Cup Soccer Games and Conferences with common rules and regulations for 1997. Independently from this, Kim founded the *Federation of International Robot-soccer Association (FIRA)* [55] which organizes the annual FIRA Robot World Cup and Congress.

As a testbed and benchmark for the robots and algorithms described in this thesis, Robo-Cup and especially the *RoboCupSoccer Middle-Size League (MSL)* are introduced in the next section.

1.1   RoboCup

> *RoboCup is an attempt to foster AI and intelligent robotics research by providing a standard problem where a wide range of technologies can be integrated and examined.*

Hiroaki Kitano [114]

Over the past 10 years robot soccer gained a high level of interest both in the scientific community and the public. As the main driving force, RoboCup celebrated this development with the 10th Robot Soccer World Cup held in Bremen in Germany in 2006. Meanwhile, RoboCup is no longer limited to robot soccer, as *RoboCupRescue* and *RoboCupJunior* were established as further research and educational disciplines. Robots competing in the RoboCupRescue are supposed to explore unknown and cluttered environments that are inaccessible for humans to simulate a search and rescue mission in large scale disaster areas, such as a city struck by a strong earthquake. RoboCupJunior on the other hand is an educational initiative designed to introduce RoboCup to primary and secondary school children [166].

Yet, *RoboCupSoccer* with its five leagues is still the main part of RoboCup. These leagues place emphasis on different aspects of robot soccer. While the *Simulation League* mainly focuses on cooperative and strategic team play in a simulated multi-agent system, all other leagues play with real robots including the tasks of processing sensor data and controlling the robots. However, the design of the robots concerning their sensors and actuators and also the degree of autonomy differs over the leagues. In the *Small-Size League* robots are of a maximum diameter of 18 cm and usually contain an omni-directional wheel drive and no external sensors. Sensor data processing and control of the robots is done on a central computer that receives images from an overhead camera above the field. Although some teams in the Small-Size League now start to build local sensor systems on the robots, the main impact of this league compared to the others is the miniaturization of the robots and components. The *Four-Legged League* was the first league featuring walking robots by using the Sony *AIBO* four-legged robot dog [179]. The challenges in this league include the control of a slipping and sliding walking robot and autonomous play using the limited sensory and computational resources of the AIBO. The use of a standard hardware helps teams to start their research quickly without having to design and build new hardware. Furthermore, the teams can share their code because they share the same hardware. On the other hand, an integrated approach to robotics using a hardware-software co-design is not possible. Since the year 2002 RoboCupSoccer includes the new *Humanoid League* which was introduced to further approach the provocative goal to build a team of humanoid robots able to play or even win against a human soccer team. In contrast to the Four-Legged League, developers of the humanoid robots in this league must cope with the problems of dynamically stable walking which is still the main problem of the league especially when kicking the ball. Additionally, some researchers develop and improve stereo vision systems for their robots.

Prior to the introduction of the Humanoid League, the *Middle-Size League (MSL)* was the most sophisticated league. Here, robots of up to $50x50\,cm^2$ floor space and 80 cm height are large enough to carry different sensors and powerful computer and motor systems including their energy supply. The MSL still has the widest variety of different sensor and actuator systems in the RoboCup community, although there was a clear trend towards omni-directional drive types and camera systems over the last four years. Furthermore, besides the Four-Legged League, the MSL is the only league with distributed control on truly autonomous robots.

To enforce constant improvement in the research, the rules of the MSL and other leagues were constantly revised. In the MSL those revisions comprised a major modification of the environment, developing from a synthetic field bounded with walls under constant bright lighting to an open field with varying lighting conditions or even daylight. Unfortunately, this also enforced the teams to change their sensor systems, as distance sensors such as infrared laser scanners or ultrasonic transducers became useless for self-localization with the walls. Nowadays, nearly all MSL teams use vision as their main sensor system [181]. Apart from the challenges introduced to the image processing algorithms by removing the walls and relaxing the lighting specifications, the environment is still simplified by using an orange colored ball as well as blue and yellow colored goals and corner poles. Nevertheless, even that will change in the near future, as the Technical Committee of the MSL already plans to remove the solid goals by nets and to replace the orange ball with a standard black and white FIFA ball. Some researchers are already preparing for these challenges by tracking non-colored balls using algorithms based on features [191, 192] or form [75, 76].

Although the MSL currently uses the largest field in the RoboCup competitions with a size of 8x12 m^2, the field will constantly grow to reach the size of a human soccer field, starting with a doubled size of 12x16 m^2 at the RoboCup 2007. The number of robots competing on an MSL field is depending on the space the robots occupy on the field. At the RoboCup 2006, where most teams used four to six robots, all robots had to fit into an area of 1 m^2. At the same time, the duration of a RoboCup MSL game will be constantly increased. From 2003 to 2005 the duration was ten minutes per half, while since 2006 the duration was raised to fifteen minutes per half, already posing a challenge for the power supply of many teams.

As MSL robots should play their game completely autonomously, no human interaction is allowed during normal game play except for stopping the robot in an emergency situation to prevent it from doing harm to humans, other robots or the field. Furthermore, a robot can be exchanged or removed from the field at every game stop with permission of the referee. These commands are transmitted to the robot via wireless network according to the *IEEE 802.11a/b Wireless LAN Standard* [93].

This communication is also used to submit the commands of the referee to the robots. All decisions of the referee are entered by an assistant referee into a graphical user interface called *Referee Box* [49] which transmits the commands to the robots. Every time the referee stops the game, all robots have to stop immediately. Then, a new game command is given by the referee (e. g. goal kick, free kick, penalty, throw-in etc.) and the robots can move to their intended position from where the game is restarted.

A detailed description of the field setup and the rules and regulations for the RoboCup 2006 in Bremen can be found in [167]. Figure 1.1 shows an image of a typical RoboCup MSL setup from the RoboCup 2006 in Bremen.

Figure 1.1: A typical RoboCup MSL setup from the RoboCup 2006 in Bremen.

1.2 Contributions and Organization of this Thesis

This thesis presents the hardware and software designed to build a new team of cooperating soccer robots that was able to reach the quarter finals of the RoboCup Middle-Size League in the Robot Soccer World Cup 2006 in Bremen. Although the *Attempto Tübingen Robot Soccer Team*[1] is active in the RoboCup MSL since 1998, the robot and software system needed to be completely revised in the year 2003 for several reasons.

On the one hand, the *Pioneer* robots from *ActivMedia Inc.* [146, 147] with their low acceleration and top speed used by the team till 2005 were too slow to be competitive against the fast and reactive robots of other teams. Even without the 10 kg extra weight for the laser scanner and its battery system that was used for self-localization with the walls and object detection, the nonholonomic [120] differential drive of these robots was too restricted to compete against omni-directional robots. Therefore, a new omni-directional robot platform with a top speed of 2.2 m/s was designed and built. The details of this platform including the sensor and on-board computer systems are given in Chapter 2.

On the other hand, the whole software system at that time was depending on the sensor data of the very accurate laser scanner which had to be replaced for two reasons. Firstly, as the walls around the field were removed, the main advantage of the laser scanner, i.e. the efficient and accurate self-localization method using the distances to the field boundaries,

---

[1]Before 2004 the team was also named *Attempto!* or *T-Team*.

disappeared. Secondly, the laser scanner system made up nearly half the weight of the robot. Thus, the software system had to be rewritten using vision as the main sensor with some basic parts being reused from the former system, especially concerning the client-server architecture. The modular design of this architecture is presented in Chapter 3 as a framework where all the components of the software system are embedded.

Since the first and basic module of the software system, the robot control algorithms are presented in Chapter 4, including the low-level connection to the robot platform and the hardware abstraction layer introduced to use the same high-level interface for controlling the old differential drive robots as well as the new omni-directional ones.

Starting with an efficient algorithm to detect landmarks and objects on the RoboCup field based on their color and followed by the algorithms developed for automatic camera calibration and for making the image processing insensitive to changing lighting conditions, Chapter 5 covers one of the main topics of this thesis.

Chapter 6 describes the process of incorporating the data from the image processing and remote data from teammates into a consistent model of the robot's environment. In contrast to the work of many other teams in RoboCup MSL [181], this *Environment Model* keeps track of the objects on the field over time to extract information on the speed and direction of movement. As another major topic of the thesis, the algorithms presented in this chapter also include robust and efficient self-localization of the robot.

The high-level control of both the goalkeeper and the field player robots is covered in Chapter 7, describing algorithms for adaptive path planning and cooperative team play.

To conclude the thesis, Chapter 8 reviews the results given in the different chapters regarding the competition results of the Attempto Tübingen Robot Soccer Team, closing with a classification of the developed multi-robot system concerning the taxonomy given in [97, 36, 47].

Finally, Chapter 9 concludes this thesis and contains an outlook to future work that needs to be done to stay competitive in the RoboCup domain.

While the work presented in this thesis covers all aspects of the design of a multi-robot system, the image processing, self-localization and high-level control algorithms constitute the main part. As any of these topics could be investigated in a thesis of its own, the related chapters contain an introduction to the topic and a section addressing the related work. For the same reason, the key contribution of this thesis is the efficiency of the complete system including these algorithms, rather than an in-depth research of the single subjects. As the primary reason for developing a new hardware and software system was increased speed and reactivity of the soccer robots, the whole software system was tuned to fit in a 20 ms cycle time while still keeping a high accuracy of the single algorithms. Many of the problems in RoboCup and service robotics are solved by other researchers at least as accurately as with the algorithms presented in this thesis. However, only a few researchers are able to keep this accuracy in a 20 ms cycle for the complete system.

Chapter 2

Hardware Design

This chapter presents the evolution of the robot platform of the Attempto Tübingen Robot Soccer Team evolving from a differential drive to an agile omni-directional robot during the past three years. The previous differential drive hardware of both the goalkeeper and the field players is briefly described in the next section. Afterwards, Section 2.2 examines the considerations that led to the design of the new omni-directional robot and introduces the robot in full detail.

2.1 Previous Hardware

The robots described in this section were used by the Attempto Tübingen Robot Soccer Team to participate in international robot soccer competitions from 1999 to 2005.

2.1.1 Platform and Actuators

As the requirements of a goalkeeper differ considerably from the requirements of a field player, two different robot platforms were used for the different players. The following paragraphs describe the major requirements and main diversities of the two player classes.

Goalkeeper
With the speeds of the robots being less than 1 ᵐ/s in 1998 [156] and a speed of the ball of about 2 ᵐ/s, it was a good strategy for a goalkeeper to stay on the goal line inside the goal and move in parallel to the goal line to defend the goal. Therefore, the goalkeeper robot was based on the commercial *Pioneer 1-AT* skid-steering platform from *ActivMedia Inc.* [146] with a top speed of 0.6 ᵐ/s. The two wheels at each side of this robot were coupled by a belt and controlled by one motor. As kicking device, this robot used a spring mechanism wound up by a strong motor to accelerate the kicker when released [157].

Figure 2.1: The Goalkeeper that was used until 2003.

Figure 2.2: A field player that was used until 2005.

Figure 2.1 shows an image of this goalkeeper.

Field Players

The field players, however, had to be more versatile and were thus based on the *Pioneer 2-DX* platform from *ActivMedia Inc.* [147] with a 1.6 m/s top speed differential drive. Both Pioneer robots were controlled by the on-board computer via a *RS232* serial interface running at 9,600 baud. To kick the ball, these robots were equipped with a tank for compressed air that actuated two pneumatic cylinders connected by a metal bar [157]. For better control of the ball while dribbling, the RoboCup MSL rules [167] allow robots to embrace a maximum of a third of the ball's diameter. The robots therefore had special fingers attached to their front to keep the ball from rolling away when driving curves. Figure 2.2 shows an image of a field player.

2.1.2   Sensors

Both Pioneer platforms included a sonar ring with seven ultrasonic transducers by default. Furthermore, the robots were upgraded with two *SICOLOR C810* PAL color cameras from *Siemens AG* with a resolution of 768x576 pixels and 5 bit color depth per channel. One of these cameras was used as a front camera with a wide angle lens observing the area in front of the robot. The other camera was mounted on top of the robot pointing upwards into a convex mirror giving a 360° view of the complete surrounding of the robot. The field players were additionally equipped with an *LMS 200* laser scanner from

SICK AG [175], which senses distances to obstacles using the time-of-flight principle. A rotating mirror inside the LMS 200 deflects short pulses of an infrared laser beam into 180 different angular directions with a distance of 1° each. By measuring the time from sending the pulse to receiving the response of the signal reflected at the nearest obstacle, the sensor can precisely compute the distance to the obstacle.

2.1.3 On-Board Computer

The robots carried an industrial PC using a *coolMONSTER/P3* PISA slot CPU from *JUMPtec AG* [115] equipped with an *Intel Pentium-III* 850 MHz CPU, 512 MB RAM, and several extensions for graphics, sound and periphery. To retrieve the images from the two PAL cameras, these computers were upgraded with two frame grabbers based on the *Brooktree BT848* chip set.

Scientific Linux was used as operating system for the on-board computer with a minimalist installation that was compiled and loaded into a *RAM disk* at the startup of the computer. A RAM disk is a specially reserved part of the computer's RAM that can be addressed like a normal disk drive. It is thus possible to run the computer completely from this RAM disk without the need of a hard disk. After the content of the system RAM disk was loaded into the memory, the hard disk of the computer can thus be switched off, bringing it into a safe state that withstands the shocks of a tough game of robot soccer. The size of the RAM disk was 16 MB both for the system disk containing the kernel and the rest of the operating system and for the user disk containing the programs that controlled the robot plus some extra space for logging test data.

To distribute data from the robot to the teammates and to receive commands from the referee box, the computer was equipped with an external IEEE 802.11b compatible WLAN bridge. Using this external device, the robot can be accessed by a control computer using either wireless connection by plugging in the bridge or wired LAN by plugging in a cable, without changing the network configuration of the on-board computer. This turned out to be very useful as during the tournament setup it was often impossible to use WLAN as there were constantly problems of limited bandwidth or no connection at all.

2.1.4 Power Supply

To supply the robots with enough power maintenance-free lead gel batteries with 12 V and 7.2 Ah were used. Both robots carried two batteries, one for the platform and one for the computer. The field players, however, had to carry an extra battery to supply the laser scanner with 24 V using a DC-DC converter. Depending on the game flow and the age of the batteries the power supply was sufficient for playing one halftime of ten minutes playing time.

2.2 The New Omni-Directional Robot Platform

After four years of progress in RoboCup with a growing number of fast and agile omni-directional robot platforms the hardware of the Attempto Tübingen Robot Soccer Team had to be completely revised. Not only the robot platform but also the sensors and computational systems needed a modernization to cope with the increased dynamics of a game against such omni-directional robots. As the annual international competitions yield the ideal testbed to collect in-game experience needed to compare and revise the developed algorithms, the Attempto Tübingen Robot Soccer Team constantly participated in the tournaments. However, this policy required a gradual redesign of the robots to keep the team running, which was sometimes sensed as disadvantage. On the other hand, the development and construction of the new robot chassis with the workshop of the Department of Astronomy of the Institute of Astronomy and Astrophysics, University of Tübingen, could not have been completed in only one year.

2.2.1 Platform and Actuators

First of all, the Pioneer 1-AT goalkeeper was renewed in 2003. However, while the platform changed, most of the periphery from the old robots was still in use until 2005.

Goalkeeper
As faster robots and higher ball speeds emerged in the MSL, the concept of staying on the goal line became inefficient, although still used by some teams in 2006. As a new defensive behavior the goalkeeper should actively defend on a circular arc in front of the goal, keeping its direction constantly towards the ball. These requirements could only be fulfilled with an omni-directional drive.

At the RoboCup in Padova 2003 the *Brainstormers Tribots* MSL team [196] was already quite successful with their new omni-directional robot platform [7]. The triangular basis of this platform was adopted and adjusted to fit the need for a new omni-directional goalkeeper.

Three *RE 30* DC motors with a power of 60 W and a maximum of 8200 revolutions per minute from *Maxon Motor AG* [137] equipped with a *GP 32 C* ceramic planetary gear box with a gear ratio of 18:1 and a *MR* wheel encoder with 500 impulses per revolution are the foundation for the omni-directional drive. These motors were extended with a custom built hexagonal brass axle carrying an *ARG 80* special transport wheel from *TRAPOROL GmbH* with a diameter of 80 mm. The special transport wheel functions as a normal wheel but further contains three single rollers at each side that are pivoted, as shown in Figure 2.3, to allow a movement perpendicular to the normal running direction of the wheel. Such wheels are also known as *Swedish 90-degree* wheels [176]. If these motor-wheel combinations are built into a solid frame at an angle of 120°, as shown in Figure 2.4, this forms a perfect omni-directional drive. The three motors can be controlled such that this

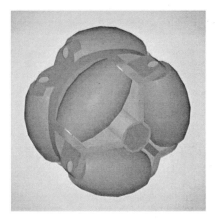

Figure 2.3: The ARG 80 special transport wheel.

frame moves into any direction while rotating around its own axis. To move forwards or backwards the two front motors are controlled to rotate with the same speed in opposite directions, while the back wheel rolls freely on its special rollers.

The triangular frame around the motors is built of three rectangular aluminum profiles that were chosen to form a stable but lightweight body. The flattened edges of the triangle carry the motors and the counter bearing of the axles. In contrast to the plain bearings used by the Brainstormers Tribots, ball joint bearings are used for better slippage and durability. With the caps of the wheel box and the cover plate tightly screwed to the frame profiles and the motor and axle mountings this frame provides an extremely robust basis for a robot.

The size of the frame had to be fixed by choosing the distance l from the wheels to the robot center. This distance was limited to a minimum by the length of the motor-wheel combination and to a maximum for which the robot was still fitting into the maximum size of 50x50 cm^2. Additionally, the existing lead batteries should fit into the space between the motors to establish a low center of gravity, thus further restricting l. To passively occlude as much of the goal as possible a vertical lattice was planned through the center of the robot along its Y_r-axis with a length of nearly 70 cm fitting into the diagonal of the 50 cm square. Thus, l was chosen as 21 cm maximizing the size of the robot frame according to the drawing in Figure 2.5.

Unfortunately, although the vertical lattice was planned right from the beginning, it was not until the upper body of the new field players was adopted that the lattice was built and attached to the robot. Until the completion of the new field players in 2006, the goalkeeper was equipped with the computer and sensors of the old goalkeeper. A kicking

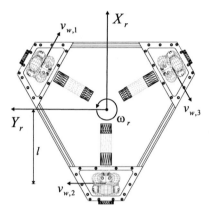

Figure 2.4: The triangular motor frame of the new omni-directional goalkeeper.

system was also missing until 2006. At that time, the robot was upgraded with three tanks for compressed air with a total volume of $1,500\,\text{cm}^3$ and a maximum pressure of $10\,\text{bar}$ connected via a solenoid valve to two pneumatic cylinders driving a shovel-shaped aluminum sheet that can kick the ball up to 1 m high. This kicker was especially designed for the goalkeeper to resolve critical game situations in front of the own goal by kicking the ball over the nearest robots.

To control the speed of the motors and wheels the *TMC200* motor controller board of the *Fraunhofer Institute for Autonomous Intelligent Systems* [117] was used. This controller contains three independent 200 W channels and is connected to the on-board computer via an *RS232* serial interface running at 57,600 baud. It is able to react to fifty commands per second, which perfectly fits into the favored 20 ms cycle time for the whole system. The most important response to the commands is information of the current speeds of the motors sensed through the wheel encoders. This can be used to compute basic odometry information[1]. Additionally, the TMC200 controller board features an 8 bit programmable I/O port plus two designated output pins that are used for the kicker.

Figure 2.6 shows an image of the new goalkeeper in the version used until 2005, while Figure 2.7 presents the final version including the upper body of the field players, the lattice and the pneumatic kicking system.

---

[1]Unfortunately, the serial communication to the TMC200 is realized with plain text commands thus limiting the usable bandwidth depending on the length of the command and the response. As with the standard firmware of the TMC200 the announced update rate of 50 Hz was not possible, a special version of the firmware with the version number *1.20* was used, that kept the 20 ms cycle time by reducing the command response to the minimal necessary length.

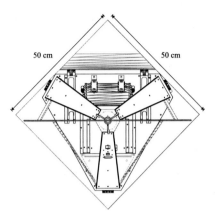

Figure 2.5: The size of the goalkeeper was maximized under the constraint that a lattice occluding as much of the goal as possible still fits into the maximum size of 50x50 cm^2.

Field Players

As a result of the very good experience made with the new goalkeeper, a series of omni-directional field players was planned and designed after the RoboCup in Lisbon in 2004, where a good performance of the old field players (cf. Section 8) was still not enough to cope with the faster teams. In contrast to the goalkeeper, this time the complete robot was renewed including the sensors, computer system and power supply.

The basic triangular form of the motor frame was retained in the design of the new field players. However, as the field players have to dribble, the ball should be kept as near to the robot center as possible. Therefore, an indentation in the triangle at the front of the robot was introduced with a depth of one third of the ball's diameter. This indentation should further improve the ability of the robot to center the ball in front of a kicking system even throughout a dribbling[2]. Figure 2.8 shows the motor frame of the field players.

A major drawback of the goalkeeper design is the position of the batteries. Although the extremely low center of gravity is an essential advantage concerning the stability of the new goalkeeper, the necessity to change the batteries through the bottom of the robot is impractical. A change of the goalkeeper's batteries takes at least five minutes and two experienced students. It was therefore decided to place the new batteries outside the motor frame of the new field players where they are easily accessible. As the batteries were removed from the frame, the distance l of the wheels to the robot center was lowered to 19.5 cm for the field players to permit higher rotational speeds needed for ball handling. In its final shape the chassis of the field players was small enough to play with four field

---

[2]It turned out later that for a perfect ball dribbling an extra rubber foam pad was needed pressing onto the ball from above to keep it from rolling away.

Figure 2.6: The new omni-directional goalkeeper in the version used until 2005 with the
old computer and sensors.

Figure 2.7: The final version of the omni-
directional goalkeeper with the upper body of
the field players, the lattice and the pneumatic
kicking system.

players plus the maximum sized goalkeeper without exceeding the limit of 1 m^2 of space
per team.

The free space between the motors was reserved to hold parts of the new electro-magnetic
kicking system. This kicking system was mainly designed by Dr. Jürgen Barnstedt from
the Department of Astronomy of the Institute of Astronomy and Astrophysics, University
of Tübingen. The primary reason for switching from spring-based or pneumatic systems
to an electro-magnetic kicker was the ability to quickly change the strength of the kick
which is essential for passing a ball to a teammate. As the overall goal of this work was
cooperative soccer play, the robots should not only be capable of shooting the ball at high
speeds but also to reduce the strength of the kick in the same moment the control system
decides to pass the ball. Nearly all systems of other teams are uncapable of an on-the-fly
adjustment of the kicking strength as springs have to be wound up some time in advance
and pneumatic systems can only be controlled by very expensive servo valves.

The basic part of the kicker is a coil with an inductance of 9.6 mH made of a plastic tube
of 100 mm length and 40 mm diameter with 690 windings of magnet wire of a diameter of
0.8 mm. Located inside this coil is a rod composed of a steel cylinder of the same length
as the coil, a nylon cylinder in the front and a thin appendix in the back. In the home
position of the rod the majority of the steel part is outside of the coil. If a high current is
sent through the windings of the coil, the steel part of the rod will be accelerated into the
coil by the produced magnetic field and finally passes through the coil if the current flow
is stopped on time. The nylon part of the rod is well outside the coil at the position of the
highest speed and kicks the ball. Figure 2.9 shows a CAD model of the kicker.

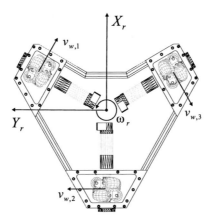

Figure 2.8: The triangular motor frame of the new omni-directional field players.

With an electronic circuit consisting of a high voltage unit and an interval timer this kicker is able to accelerate the ball to a maximum speed of nearly 10 m/s. For this, the coil is connected to a 300 V capacitor with a capacitance of 8200 μF loaded via a single phase bridge rectifier by a power converter generating 230 V AC from the battery voltage. The interval timer controls the duration of the current flow by means of a power MOSFET switch that withstands the currents of up to 100 A. This duration is set according to a 6 bit value applied to the I/O port of the motor controller. Using one of the special output pins of the TMC200 the timer can be started to kick the ball. Thus, with a maximum total delay of 40 ms for sending the 6 bit duration value and for sending the kicking command the robot is able to kick the ball in 64 different strengths. As the strength of the kick not only depends on the duration of current flow but also on the state of charge of the capacitor, the remaining two bits of the 8 bit I/O port of the TMC200 motor controller were used to control the capacitor voltage indicating the excess of 85% and 95% of the maximum voltage. While the interval timer electronics is located above the motor frame, the complete high voltage unit is tucked into the hardly accessible space between the motors to prohibit unintentional contact. Only the coil itself protrudes out of the motor frame to achieve the exact height to hit the ball centric. As the top plate of the chassis had to be raised accordingly, additional space to the left and right of the coil emerged that is used to store the new batteries.

However, one of the most complex design issues was to build a mechanism that returned the rod into its home position. To transfer the whole momentum from the rod to the ball, the rod has exactly the same weight as the standard FIFA ball, but the rod ends up at the exact position where it hit the ball. To return the rod to its home position it was considered

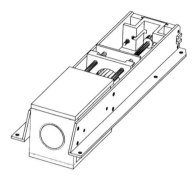

Figure 2.9: A CAD model of the electro-magnetic kicker of the new field players.

to activate the coil a second time to accelerate the rod backwards into the other direction but as the end position of the rod was depending on the kicking strength this was not always successful. The most obvious solution is to connect a spring to the rod that returns it into the home position. Here, the problem is the spring force rising linearly with the deflection of the spring thus counteracting the acceleration of the coil. The final solution is a rubber spring used in space technology that has a nearly constant spring force for a certain range of deflection. This rubber spring is attached to the thin appendix of the rod and adjusted such that it can just return the rod from every position. To keep the rod in its home position even during a tough game a small permanent magnet was fixed at the rear side of the kicker frame.

To complete the new design of the field players a tripod for the new omni-directional camera system was designed and attached to the top plate of the motor frame. Inside the tripod a small podium contains the interval timer electronics, the motor controller board and the power splitter. The on-board computer is mounted on top of this podium. Figure 2.10 shows a CAD model and an image of one of the new omni-directional field players.

2.2.2   Sensors

With the development of efficient image processing algorithms for the omni-directional camera after removing the laser scanner, the front camera of the goalkeeper was merely used to roughly estimate the direction towards the ball at higher distances. Therefore, the new field players were equipped with an omni-directional camera system as the only sensor. Thereby, the Attempto Tübingen Robot Soccer Team followed a general paradigm shift away from heterogeneous robot and sensor systems to omni-directional robots with one omni-directional sensor which seems to become a standard in the MSL, giving up or at least decreasing the diversity that was characteristic for the league. However, as

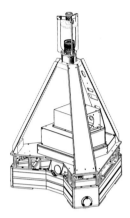 

Figure 2.10: A CAD model and an image of the new omni-directional field player.

this thesis shows, all necessary components of a cooperating robot soccer team can be successfully based on such an architecture. Furthermore, all eight teams of the final round robin of the RoboCup 2006 in Bremen were using this hardware [11], showing the present predominance of such systems.

Yet, the selection of an adequate vision system is certainly a crucial task. Only the hyperbolic mirror of the *AIS Vision System* from the *Fraunhofer Institute for Autonomous Intelligent Systems* [206] was taken over from the old vision system. The PAL camera with a frame grabber used in the old robots was of limited use for the new agile robots, as the frame rate of the PAL standard is defined at 50 half frames per second that are interleaved line by line resulting in 25 full frames per second (25 fps). In addition to the fixed low frame rate the interleaving of the lines of two consecutively captured images results in a very distorted full frame as the ball moves up to 20 cm from one half frame to the other. Finally, the transmission of the analog video signal to the frame grabber was very prone to interferences resulting in a low image quality despite the shielded *S-Video* cables that were used.

Therefore, a camera with a digital output signal was chosen. Only two different standard bus systems were considered for the connection of the camera to the computer, *USB 2.0* and *IEEE 1394a FireWire*, as high speed broadband standards like *Camera Link* were too expensive and again required additional frame grabber hardware.[3] While the bandwidth of USB 2.0 and IEEE 1394a FireWire is roughly the same with 480 Mbit/s and 400 Mbit/s, respectively, there are big differences concerning the data transfer protocol. Most cameras

---

[3]Cameras with a Gigabit Ethernet connection to the computer were unfortunately still in the experimental stage and unaffordable at that time.

with a USB 2.0 interface use a proprietary protocol to transfer the data to the computer, requiring special device drivers usually only available for *Microsoft Windows*. On the other
hand many FireWire cameras support the *IIDC 1394-based Digital Camera Specification
(DCAM)* standard that defines a common protocol for uncompressed image data transmission and parameterization of the camera features (e. g. exposure time, white balance etc.).
In order to stay flexible concerning the camera used on the robot, it was decided to use a
DCAM compatible FireWire camera.

Besides a good image quality, the new camera needed a high resolution for a good accuracy of the image processing algorithms and a high frame rate to achieve a highly reactive
control system based on the image data. Unfortunately, these properties are contradictory
at least concerning the limited bandwidth of the FireWire bus system. Several cameras
were thoroughly tested, considering quality, resolution, and frame rate. In those tests most
of the cameras could not keep the theoretical frame rate denoted in their specifications, as
the camera hardware was not able to simultaneously capture a new image while transmit-
ting the old frame over the FireWire bus. Thus, depending on the exposure time the frame
rate drastically dropped.

Finally, the *Marlin F-046C* camera from *Allied Vision Technologies GmbH* [5] offered
the best compromise. As expected, the Sony CCD chip of the F-046C with a diagonal of
8 mm yielded brighter images than the 6 mm Sony chip of the F-080C that would have
had a higher resolution. The F-131C with a CMOS chip providing a resolution of over
one million pixels would have been most interesting for selecting small regions of interest
that could be tracked at very high frame rates. However, the transmissible range of the
color filters of the CMOS chip were overlapping, resulting in a low contrast image that
was useless for the color based image processing algorithms needed in RoboCup.

The Marlin F-046C has a resolution of 780x580 pixels and is able to capture and transmit
50 fps at a reduced resolution of 580x580 pixels in the 16 bit *YUV4:2:2* format. This is
ideal for the target cycle time of 20 ms and at the same time represents the maximum
resolution that can be transmitted 50 times per second via the IEEE 1394a FireWire bus[4].
Figure 2.11 shows a close-up view of the final omni-directional camera system.

2.2.3   On-Board Computer

The on-board computer system is a *Thunderbird Mini-ITX* motherboard from *Lippert
GmbH* [128] equipped with an Intel Pentium M processor running at 2.0 GHz, 1 GB
RAM, and on-board support for graphics, network, sound and other periphery. A *mini-
PCI* slot is used to extend the board with two IEEE 1394a FireWire ports. As operating
system *Scientific Linux 4.0* was installed on a RAM disk of 32 MB size.

The computer system is fast enough to process the current version of the software in a

---

[4]With a maximum of approximately 32 MB/s of user data this frame size and rate consumes 100% of the
IEEE 1394a FireWire bandwidth.

Figure 2.11: A close-up view of the omni-directional camera system with the Marlin F-046C color camera below and the hyperbolic mirror on top.

stable 20 ms cycle at a power consumption of only 25 W. However, using the dual core successor of the Intel Pentium M CPU that was launched in 2006, a huge performance gain can be expected, as the client-server based software architecture presented in Chapter 3 is predestined for assigning the different processes to different CPUs. The spare computational power could then be used for more accurate algorithms.

In contrast to the old computer system, the new on-board computer is equipped with external WLAN bridges that are IEEE 802.11b and 802.11a compatible. To use the newly allowed IEEE 802.11a standard is not only advantageous because of a possibly higher bandwidth of maximally 54 Mbit/s instead of a maximum of 11 Mbit/s, but also as there are more different channels and less interference from other leagues at RoboCup tournaments.

2.2.4   Power Supply

With the low power consumption of the embedded computer and the omni-directional drive, the battery power was reduced to a set of batteries with 24 V and 9.0 Ah. As it took up to fifteen hours to recharge the old lead batteries the new batteries are composed

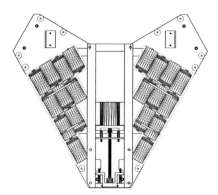

Figure 2.12: The new battery packs in the custom steplike design fitting perfectly into the new triangular robot.

of two packs with ten nickel-metal hydride D cells of 1.2 V each. These two battery packs are operated in series connection to deliver the 24 V needed for the motors, the motor controller, the kicking system and the computer. The custom steplike design of the battery packs (cf. Figure 2.12) fits perfectly into the open space besides the coil of the kicker and between the motor frame and the top plate where they can be easily exchanged from both sides. With special express chargers using a current of 5 A these batteries can be recharged in less than two hours for a play time of nearly an hour being the ideal power supply for use in a RoboCup tournament.

Chapter 3

Software Design

As the software system of the Attempto Tübingen Robot Soccer Team was not only designed to play robot soccer in RoboCup tournaments but also to serve as a common *advanced programming interface (API)* to the mobile robots for other tasks, like student teaching in practical trainings, the system was divided into several functional processes that provide data to other processes according to a client/server architecture [198]. Although there is an overhead for the *inter-process communication (IPC)* and the context switches between the processes, when compared to a monolithic system with only one complex process [68], there are many advantages of this subdivision. First of all the partitioning of the system into several functional processes simplifies the design and testing of such a large system. As each process runs in its own address space, the risk of undiscovered data corruption by programming errors is reduced. Secondly, the client/server character of these processes allows common access to data sources like images, preprocessed image data, or a complete model of the environment. On the other hand, the substitution of the low level data services by means of a simulator permits an easy interface for testing the higher level components in a simulated environment (cf. [16]). Thirdly, the multi process software system allows parallel computation on a multi-processor system like the new dual core technology CPUs. However, the performance gain from using such an MIMD architecture [154] with the current system would be low, as there is mainly a single data flow in a global 20 ms cycle which already matches the frame rate of the only data source. Yet, if the system contains more than one sensor or the global cycle time rises above the frame rate of the camera with more complex algorithms, the multiprocessor system could provide a higher throughput by processing the data in a pipeline fashion.

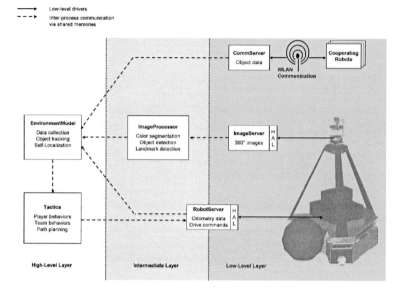

Figure 3.1: An overview of the software system.

3.1   System Overview

Figure 3.1 gives an overview of the data flow in the current software system of the At-tempto Tübingen Robot Soccer Team. The system can be divided into three functional layers, the low-level data layer containing all processes that provide the low-level access to sensor systems and serve basic sensor data, the intermediate layer with processes that preprocess the basic sensor data and extract features like landmarks and obstacles, and finally the high-level layer that includes the collection of the preprocessed data in a model of the environment and the high-level control of the robot.

3.1.1   Low-Level Layer

The low-level layer of the software system currently contains two processes that provide access to the raw sensor data through appropriate low-level drivers.

The `RobotServer` is responsible for the communication with the TMC 200 motor con-troller board and has thus two different tasks to fulfill, which are encapsulated in two synchronized threads. One thread serves as client to the system receiving commands from the robot control process `Tactics` and sending them to the controller board. The other one works as server of basic data from the robot. For each command that is sent to the board information about the current rotational speed and the encoder count of the three motors is returned. This data is used by the server thread to compute and serve odometry information on the traveled distance of the robot. Furthermore, it collects and serves information on the battery voltage and the kicker capacity once every second. This `RobotServer` is presented in detail in Chapter 4.

The `ImageServer` uses *libdc1394* [44], an open source API for controlling IEEE 1394 FireWire cameras that conform to the DCAM standard to capture the raw images from the omni-directional camera system and serves the data to the other processes. This process is presented in detail in Chapter 5.

3.1.2 Intermediate Layer

The main process of the intermediate layer is the `ImageProcessor`. This process acts as a client to the `ImageServer` to get the raw image data and then processes the raw data to extract all necessary features like landmarks and objects. These features are provided in a server function to other processes. The `ImageProcessor` is presented in detail in Chapter 5.

The new robot system contains only one `Server/Processor` pair for the camera system. The old system and the preliminary omni-directional goalkeeper, however, were equipped with more sensors thus, containing more `Server/Processor` pairs concurrently processing the data from all sensors. In the case of the two camera systems, the two `ImageServer` processes were even identical for both cameras only working on a different device.

Similar to the `RobotServer` the `CommServer` has two different functions. On the one hand, it collects data from the `EnvironmentModel` of the own robot to send it to the teammates, being a client to the `EnvironmentModel`. On the other hand, it receives messages from the teammates containing data of their `EnvironmentModel` which it serves to the local processes. As such, the `CommServer` has a special role in the software system layout, as it acts as a server for preprocessed data from a high-level layer process instead of a low-level data source. The `CommServer` is detailed as part of the environment modeling in Chapter 6.

3.1.3 High-Level Layer

The high-level layer contains the `EnvironmentModel` that integrates the preprocessed information of the local sensors and remote data from other robots into a consistent model of the robot's environment. By tracking the position of obstacles over time, it also generates information on the velocity of the obstacles. Using the landmarks from the omni-directional camera system, self-localization of the robot in its environment is done as one of the most important tasks for the mobile robot. These algorithms of the `EnvironmentModel` are explained in full detail in Chapter 6.

Based on the data from the `EnvironmentModel` the robot control process `Tactics` is driving the robot by planning paths, specifying way points on the path and assigning driving commands to the `RobotServer`, thus closing the control loop of the robot. This last process of the control software is presented in Chapter 7.

3.1.4   Graphical User Interface and Tools

Besides the control processes which run on the robot during a game, there are some other processes that help to calibrate the robot or serve as a *graphical user interface (GUI)* to monitor the game state of the team of robots during a game.

The `NewTrainingCenter` is a GUI with three main views that are used for calibrating and testing the camera system and the image processing algorithms. One of the views shows the raw image providing support to measure distances in the image and to map the image colors to different color classes needed to calibrate the camera by hand. Additionally, the parameters of the camera system can be adjusted on-line to adapt the camera to different lighting conditions. A second view of the GUI shows the color segmented camera image as seen by the `ImageProcessor` to control the color mapping (cf. Figure 3.2). A third view shows the extracted and undistorted white lines that are used as landmarks in the self-localization algorithm. Here, the accuracy of the geometric calibration of the camera can be tested. To send the user-selected camera parameters and the new geometric and color mappings to the `ImageServer` and `ImageProcessor`, both processes also have a client part that receives commands from the GUI.

To visualize the robots at their computed position in the global coordinate system of the field, one remote process collects all data sent by the robots and shows them in a GUI called `Visualization` (cf. Figure 3.3). This process also contains a panel for each robot to remotely start and stop the robot as well as a local version of the referee box for testing particular game situations.

3.2   Inter-Process Communication

For a fast inter-process communication throughout the control system the server processes provide their data in shared memory segments, while one or more client processes connect to these shared memories to read the data. In order to eliminate the risk of race conditions [189], the access to the shared memory segments is synchronized and protected by semaphores. Additionally, to allow the server process write new data to the shared mem-

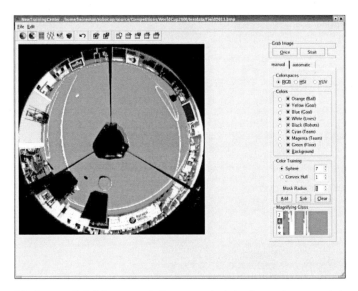

Figure 3.2: A screenshot of the `NewTrainingCenter` tool showing a color segmented camera image.

ory while clients are still reading the old data, the shared memory is organized as a ring buffer. Every time the server has new data available a free buffer in the ring buffer with no attached clients is retrieved and locked for exclusive access to write the data. On the other hand the clients have three different possibilities to retrieve a data buffer. The first is to get the newest buffer in the ring buffer structure. The second retrieves the newest buffer only if this buffer was not already read by the client, otherwise the client is blocked until a new buffer was written. In the third mode of access the client is always blocked until new data was written, even if there is a buffer the client has not read so far.

The software library providing an interface to the inter-process communication based on shared memory ring buffers is shown as class diagram in Figure 3.4. Two template classes for read and write access to a shared memory ring buffer, `ReadRingBuffer` and `WriteRingBuffer`, respectively, are derived from `ShmRingBuffer`, the abstract base class that implements the basic support for the ring buffer structure using the efficient shared memory and semaphores support of Linux [136]. These classes were already implemented by Michael Plagge before 2003 [83] and were reused for the current system.

The template parameter for the `ReadRingBuffer` and `WriteRingBuffer` classes is a structure that defines the layout and type of data of the shared memory for a specific

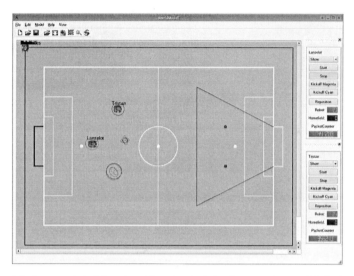

Figure 3.3: A screenshot of the `Visualization` tool showing two robots and their observed objects.

server process. The `ImageServerDataShmLayout` structure, for example, contains the plain image data, the width and height of the image in pixels and a specifier for the pixel format and the camera type. Furthermore, each shared memory layout structure includes a time stamp that is used to store the time when the data was collected, as this information is crucial for object tracking and data fusion.

To differentiate the shared memories of several servers, two parameters are given to the constructor of `ReadRingBuffer` and `WriteRingBuffer`. The first one is a unique type specifier for the type of shared memory buffers to create or to connect to, while the second one is a unique key generated from the filename of the device the data comes from. Although some servers in the system are not associated with a data device and therefore use a special filename to generate the key, this key is very useful to distinguish the shared memories from two different camera systems that have the same type specifier for the shared memory, but act on a different device. In addition, this key is also used to initialize the semaphores for the shared memory access.

While the servers directly create the shared memory using the `WriteRingBuffer` class, the client access to the shared memory is packaged in classes that provide a simple access to the data of the shared memory by abstracting from the underlying mechanism to attach to the shared memory using the `ReadRingBuffer` class.

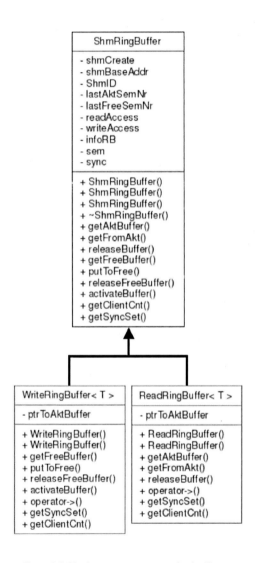

Figure 3.4: The inter-process communication library.

Chapter 4

Robot Control

As the motor controllers of robots usually only have a generic low-level interface to control the different wheels instead of a high-level interface that directly controls the movement of the specific robot, the `RobotServer` needs to decompose the high-level driving commands into the speeds of the different wheels and to combine the wheel speeds to position and movement data of the whole robot. For this, knowledge of the robot's kinematics is required as it describes this relationship between the single wheel speeds and the motion of the robot system as a whole. Therefore, the kinematics of the two robot types presented in Chapter 2 is introduced in the next section. Afterwards, the interfaces to the `RobotServer` and their implementation is addressed.

4.1 Robot Kinematics

A few assumptions are made concerning the kinematic modeling of the robots. The robots are modeled as a rigid body moving on a two-dimensional plane with vertical wheels that contact the ground plane in a single point. Furthermore, it is assumed that there is no slippage when accelerating or decelerating the wheels and the rotation around the vertical axis of the wheel is possible without friction.

4.1.1 Differential Drive

Forward Kinematics

Generally, the *forward kinematics* of a mobile robot describes the velocity of the robot body as a function of its geometry and the speeds of its n wheels

$$\mathbf{v}_r = \begin{bmatrix} v_{r,x} \\ v_{r,y} \\ \omega_r \end{bmatrix} = \mathbf{V} \begin{bmatrix} v_{w,1} \\ v_{w,2} \\ \vdots \\ v_{w,n} \end{bmatrix} \tag{4.1}$$

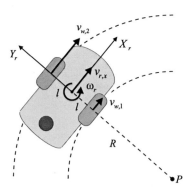

Figure 4.1: The general movement of a differential drive robot.

Here, $\mathbf{v}_r$ is a vector containing the speeds $v_{r,x}$ and $v_{r,y}$ of the robot along its X_r- and Y_r-axis, respectively, and an angular speed ω_r around its vertical axis, $\mathbf{V}$ is a $(3 \times n)$ matrix mapping the wheel speeds $v_{w,i} = \omega_{w,i}R_{w,i}$, consisting of the angular speeds $\omega_{w,i}$ and the wheel radii $R_{w,i}$, to the velocity of the robot body. For differential drive robots, like the Pioneer robots, solving the forward kinematics is equivalent to finding a (3×2) matrix that solves equation (4.1) with $n = 2$. Although this matrix can be developed straightforwardly for a differential drive robot by analyzing a generalized movement shown in Figure 4.1, the formal approach of Siegwart $et\,al.$ [176] is presented in this thesis to serve as a common method to compute the kinematics of both robot types.

Siegwart $et\,al.$ combine the kinematic constraints of each wheel on the motion of a robot to describe the kinematics in a system of equations. Given the assumptions presented earlier, each wheel imposes two constraints. Firstly, the wheel must roll without slippage when motion takes place in the appropriate direction and secondly, the wheel cannot slide orthogonal to the wheel plane. For a *fixed standard wheel* as shown in Figure 4.2, the first constraint can be expressed as

$$v_1 - v_2 - v_3 = \omega_{w,i}R_{w,i} \tag{4.2}$$

where v_1 is the robots speed along its X_r-axis projected into the wheel plane

$$v_1 = v_{r,x}\,sin(\alpha + \beta) \tag{4.3}$$

v_2 is the robots speed along its Y_r-axis projected into the wheel plane

$$v_2 = v_{r,y}\,cos(\alpha + \beta) \tag{4.4}$$

and v_3 is the robots angular speed resulting in a speed along the wheel plane

$$v_3 = \omega_r\,l\,cos(\beta) \tag{4.5}$$

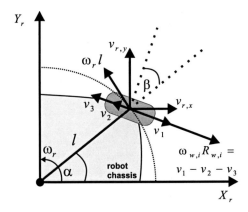

Figure 4.2: A fixed (non-steerable) standard wheel and its parameters.

Combining these terms results in the final form of the first constraint

$$\left[sin(\alpha + \beta) \quad -cos(\alpha + \beta) \quad -l\, cos(\beta)\right] \mathbf{v}_r - \omega_{w,i} R_{w,i} = 0 \qquad (4.6)$$

meaning that sum of the effective translational and rotational body movements along the wheel plane must be completely anticipated by the wheel's rotation. Accordingly, the sliding constraint enforcing zero motion orthogonal to the wheel plane can be expressed as

$$\left[cos(\alpha + \beta) \quad sin(\alpha + \beta) \quad l sin(\beta)\right] \mathbf{v}_r = 0 \qquad (4.7)$$

The differential drive Pioneer robot shown in Figure 4.1 consists of one fixed standard wheel at each side and one caster wheel in the back stabilizing the robot. As the castor wheel is not actuated and can freely move into any direction, it imposes no constraint to the robot motion and is thus neglected leaving only the two standard wheels influencing the robot motion. According to Figure 4.1, the angles are $\alpha_1 = -\frac{\pi}{2}$, $\beta_1 = \pi$ and $\alpha_2 = \frac{\pi}{2}$, $\beta_2 = 0$ for wheel number 1 and 2, respectively, reducing the constraints to

$$\begin{aligned}
\left[1 \quad 0 \quad l\right] \mathbf{v}_r - \omega_{w,1} R_{w,1} = 0 \\
\left[1 \quad 0 \quad -l\right] \mathbf{v}_r - \omega_{w,2} R_{w,2} = 0 \\
\left[0 \quad 1 \quad 0\right] \mathbf{v}_r \qquad\qquad = 0
\end{aligned} \qquad (4.8)$$

as the second constraint is identical for both wheels. Rewriting and transforming this system of equations using matrices yields

$$\begin{bmatrix} 1 & 0 & l \\ 1 & 0 & -l \\ 0 & 1 & 0 \end{bmatrix} \mathbf{v}_r = \begin{bmatrix} v_{w,1} \\ v_{w,2} \\ 0 \end{bmatrix} \qquad (4.9)$$

The inverted version of this equation is very similar to equation (4.1)

$$\mathbf{v}_r = \begin{bmatrix} 1 & 0 & l \\ 1 & 0 & -l \\ 0 & 1 & 0 \end{bmatrix}^{-1} \begin{bmatrix} v_{w,1} \\ v_{w,2} \\ 0 \end{bmatrix} = \begin{bmatrix} \frac{1}{2} & \frac{1}{2} & 0 \\ 0 & 0 & 1 \\ \frac{1}{2l} & -\frac{1}{2l} & 0 \end{bmatrix} \begin{bmatrix} v_{w,1} \\ v_{w,2} \\ 0 \end{bmatrix} \tag{4.10}$$

except for the three dimensional vector containing the wheel speeds. As the third element of this vector is zero, we can simplify the equation to

$$\begin{bmatrix} v_{r,x} \\ v_{r,y} \\ \omega_r \end{bmatrix} = \begin{bmatrix} \frac{1}{2} & \frac{1}{2} \\ 0 & 0 \\ \frac{1}{2l} & -\frac{1}{2l} \end{bmatrix} \begin{bmatrix} v_{w,1} \\ v_{w,2} \end{bmatrix} \tag{4.11}$$

representing the forward kinematics of the differential drive.

Equation (4.11) shows three results. Firstly, the forward speed of the robot along its X_r-axis is simply the mean of the two wheel speeds. According to the general movement shown in Figure 4.1 this solution can be verified geometrically. At any instant in time, the differential drive robot moves on a circular path centered in a point P that is located somewhere on the common axis of the two wheels. This point is also called *instantaneous center of rotation (ICR)* [46]. The rigid robot body assumption demands that both wheels move at the same angular rate ω around P resulting in

$$\begin{aligned} \omega(R + l) &= v_{w,1} \\ \omega(R - l) &= v_{w,2} \end{aligned} \tag{4.12}$$

Solving this equation for the circular speed ωR of the reference point of the robot centered in the origin of the robot's coordinate system I_r yields

$$\omega R = \frac{v_{w,1} + v_{w,2}}{2} = v_{r,x} \tag{4.13}$$

which is exactly the first result of equation (4.11).

Secondly, the speed of the robot along its Y_r-axis is always zero, as the wheels do not allow such a motion without slipping and thirdly, the rotational speed of the robot is proportional to the difference of the wheel speeds. In solving equation (4.12) for R and the angular rate ω that equals the rotation of the robot around its reference point, this result can be verified, too,

$$R = l\frac{v_{w,1} + v_{w,2}}{v_{w,1} - v_{w,2}} \tag{4.14}$$

$$\omega = \frac{v_{w,1} - v_{w,2}}{2l} = \omega_r \tag{4.15}$$

Two special movements of a differential drive robot can be derived from the forward kinematics described in equation (4.11). Firstly, at any instant in time, if the wheel speeds of the robot are identical, $v_{w,1} = v_{w,2}$, the robot moves on a straight line without turning, i. e. on a circle with infinite radius, which is consistent with the result of equation (4.14). Secondly, if at any instant in time, the wheel speeds are exactly opposite $v_{w,1} = -v_{w,2}$, the robot rotates on the spot.

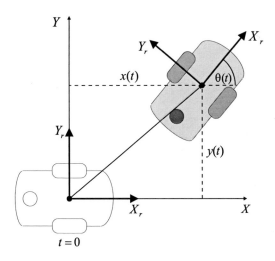

Figure 4.3: A Pioneer robot in the global reference frame I.

Inverse Kinematics

The *inverse kinematics* of a mobile robot describes the decomposition of the robot body movement into the speeds of its n wheels

$$\begin{bmatrix} v_{w,1} \\ v_{w,2} \\ \vdots \\ v_{w,n} \end{bmatrix} = \mathbf{W} \begin{bmatrix} v_{r,x} \\ v_{r,y} \\ \omega_r \end{bmatrix} \tag{4.16}$$

where $\mathbf{W}$ is a $(n \times 3)$ matrix containing the fractions that the single wheels contribute to the total speed of the robot. Actually, equation (4.9) already contains the solution to the inverse kinematics problem if the zero valued third dimension is eliminated

$$\begin{bmatrix} v_{w,1} \\ v_{w,2} \end{bmatrix} = \begin{bmatrix} 1 & 0 & l \\ 1 & 0 & -l \end{bmatrix} \begin{bmatrix} v_{r,x} \\ v_{r,y} \\ \omega_r \end{bmatrix} \tag{4.17}$$

Position Estimation

With the equations presented so far the motion of the robot at each instant in time can be computed from the instantaneous rotational speeds of the robot's wheels and vice versa. The `RobotServer` interface, however, also contains information on the position of the robot in a local frame that is fixed at the position where the robot started and the position difference compared to the last cycle. For simplicity it is assumed that the local coordinate frame of the robot is coincident with the global reference frame I. Figure 4.3 shows the robot in the global reference frame I.

To compute the distance traveled and the position of the robot in I, the velocity of the robot is integrated over time[1]

$$x(t) = \int_0^t v_x(\tau)\,d\tau$$

$$y(t) = \int_0^t v_y(\tau)\,d\tau \tag{4.18}$$

$$\theta(t) = \int_0^t v_\theta(\tau)\,d\tau$$

By applying a simple rotation matrix depending on the orientation of the robot in I the robot's velocity $\mathbf{v}_r(t)$ in the robot-centered frame I_r is transformed into the robot's velocity $\mathbf{v}(t)$ in I

$$\begin{bmatrix} v_x(t) \\ v_y(t) \\ v_\theta(t) \end{bmatrix} = \begin{bmatrix} cos(\theta(t)) & -sin(\theta(t)) & 0 \\ sin(\theta(t)) & cos(\theta(t)) & 0 \\ 0 & 0 & 1 \end{bmatrix} \begin{bmatrix} v_{r,x}(t) \\ v_{r,y}(t) \\ \omega_r(t) \end{bmatrix} \tag{4.19}$$

Using the results of equation (4.11) and equation (4.19) to rewrite equation (4.18) for the differential drive Pioneer robot yields

$$x(t) = \int_0^t v_{r,x}(\tau)cos(\theta(\tau))\,d\tau = \frac{1}{2}\int_0^t (v_{w,1}(\tau) + v_{w,2}(\tau))\,cos(\theta(\tau))\,d\tau$$

$$y(t) = \int_0^t v_{r,x}(\tau)sin(\theta(\tau))\,d\tau = \frac{1}{2}\int_0^t (v_{w,1}(\tau) + v_{w,2}(\tau))\,sin(\theta(\tau))\,d\tau \tag{4.20}$$

$$\theta(t) = \int_0^t \omega_r(\tau)\,d\tau \qquad = \frac{1}{2l}\int_0^t (v_{w,1}(\tau) - v_{w,2}(\tau))\,d\tau$$

As the exact mathematical function of the wheel speeds is unknown and can only be sampled at specific instants in time, the position of the robot cannot be calculated correctly. With an adequately high sample rate compared to the maximum speed of the robot, however, the position can be estimated with rather small errors by linear interpolation. Let $u_{w,i}(t_j)$ be the total number of revolutions of wheel i at time t_j coming from the wheel encoders. Then, the speed of wheel i during the sampling interval Δt_j between two samples at time t_{j-1} and time t_j is assumed to be

$$\widehat{v}_{w,i}(t_j) = 2\pi R_{w,i}\frac{u_{w,i}(t_j) - u_{w,i}(t_{j-1})}{\Delta t_j} \tag{4.21}$$

---

[1]Please notice that the speeds used in the kinematic equations are all functions of time. So far these speeds were only examined at an instant in time.

The position of the robot can thus be estimated as

$$\widehat{x}(t_j) = \frac{1}{2} \sum_{n=1}^{j} \left[\left(\widehat{v}_{w,1}(t_n) + \widehat{v}_{w,2}(t_n)\right) \cos(\theta(t_n)) \, \Delta t_n\right]$$

$$\widehat{y}(t_j) = \frac{1}{2} \sum_{n=1}^{j} \left[\left(\widehat{v}_{w,1}(t_n) + \widehat{v}_{w,2}(t_n)\right) \sin(\theta(t_n)) \, \Delta t_n\right] \qquad (4.22)$$

$$\widehat{\theta}(t_j) = \frac{1}{2l} \sum_{n=1}^{j} \left[\left(\widehat{v}_{w,1}(t_n) - \widehat{v}_{w,2}(t_n)\right) \, \Delta t_n\right]$$

This process of estimating the robot's position by addition of single movements is known as *dead reckoning*. The larger the sampling interval Δt_j, i.e. the lower the sampling rate, the higher is the error in position estimation by dead reckoning, as the real movement of the robot between the two samples is unknown. Furthermore, the position estimation suffers from the idealized assumption that there is no slippage between the wheels and the ground. These errors accumulate over time, making dead reckoning unsuitable for position estimation over longer periods. For a correct estimation of the robot's position during a complete mission such as a soccer play, self-localization methods are needed that use external sensor data, as presented in Chapter 6.

4.1.2   Omni-Directional Drive

Forward Kinematics

The first constraint concerning the rolling of the robot wheels also applies to the Swedish wheels of the omni-directional robot. Thus, equation (4.6) must be fulfilled for all three wheels. As the rollers of the Swedish 90-degree wheels used for the omni-directional robot are oriented orthogonal to the wheel plane, the wheel does not constrain the movement of the robot body perpendicular to the wheels. Therefore, the sliding constraint expressed in equation (4.7) does not apply for the omni-directional wheels. For a study of the constraints of a general Swedish wheel with rollers at arbitrary angles see [176].

With $(\alpha_1 = \frac{\pi}{3}, \beta_1 = 0)$, $(\alpha_2 = \pi, \beta_2 = 0)$, and $(\alpha_3 = -\frac{\pi}{3}, \beta_3 = 0)$ as the values for the angles of wheel 1, 2, and 3, according to the illustration in Figure 4.4, the constraints for the omni-directional robot are

$$\begin{bmatrix} \frac{\sqrt{3}}{2} & -\frac{1}{2} & -l \end{bmatrix} \mathbf{v}_r - \omega_{w,1} R_{w,1} = 0$$

$$\begin{bmatrix} 0 & 1 & -l \end{bmatrix} \mathbf{v}_r - \omega_{w,2} R_{w,2} = 0 \qquad (4.23)$$

$$\begin{bmatrix} -\frac{\sqrt{3}}{2} & -\frac{1}{2} & -l \end{bmatrix} \mathbf{v}_r - \omega_{w,3} R_{w,3} = 0$$

Combining and inverting this system of equations results in the forward kinematics equa-

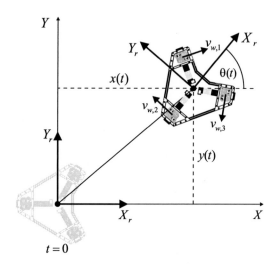

Figure 4.4: The new omni-directional robot in the global reference frame I.

tion for the omni-directional robot

$$
\begin{bmatrix} v_{r,x} \\ v_{r,y} \\ \omega_r \end{bmatrix} = \begin{bmatrix} \frac{\sqrt{3}}{2} & -\frac{1}{2} & -l \\ 0 & 1 & -l \\ -\frac{\sqrt{3}}{2} & -\frac{1}{2} & -l \end{bmatrix}^{-1} \begin{bmatrix} v_{w,1} \\ v_{w,2} \\ v_{w,3} \end{bmatrix} = \begin{bmatrix} \frac{1}{\sqrt{3}} & 0 & -\frac{1}{\sqrt{3}} \\ -\frac{1}{3} & \frac{2}{3} & -\frac{1}{3} \\ -\frac{1}{3l} & -\frac{1}{3l} & -\frac{1}{3l} \end{bmatrix} \begin{bmatrix} v_{w,1} \\ v_{w,2} \\ v_{w,3} \end{bmatrix} \tag{4.24}
$$

Three special movements of the omni-directional robot can be derived from equation (4.24). Firstly, if the wheel speeds are equal in all wheels, $v_{w,1} = v_{w,2} = v_{w,3}$, the robot rotates on the spot. Secondly, if $v_{w,1} = -v_{w,3}$ and $v_{w,2} = 0$, the robot translates along its X_r-axis, and thirdly, if $v_{w,1} = v_{w,3} = -\frac{1}{2}v_{w,2}$, the robot translates along its Y_r-axis. With the correct adjustment of the wheel speeds, the robot can translate into any direction. Given the maximum speed of a wheel

$$
v_{w,\max} = 2\pi \cdot \frac{8200}{18} \text{1/min} \cdot \frac{80}{2}\text{mm} = 1.9\,\text{m/s}
$$

computed from the maximum number of revolutions of the motor, the gear ratio, and the wheel diameter, as defined in Chapter 2, the robot can reach a full forward speed of

$$
v_{r,x,\max} = \frac{2}{\sqrt{3}}\,v_{w,\max} = 2.2\,\text{m/s}
$$

but only a sidewards speed of

$$
v_{r,y,\max} = v_{w,\max} = 1.9\,\text{m/s}
$$

Comparing equations (4.11) and (4.24) the restricted movement of the differential drive Pioneer robots compared to the new omni-directional robots becomes clear. The *degree of mobility* [176] of the omni-directional robots is $\delta_m = 3$ in contrast to the Pioneer robots with impossible movement along the Y_r-axis resulting in a degree of mobility of $\delta_m = 2$. Although both robots can reach any pose $\mathbf{l} = \begin{bmatrix} x & y & \theta \end{bmatrix}^T$ in the global reference frame I, the Pioneer robots have to reach these poses by specific maneuvers. With the translational and rotational movement being independent of each other, the omni-directional robots can drive directly to the desired position $\begin{bmatrix} x & y \end{bmatrix}^T$ while simultaneously turning to the correct orientation θ.

Inverse Kinematics

Combining and transforming the system of equations (4.23) yields the inverse kinematics equation for the omni-directional robot

$$\begin{bmatrix} v_{w,1} \\ v_{w,2} \\ v_{w,3} \end{bmatrix} = \begin{bmatrix} \frac{\sqrt{3}}{2} & -\frac{1}{2} & -l \\ 0 & 1 & -l \\ -\frac{\sqrt{3}}{2} & -\frac{1}{2} & -l \end{bmatrix} \begin{bmatrix} v_{r,x} \\ v_{r,y} \\ \omega_r \end{bmatrix} \tag{4.25}$$

Position Estimation

According to equations (4.18) and (4.19) the distance traveled by the omni-directional robot is

$$x(t) = \int_0^t v_{r,x}(\tau) \cos(\theta(\tau)) - v_{r,y}(\tau) \sin(\theta(\tau)) \, d\tau$$
$$y(t) = \int_0^t v_{r,x}(\tau) \sin(\theta(\tau)) + v_{r,y}(\tau) \cos(\theta(\tau)) \, d\tau \tag{4.26}$$
$$\theta(t) = \int_0^t \omega_r(\tau) \, d\tau$$

Inserting equation (4.24) yields

$$x(t) = \int_0^t \frac{1}{\sqrt{3}}(v_{w,1}(\tau) - v_{w,2}(\tau)) \cos(\theta(\tau))$$
$$- \frac{1}{3}(-v_{w,1}(\tau) + 2v_{w,2}(\tau) - v_{w,3}(\tau)) \sin(\theta(\tau)) \, d\tau$$
$$y(t) = \int_0^t \frac{1}{\sqrt{3}}(v_{w,1}(\tau) - v_{w,2}(\tau)) \sin(\theta(\tau)) \tag{4.27}$$
$$+ \frac{1}{3}(-v_{w,1}(\tau) + 2v_{w,2}(\tau) - v_{w,3}(\tau)) \cos(\theta(\tau)) \, d\tau$$
$$\theta(t) = -\frac{1}{3l} \int_0^t v_{w,1}(\tau) + v_{w,2}(\tau) + v_{w,3}(\tau) \, d\tau$$

Finally, the position of the omnidirectional robot can be estimated using the approximation of the wheel speeds in equation (4.21)

$$
\begin{aligned}
\widehat{x}(t_j) &= \sum_{n=1}^{j} \left[\frac{1}{\sqrt{3}} (\widehat{v}_{w,1}(t_n) - \widehat{v}_{w,2}(t_n))\, cos(\theta(t_n)) \right. \\
&\qquad \left. -\frac{1}{3}(-\widehat{v}_{w,1}(t_n) + 2\widehat{v}_{w,2}(t_n) - \widehat{v}_{w,3}(t_n))\, sin(\theta(t_n))\, \Delta t_n \right] \\
\widehat{y}(t_j) &= \sum_{n=1}^{j} \left[\frac{1}{\sqrt{3}} (\widehat{v}_{w,1}(t_n) - \widehat{v}_{w,2}(t_n))\, sin(\theta(t_n)) \right. \\
&\qquad \left. +\frac{1}{3}(-\widehat{v}_{w,1}(t_n) + 2\widehat{v}_{w,2}(t_n) - \widehat{v}_{w,3}(t_n))\, cos(\theta(t_n))\, \Delta t_n \right] \\
\widehat{\theta}(t_j) &= -\frac{1}{3l} \sum_{n=1}^{j} \left[(\widehat{v}_{w,1}(t_n) + \widehat{v}_{w,2}(t_n) + \widehat{v}_{w,3}(t_n))\, \Delta t_n \right]
\end{aligned}
\tag{4.28}
$$

4.2 User Interface

Although the robot control process is called `RobotServer`, it not only serves the odometry data generated from the wheel encoder sensors of the robot but also receives driving commands from the `Tactics` by reading from a shared memory. Nevertheless, both tasks can be seen as a service to the other processes and accordingly both tasks handle the complex shared memory creation in the `RobotServer`. Two different client interfaces connect to the existing shared memories providing high-level access to the robot for reading data and for giving commands.

These interfaces were defined as a platform independent interface. A special *hardware abstraction layer (HAL)* was introduced in the `RobotServer` not only to hide the different communication protocols used by different robots, but also to process the data coming from the robot and the commands going to the robot. With this HAL the common interface works for all kinds of robots. The current version of the `RobotServer` is able to access two types of Pioneer robots and the omni-directional robot with the TMC200 motor controller using exactly the same interface.

RobotServerCommandClient

Processes have to create an instance of the `RobotServerCommandClient` to control the robot. Although only one command can be processed at each cycle, it is possible that more than one client has access to the robot at the same time. At the creation of the `RobotServerCommandClient`, however, it is possible and most usual to try to gain exclusive access to the robot. If a process has exclusive access to the robot, each subsequent attempt to create an instance will fail.

The most important commands to control a mobile robot are the commands to set the velocity of the robot. Four commands are contained in the interface definition, one that sets the translational velocity specified as a vector in I_r, one that sets the rotational speed, one that simultaneously sets translational velocity and rotational speed and finally one that sets the speeds of the single wheels. A special stop command was also included for an emergency stop using special brakes where applicable. As long as no other command is given by the client, the robot is expected to perform the last command.

In addition to the driving commands there exists a series of commands setting internal parameters of the `RobotServer` or the motor controller, such as the maximum allowed translational and rotational speed and acceleration, the maximum speed per wheel, and the digital output lines.

RobotServerDataClient

To get data from the `RobotServer` other processes have to create an instance of the `RobotServerDataClient`. Besides the obligatory time stamp, the client delivers data of the robot's movement, including the translational velocity and the rotational speed in I, the wheel speeds, the position in a local frame that is fixed at the position where the robot started, and the position difference compared to the last cycle.

Furthermore, information on the internal state of the robot or motor controller can be queried, such as the state of the digital input lines, the supply voltage, and whether a wheel stall occurred in one of the wheels.

4.3 Implementation

When the `RobotServer` process is started, it tries to open a serial connection to the robot. As all robots have different communication protocols and speeds, several configurations are tested until the connection with the robot is established. From the configuration the `RobotServer` then knows the type of robot that is connected to the on-board computer.

The two tasks of the `RobotServer` are executed in two different threads to be able to write commands to the robot and read the answers containing the wheel encoder data in full duplex, i. e. reading and writing simultaneously. Figure 4.5 shows a flow chart of the two threads.

Command Thread

The command thread is started after the `RobotServer` has connected to the robot. In the beginning it waits for a command of a client that can be read from the shared memory. If there is a new command it decomposes the desired velocity into the wheel speeds according to the inverse kinematic equations of Section 4.1 and tries to send the command to the robot. In order not to send too many commands to the robot without receiving

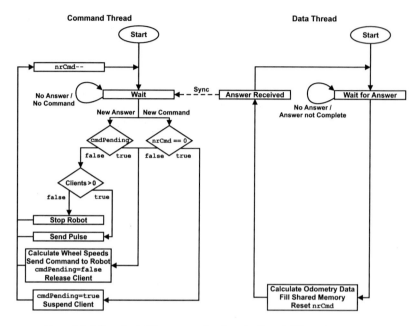

Figure 4.5: A flow chart of the command and receive thread of the RobotServer.

an answer of the robot, there is a shared variable called nrCmd that is used to loosely synchronize the command thread and the data thread. If nrCmd = 0 when a new command is issued by a client, there were already too many commands sent to the robot without receiving an answer. Then, the client is suspended, cmdPending is set to true, and the command thread waits for the data thread. This wait mode is left as soon as a new answer from the robot is received. In that case, if there is an old command to be sent (cmdPending=true) this command is sent to the robot, the suspended client is released, cmdPending is set to false, and the thread returns into the wait mode until a new command was given by a client or a new answer was received by the data thread. Otherwise (cmdPending=false), the command thread checks if there are still clients connected to the shared memory and if not it immediately stops the robot by sending a stop command. If there are still clients connected, however, it sends a special Pulse command which has two different purposes on the different robot platforms. After the connection to the RobotServer, the Pioneer robots constantly send data of their sensors even without a command coming from the RobotServer. However, they have a watchdog timer that safely stops the robot and the communication if the connection to the computer is lost and no more commands are sent. To circumvent the shutdown, the

`Pulse` command is sent to show that the computer is still active. On the other hand, the TMC200 motor controller only sends the data of the wheel encoders as an answer to a driving command [116] so that the special command in this case is just a repetition of the old driving command to get current data of the motors. Regardless of the specific command, `nrCmd` is decreased after a command was sent to the robot.

Data Thread

The data thread is started after the `RobotServer` has connected to the robot and listens at the serial port for data packets coming from the robot. Whenever a new data packet was received as an answer to the commands sent by the command thread, the data thread calculates the odometry data from the wheel encoder values according to the robot's forward kinematic and position estimation equations presented in Section 4.1. This data is then copied to the shared memory where the connected clients can read it for further use. Additionally, `nrCmd` is reset to the number of commands that can be sent without receiving an answer from the robot. This number is two for the Pioneer robots and one for the omni-directional robots, resulting in fully synchronized, though parallel threads for the omni-directional robots. As `nrCmd` is a shared resource, the access to the variable is protected by semaphores. Finally, the data thread releases the command thread using a different semaphore in order to send a `Pulse` or a stop command, if there are no new commands from the client.

Hardware Abstraction Layer

The class diagram in Figure 4.6 presents the structure of the hardware abstraction layer used to control different robot types with one common interface and `RobotServer` code. The `RobotServer` communicates with the robot using a pointer to the abstract `robotDataPacket` class. This base class is used to derive a class for each type of robot that handles the special communication with the specific robot or motor controller. As all of the derived classes implement the same interface, the `RobotServer` can transparently use this interface to send commands to the robot or to receive wheel speeds from the robot without knowledge about the specific robot type in use. At startup, when the connection to a specific robot type is established, the `RobotServer` instantiates the correct subclass according to the connection parameters.

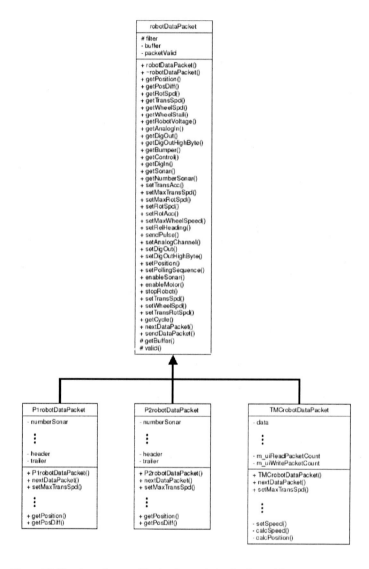

Figure 4.6: The class diagram of the hardware abstraction layer of the `RobotServer`.

Chapter 5

Image Processing

As the only external sensor of the new omni-directional robots is an omni-directional camera system, the image processing task is crucial for the robot control system. From the image data served by the `ImageServer`, the `ImageProcessor` extracts landmarks and objects in the surrounding of the robot that are needed for building a model of the robot's environment (cf. Figure 5.1). The following section contains an introduction to the challenges of object and landmark detection in a camera image by giving an overview of the related work. The remainder of the chapter presents the image processing algorithms of the Attempto Tübingen Robot Soccer Team including detailed experimental results, the user interface to the image and feature data, and the implementation of the `Server/Processor` pair.

5.1 Related Work

Object and Landmark Detection

While robots and the ball are the only objects to be extracted for a RoboCup robot, several features of the RoboCup environment might be considered as landmarks. First of all, the field contains the white field markings that can be used to localize the robot. To resolve the symmetry problem of both field halves the two goals and the four corner posts that are differently colored on each half field form perfect landmarks.

Zhang and Zelinsky [209] identified two classes of object detection approaches, appearance based approaches and feature based approaches. Appearance based approaches work directly on the pixel intensities of an image. Using a set of training images containing the object to be identified, a classifier is trained which detects the objects in the final object detection system. Feature based approaches try to detect objects based on features, including texture and shape, that are typical for the given object. While extracting the shape of an object is relatively easy using existing edge detection methods, the selection of sig-

43

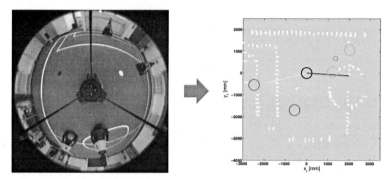

Figure 5.1: The Image Processing Task. From a camera image (left) landmarks and objects are extracted and are mapped back to robot-centered coordinates (right) as input for a process that builds a model of the robot's environment.

nificant texture or gray level features is usually not straightforward. Therefore, Viola and Jones proposed to learn such features on a training set [201].

However, all these approaches suffer from the necessity of knowing the form or texture of the object in advance, which in RoboCup is fine for detecting the ball according to its shape [75, 76] or gray scale features [191, 192], but is impractical concerning the robots of other MSL teams, as these robots not only differ from team to team but also sometimes change their form from tournament to tournament. Only the color is a feature for detecting the robots that remains constant in time, because it is stated in the rules that the robot has to be mainly black. Since the ball and all landmarks are coded in a special color as well, color based methods to object and landmark detection are predominant in the RoboCup MSL.[1]

For a fast detection of the color coded elements in the image, the image is first segmented into several regions of a common color class. For this, the color of the image pixels has to be mapped to one of the color classes *Green, White, Blue, Yellow, Orange, Black, Cyan,* or *Magenta.*

Color Segmentation

The way of segmenting the image and the number of image pixels used differ over the proposed algorithms. Some early approaches classified every pixel of the image to extract regions of the same color class [14, 27, 105, 139, 34]. As this method is very time consuming, the image size had to be low or a sub-sampled image had to be used for object detection. The regions were then extracted using topological information on the 8-neighborhood of the pixels [14] or using a run length encoding method [27].

---

[1]Color information is also used in many driver assisting systems for intelligent vehicles to detect traffic signs [161] or traffic lights [64].

To reduce the amount of pixels inspected to extract the regions Jamzad *et al.* [100, 99] defined a set of *jump points* that cover the image and serve as starting points for a region growing algorithm [210] that fills regions of the same color class. Although the region growing is only started if a jump point belongs to one of the considered color classes (here: *Blue*, *Yellow*, *Orange*, and *Black*), this method is inefficient since it visits every pixel of a region several times. In the worst case, when the robot is surrounded by objects, this method is even worse than simply classifying the whole image. Hundelshausen *et al.* [91] presented a very similar method of extracting the color regions, however, the regions are tracked over time. Once initialized in the first frame, the regions merely have to be adapted to their new position in the following frames, resulting in a very efficient method if the overlap of the regions is large between two consecutive frames. For both methods, the distribution of the jump points in the image is crucial for finding the correct regions. If a region is not hit by any jump point, it will not be detected. Jamzad *et al.* [100, 99] address the coverage of the relevant image parts by selecting the distance between two adjacent jump points small enough to cover the ball as the smallest object with at least one of the two points. In their biologically inspired *receptor* approach, which is eventually very similar to the method of Jamzad *et al.*, Bonarini *et al.* [22] already proposed the same for an omni-directional camera.

Another method to significantly reduce the number of inspected pixels was presented by Jüngel *et al.* [103, 102] and Röfer *et al.* [163, 164] which classifies only the pixels of different scan lines. Transitions from one color class to another along the scan lines determine the border of the relevant objects in the camera image. Objects are detected combining the transitions of one or more scan lines. Compared to the method using jump points and region growing, it is thus even more important to distribute the scan lines to the important parts of the image to cover the objects in their full extension.

The extracted color regions are usually directly related to the objects and landmarks. However, finding the correct position of the ball is crucial for soccer playing and many robots in the RoboCup MSL still track down young spectators because the robots confuse their orange shirts with the ball. Therefore, some teams additionally use context information [103, 69] and/or a special form detection [14, 105, 103, 69] to assure that the orange region really represents the ball.

Color Calibration

Besides the method of segmenting the image into regions of the same color class, the mapping of different colors to one of the color classes is the most important part of the image processing algorithms, mainly influencing the segmentation process. As for the segmentation, there exist several different approaches to subdivide the three-dimensional color space into areas that are mapped to the color classes. Even the type of color space *RGB*, *HSI*, or *YUV* [50, 56] that is suited best for the subdivision is discussed.

The majority of the approaches presented so far simply defines sub-cuboids of the color space to represent the color values to be mapped to one of the color classes [22, 27, 105,

100, 139]. The process of classifying a pixel is thus limited to two simple threshold checks per color channel and per color class. However, for a large number of pixels to be classified these checks can still be very inefficient. In addition, depending on the color space in use, the distribution of the color values of the different classes cannot always be modeled with cuboids without including color values of other classes. Therefore, Bandlow *et al.* [14] use prisms composed of arbitrary shapes in the two color dimensions of the YUV color space and thresholding in the third which represents the intensity of the color. To avoid extensive tests if a color value belongs to one of the prisms defining a color class, they fill a look-up table containing the correct color class for each color value of two dimensions in advance, resulting in a fast table look-up and two threshold checks in the third dimension of the color space to classify a pixel. To model completely arbitrary clusters of color values belonging to a color class Hundelshausen *et al.* [91] use a look-up table for the full color space. Although this table can be very large, depending on the color depth of the camera system, the process of classifying the image pixels reduces to a very fast table look-up.

The methods for color calibration mentioned so far were all depending on a user specifying the thresholds and parameters of the subdivision of the color space according to the analysis of many images taken on site. This is the main reason for the multiple days of setup time needed by the teams before a RoboCup competition can start, as the process of manual color calibration is very tedious. In [183] Sridharan and Stone present an automatic color calibration technique that searches images taken by the robot standing at predefined poses for given shapes of landmarks from which the colors can be learned. During the learning phase, the regions of the color classes in the color space are modeled as three-dimensional Gaussian density functions with a mean value and a standard deviation. To reduce the classification time, the mapping itself is stored in a look-up table mapping each color to the class with the highest probability value of the Gaussian density function. According to the authors, the time to generate a color table can be reduced to 2-4 minutes when using this approach.

The type of color space used differs as much as the subdivision itself. In their biologically inspired receptor approach Bonarini *et al.* [22] use RGB, presumably because it agrees with the three colors that are detected by the cones in the human eye. In combination with a simple thresholding in the three dimensions, however, this seems to be the worst selection, since at least the distribution of the ball color in RGB is conical [27]. Not only the shape of the set of color values belonging to a color class changes with the color space, but also the relative positions of the shapes under different illumination conditions. HSI and YUV color space have the chrominance coded in two dimensions and the intensity coded in the third. By using HSI [100, 99, 139] or YUV [14, 27] the teams hope to make their classification independent of the illumination by choosing the threshold in the intensity dimension very high. However, the case study in [140] shows that the position of the set of color values of one class does not only change along the intensity axis of the HSI or YUV color space as also the colors change under different illumination.

When using an arbitrary subdivision of the color space, the selection of a special color space is unnecessary. The color space used is then usually defined by the camera system to avoid conversion. The changes in illumination can be anticipated, too, even if the shape and the position of the set of color values mapped to a color class changes over the different lighting conditions, as long as the sets of different color classes do not overlap. However, since 2004 the lighting conditions in RoboCup MSL continuously changed from constant bright illumination to moderately changing illumination over the field and finally up to indirect daylight illumination at the RoboCup 2006 in Bremen. With these conditions the shapes and the positions of the color classes in the color space change drastically over time and even overlap for different illuminations [140]. Thus, the classical approach of a constant subdivision of the color space became useless for the future and automatic color calibration became one of the main research topics in RoboCup.

To determine the field illumination and adjust the color thresholds accordingly following previously defined parameters Jamzad *et al.* mounted a piece of the green field carpet on their robot [99]. A similar idea was presented by Sridharan *et al.* [182] were the field illumination is classified into one of three different classes for which a special look-up table was trained in advance. Yet, this approach does not need a reference color on the robot.

Jüngel *et al.* [103, 102] and Röfer *et al.* [163, 164] defined the predominant green color of a RoboCup field as a sub cube in the color space and the other color classes as higher or lower in relation to the green along the three color dimensions. By identifying the green pixels in the image and adjusting the position and thresholds of the green class, the method becomes less dependent on different illuminations.

Another approach to adaptive color classification was presented by Stanton *et al.* [184] who explicitly train the color look-up table at different lighting conditions to include all color values that should be mapped to a given class. Because some color values represent different classes at different illuminations, a color value can be mapped to more than one color class. The correct mapping of such a *maybe-color* for a special illumination is then identified by the surrounding in the image. If the majority of the surrounding pixels of a maybe-color is mapped to only one of the classes of the maybe-color it is likely that the maybe-color should be mapped to the same class. The exact opposite approach was proposed by Lovell [129]. Only color values that belong to a color class over a wide variety of illumination settings are mapped to this class. Thus, the method is invariant to changes in illumination. However, this mapping does not contain enough information for the standard image segmentation approach. Therefore, to identify the interesting image regions a combination of edge detection and blob forming is used. These regions are labeled according to the majority of pixels in the region classified as the same color class.

Most of the algorithms proposed to adapt to changing lighting conditions, however, directly estimate the new position of the regions in the color space based on a previous mapping [35, 69, 34, 71, 6, 112, 95]. The methods of Cameron *et al.* [35] and Gönner *et al.* [69] both use form detection mechanisms to identify pixels that should belong to an object or landmark and thus to the same color class. However, in contrast to the approach of Cameron *et al.* a rudimentary mapping of color values to classes must exist in the approach of Gönner *et al.* to roughly identify the position of the ball or landmarks. Kikuchi *et al.* [112] instead model the distribution of color values classified as the same class with a χ^2 distribution. If the lighting changes slowly, the correct distribution of the color values of a color class moves in the color space and the modeled distribution has to be adapted. As some of the color values in the new camera image still have a small *Mahalanobis distance* to the modeled distribution, these color values are expected to define the new position of the color class. The distribution of these values is then used to determine the new classification.

A different idea to cope with changes in the illumination of color coded scenes is to adapt the raw image. In [70] Grillo *et al.* exploit the possibility of the DCAM standard to adjust the parameters of a FireWire camera like exposure time and white balance to optimize the camera image for a good color classification. Mayer *et al.* [139] propose the *RETINEX* algorithm to preprocess the camera image for improved separation of the color classes within the color space. However, this approach is currently not suitable for real-time applications.

Geometry Calibration

Once the objects in the image are detected, their position in robot-centered real-world coordinates has to be calculated. For this, a mapping from image coordinates $\begin{bmatrix} x_p & y_p \end{bmatrix}^T$ to two-dimensional coordinates on the ground floor $\begin{bmatrix} x_r & y_r \end{bmatrix}^T$ is needed.[2]

One way to find the mapping function of a camera is to use calibration techniques that automatically extract the extrinsic and intrinsic parameters of the camera and build a complete physical model of the projection [193]. Although this method results in a very accurate model of the mapping, it is time consuming and furthermore requires a special calibration pattern. Egorova *et al.* [48] instead presented an automatic geometry calibration approach for a global camera system used in the RoboCup Small-Size League which fits the white field markings onto a model of these lines using conventional optimization techniques.

As omni-directional camera systems are composed of a camera pointing upwards onto a convex shaped mirror, however, calibration of the camera itself is not sufficient for such systems. On the one hand, knowing the calibrated parameters of the camera, the exact position of the camera and the mirror, and the shape of the mirror, the mapping function indeed can be derived geometrically. But on the other hand, the relative position of the mirror to the camera changes during transport or maintenance of the robot, often resulting

---

[2]Here, it should be mentioned that several RoboCup teams do not model the objects in the camera image explicitly and thus do not need this step. These teams merely consider the detected black regions as obstacles to the robots movement and extract the free space between these obstacles to reactively generate a driving command [173].

in a completely wrong mapping. An approach for automatic calibration of these extrinsic parameters of a general omni-directional camera system was presented by Colombo *et al.* [39]. However, the intrinsic parameters of the camera still have to be calibrated using a different method. For omni-directional cameras comprising of a parabolic mirror and an orthographic lens, Geyer and Daniilidis therefore presented a calibration method [67] that completely calibrates all parameters of the omni-directional camera system. Yet, the demand of a special calibration pattern is a strong disadvantage of the mentioned automatic calibration algorithms.

Most teams in RoboCup, however, roughly approximate the mapping of their omni-directional camera systems by collecting corresponding coordinate pairs in the image and robot coordinate systems (I_p and I_r) that describe the same feature on the floor level, followed by fitting a two-dimensional function through these correspondences. Yet, even with the semi-automatic approach presented in [3] this approximation procedure is still very time consuming and prone to errors.

In contrast, some researchers use the extracted camera parameters to calculate and design a special mirror shape that directly maps the ground floor without distortion [89, 132, 134]. However, these approaches suffer, too, if the position of the mirror in relation to the camera changes.

5.2 Image Processing Algorithms

The main paradigm followed in the development of the image processing algorithms of the Attempto Tübingen Robot Soccer Team presented in this section was to be as efficient as possible. As the omni-directional camera system is the only sensor system on the new omni-directional robots, the image processing cycle time is fundamental for the cycle time of the whole system. Therefore, a camera system with a 50 fps frame rate was used and the algorithms were designed to process a frame within 20 ms using less than 50% of the processor time of the on-board computer. Although some of the algorithms could achieve higher precision with more computational resources, the selected accuracy is shown to be a good compromise between a high cycle time and reactivity of the system and a sufficient precision of the extracted data. The next section describes the basic image processing algorithm of the Attempto Tübingen Robot Soccer Team that was also published in [84, 162], section 5.2.2 describes two extensions to the image processing system for automatic geometry and on-line color calibration which were also published in [172, 86, 85, 87].

5.2.1 Basic Algorithm

Similar to most of the image processing approaches in RoboCup the algorithm developed for the Attempto Tübingen Robot Soccer Team extracts landmarks and objects from the image of an omni-directional camera based on their specific color and maps them into the robot-centered frame I_r (cf. Figure 5.1). For building a complete model of the robot's environment including its pose, it is crucial to know the exact position of other robots, the ball, and the white field markings. However, to resolve the symmetry using the differently colored goals and corner posts, only the angles towards these landmarks are important. Even for a self-localization algorithm that estimates the robot's pose by triangulation, only the angles to the corner posts are needed. Therefore, the algorithm presented here only extracts the angles to these landmarks from the image.

The algorithm needs two prerequisites which depend on the camera system and the specific environment, a mapping from image coordinates in I_p to coordinates in I_r and a mapping from color values to color classes. The next two sections describe the camera calibration techniques used to manually determine these mappings for the omni-directional camera systems on both types of robots. The following sections then describe the biologically inspired algorithm for fast and accurate segmentation of the image and the extraction of objects and landmarks based on the segmented image.

Geometry Calibration

Here, the term *geometry calibration* describes the task of identifying the *inverse perspective mapping*, a function

$$f_g^{-1} : \mathbb{N}^2 \mapsto \mathbb{R}^2, \quad \begin{bmatrix} x_p \\ y_p \end{bmatrix} \to \begin{bmatrix} x_r \\ y_r \end{bmatrix} \tag{5.1}$$

that inverts the *perspective mapping* f_g of the camera system and maps two-dimensional image coordinates $\begin{bmatrix} x_p & y_p \end{bmatrix}^T$ in I_p, originated in the image center, to two-dimensional robot-centered coordinates $\begin{bmatrix} x_r & y_r \end{bmatrix}^T$ in I_r. However, the perspective mapping is only bijective and thus invertible for a specific two-dimensional plane, e. g. the floor on which the robot moves. The parts of robots and goals that extend into the third dimension are incorrectly mapped back to I_r as Figure 5.2 shows. Therefore, the inverse perspective mapping is calibrated for the floor plane and the correct position of objects in I_r is derived by mapping a point where the object contacts the floor (cf. point A in Figure 5.2).

As both the camera and the mirror of an omni-directional camera system are usually rotationally symmetric, the inverse perspective mapping is also rotationally symmetric if the optical axis of the camera and the symmetry axis of the mirror are collinear and orthogonal to the floor plane, i. e. identical to the cross product $X_r \times Y_r$ of the two axes of I_r. On both robot types a careful design and a precise production resulted in an omni-directional camera system that fulfills this assumption sufficiently. Exploiting the symmetry and the angle preserving property of such a symmetric camera system and furthermore using polar coordinates, the two-dimensional inverse perspective mapping from equation (5.1) can be simplified to

$$f_g^{-1} : \begin{bmatrix} r_r \\ \varphi_r \end{bmatrix} = \begin{bmatrix} f_r^{-1}(r_p) \\ \varphi_p \end{bmatrix} \tag{5.2}$$

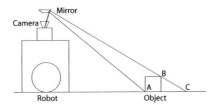

Figure 5.2: The perspective mapping can be ambiguous and is only bijective for a specific two-dimensional plane, e. g. the floor on which the robot moves. Robots and goals that extend into the third dimension are not correctly mapped by the inverse perspective mapping. Only the mapping of point A can be inverted, while point B would be incorrectly mapped onto the floor at point C.

where f_r^{-1} is the inverse perspective mapping of the radius in image coordinates I_p to the radius in robot-centered coordinates I_r

$$f_r^{-1} : \mathbb{N} \mapsto \mathbb{R}, \; r_p \to r_r \qquad (5.3)$$

Thus, the task of calibrating the inverse perspective mapping is simplified to the identification of f_r^{-1}.

During the manual calibration procedure several pairs of corresponding distances are collected, each pair consisting of the distance r_r of an artificial landmark to the robot in I_r and the distance r_p of its mapping to the image center. By fitting a polynomial of degree five through these pairs using a least-squares approach, f_r^{-1} can be approximated as $\widehat{f}_r^{-1}$. The resulting polynomial is evaluated for each $r_p \in \{1, 2, \ldots, r_{\text{max}}\}$ and the resulting values are stored in a distance look-up table (*DistanceLUT*) for efficient access. For the image resolution of 580x580 pixels used on the new omni-directional robots this means a maximum of 290 entries in the DistanceLUT. This calibration procedure is very similar to the semi-automatic method of Adorni *et al.* [3].

However, the relative position of the mirror to the camera changes during transport or maintenance of the robot, resulting in a wrong mapping since the collinearity of the symmetry axes is not achieved. Yet, experimental results with both types of robots have shown that the inverse perspective mapping is still approximately rotationally invariant if the center point of the mirror $\begin{bmatrix} x_{p,c} & y_{p,c} \end{bmatrix}^T$ in the image is extracted and used to finally compute

$$\widehat{f}_g^{-1} : \begin{bmatrix} r_r \\ \varphi_r \end{bmatrix} = \begin{bmatrix} \widehat{f}_r^{-1}(\widetilde{r}_p) \\ \widetilde{\varphi}_p \end{bmatrix} \qquad (5.4)$$

with

$$\widetilde{r}_p = \sqrt{(x_{p,c} - x_p)^2 + (y_{p,c} - y_p)^2} \qquad (5.5)$$

$$\widetilde{\varphi}_p = tan^{-1}\left(\frac{y_{p,c} - y_p}{x_{p,c} - x_p}\right) \qquad (5.6)$$

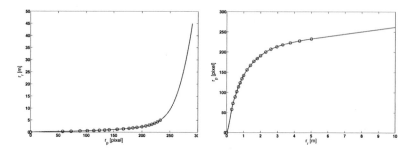

Figure 5.3: A manually calibrated mapping function $\widehat{f}_r^{-1}$ that is used to generate the DistanceLUT (left) and the inverted mapping function $\widehat{f}_r$ (right).

being polar coordinates in a frame parallel to I_p but centered in $\begin{bmatrix} x_{p,c} & y_{p,c} \end{bmatrix}^T$. The center point $\begin{bmatrix} x_{p,c} & y_{p,c} \end{bmatrix}^T$ is also stored in the look-up table. An automatic approach to calibrate the DistanceLUT and the center point $\begin{bmatrix} x_{p,c} & y_{p,c} \end{bmatrix}^T$ is presented in Section 5.2.2.

To identify pixels that correspond to points on an equally spaced grid in I_r, needed for the image segmentation step of the image processing algorithm, the perspective mapping function f_g is computed, too. For this, a second look-up table is generated for the approximation $\widehat{f}_g$ by simply inverting $\widehat{f}_g^{-1}$ and $\widehat{f}_r^{-1}$

$$\widehat{f}_g : \begin{bmatrix} \widetilde{r}_p \\ \widetilde{\varphi}_p \end{bmatrix} = \begin{bmatrix} \widehat{f}_r(r_r) \\ \varphi_r \end{bmatrix} \tag{5.7}$$

Color Calibration

The term *color calibration* describes the task of identifying a function f_c that maps all color values of a three-dimensional color space to one of nine color classes

$$f_c : \mathbb{N}^3 \mapsto \mathbb{N}, \ \mathbf{c} \to C \tag{5.8}$$

where

$$C \in \{Green, White, Yellow, Blue, Orange, Black, Cyan, Magenta, Unknown\} \tag{5.9}$$

such, that the pixels of each color coded landmark or object in the image are completely mapped to the corresponding color class (*Green* for the field, *White* for the field markings, *Yellow* and *Blue* for the goals, *Orange* for the ball, *Black* for the robots, and *Cyan* and *Magenta* for the team colors) and all other pixels that do not display one of the field elements of the RoboCup field should correspond to the special class *Unknown*. Obviously there

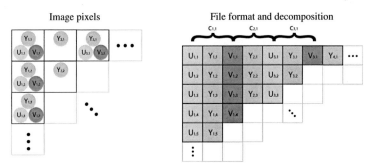

Figure 5.4: In the common YUV4:2:2 format, the color information stored in the the U- and V-component is only provided for every second pixel while the intensity stored in the Y-component is provided for all pixels (left). However, an efficient technique is used to interpolate the color information for all pixels by exploiting the data alignment in the YUV4:2:2 file stream (right).

is no ideal function f_c that fulfills these requirements as the color values that identify the objects and landmarks strongly depend on the field illumination. Furthermore, with the limited resolution of the pixel colors in each direction of the color space some color values occur in differently colored landmarks and would require a mapping to two different classes. Although this is done in the approach of Stanton *et al.* [184] and would technically be possible with the presented method since each color class is stored as one bit of a byte value (for the *Unknown* class no bit is set), the color segmentation approach presented in the next section is fault-tolerant enough to cope with an approximation $\widehat{f}_c$ of the color mapping that strictly maps one color value to only one class.

Similar to Hundelshausen *et al.* [91] the color calibration of the Attempto Tübingen Robot Soccer Team stores $\widehat{f}_c$ in a color look-up table (*ColorLUT*) to enable the user to specify arbitrary subdivisions of the color space. With a resolution of 8 bit per color channel and one byte for coding the color class, the size of the final ColorLUT is 16.7 MB. Although a look-up table of this size does not fit into the cache of typical embedded systems processors the access is still competitive if compared to a thresholding in all three color dimensions as used in many other approaches. Furthermore, for slightly varying illumination a ColorLUT with arbitrary clusters in the color space is superior to simple thresholding.

The YUV color space is used for the ColorLUT to save computational costs for conversion of the camera image that is delivered in the 16 bit *YUV4:2:2* format to transmit the full 50 fps via the IEEE 1394a FireWire bus. In this common format, the color information stored in the the U- and V-component is only provided for every second pixel while the intensity stored in the Y-component is provided for all pixels (cf. Figure 5.4). This method to reduce the data amount per pixel to 16 bit (24 bit for the first pixel, 8 bit for the second etc.) is known as *chroma subsampling*. It exploits the fact that the human eye is less sensitive to color than to luminance. In order to regain 24 bit or 8 bit per channel of each pixel without spending the computational costs for interpolating the U- and V-components of neighboring pixels, a clever addressing technique is used. As shown in Figure 5.4 the single components of the image are stored in the order $\{U_{1,1}, Y_{1,1}, V_{1,1}, Y_{2,1}, U_{3,1}, Y_{3,1}, V_{3,1}, \ldots\}$. For the first pixel and all other 'odd' pixels, the information of all three components is given as $c_{i,j} = \begin{bmatrix} U_{i,j} & Y_{i,j} & V_{i,j} \end{bmatrix}^T$. For the second pixel and all other 'even' pixels, only the Y-component is given explicitly and the two other components are taken from the two pixels preceding and succeeding the current pixel as $c_{i,j} = \begin{bmatrix} V_{i-1,j} & Y_{i,j} & U_{i+1,j} \end{bmatrix}^T$ (cf. Figure 5.4). This implicitly mixes the U-component of the preceding pixel and the V-component of the succeeding pixel, resulting in a color that is different to both the preceding and the succeeding pixels at horizontal transitions between two colors. However, this technique to regain the color information for all pixels is extremely efficient since no computation is required and works perfectly in the color coded environment of the RoboCup, where large areas of the image are occupied by similar colors.

Like most of the other calibration methods presented in Section 5.1 the calibration procedure consists of the inspection of one or more camera images by a human supervisor that manually adapts the mapping to achieve a good result. In contrast to the thresholding approaches, however, the color space used for defining the arbitrary clusters in the color space is irrelevant. In the NewTrainingCenter (cf. Section 3.1.4) the user can grab images from the camera system and is able to use a marker tool to select image pixels and specify which color class these color values should be mapped to. As it is nearly impossible with 8 bit resolution per color channel to select all shades of a color that should be mapped to a color class, not only the selected color values themselves are added to the ColorLUT, but also neighboring colors in the color space since it can be expected that these values should be mapped to the same color class. The user can therefore select either to add all color values lying inside the convex hull of all the selected color values or inside spheres with a selected radius centered at the single color values. The result of the new mappings is directly visualized in the NewTrainingCenter as all mapped colors are replaced with a common color for their corresponding color class. If too many color values were added to the ColorLUT, the user can also remove color mappings to a class using the same mechanisms. For compatibility with other approaches the user can furthermore specify the color space in which the selected color values are transformed before the convex hull or the spheres are generated, but the experience of several RoboCup tournaments showed that the selection of different color spaces is dispensable. Although during the calibration step colors can be mapped to more than one class, for generating the ColorLUT only one of these mappings is retained based on a prioritization of the different color classes. With this method it is possible for an experienced user to calibrate a good ColorLUT as shown in Figure 5.5 in less than five minutes.

By incorporating more than one image captured at different positions on the field it is also possible to reflect different illuminations occurring on the field in the ColorLUT. However, this is only possible for slight and static differences, since otherwise the same

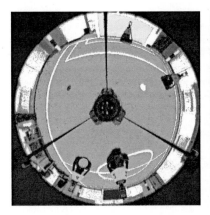 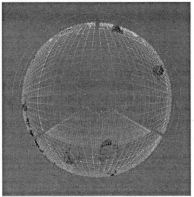

Figure 5.5: The example image of Figure 5.1 classified with a manually trained ColorLUT.

Figure 5.6: The segmented grid of the example image of Figure 5.1 representing the input data for the image processing algorithm.

color values correspond to different classes at different positions on the field and the mapping is no longer unique. Therefore, Section 5.2.2 presents an automatic approach to color calibration which can be used for on-line recalibration of the ColorLUT.

Color Segmentation

Several approaches for extracting image regions of the same color class were presented in Section 5.1. Most of them were based on the classification of all image pixels or at least all pixels of the extracted regions for methods using region growing. Classification of such a high number of pixels is too time-consuming for the given target frame rate and processor time. Furthermore, it is unnecessary to classify every pixel in an extracted region as this additional information is useless compared to the information that is given by the contour of an object. But even the exact contour of an object is not absolutely important, since it is enough to know the angular extension $[\varphi_{\min}, \varphi_{\max}]$ and the minimum distance $r_{\min}$ to the image center of an object in the omni-directional camera image. With these two parameters, the position of the object in I_r can be estimated by inserting $r_{\min}$ into the inverse perspective mapping of equation (5.4) and the radius of the object can be calculated using the angular difference $\varphi_{\max} - \varphi_{\min}$. The type of the object or landmark can be determined according to its color class.

In this section an efficient algorithm is presented, that only extracts sequences of the same color class on scan lines of the image, clusters these sequences to regions based on the center points of the sequences, and calculates the exact position of the objects in robot-centered coordinates. To achieve maximum coverage of the relevant parts of the image while keeping the number of processed pixels as low as possible, two major innovations are introduced compared to the scan line approaches of Jüngel *et al.* [103, 102] and Röfer *et al.* [163, 164]. Firstly, the scan lines are not completely classified but sampled, too, hence further reducing the number of processed pixels. Secondly, coverage of the processed pixels in the image is not merely higher where the resolution of the image is lower which is done in the receptor approach of Bonarini *et al.* [22] or for the jump points in [100, 99]. Instead, the coverage is defined on the field where the objects and landmarks reside, by using scan lines arranged in an orthogonal grid with a resolution just high enough to cover even the smallest object on the field with at least one scan line in each direction. Although the field markings with a width of only 5 cm are the smallest objects on the field, they extend in the other direction over at least 50 cm. Therefore, the ball with a diameter of 21 cm is considered as the smallest object and defines the distance of the scan lines in the grid as 20 cm. With a resolution of 2 cm along a scan line, a grid of points is defined that uniformly covers the surrounding of the robot (cf. left side of Figure 5.7). Since the exact ball position in front of the robot is extremely important for ball handling and approaching the ball for passing and shooting, the resolution of the grid is raised to 2 cm distance between the scan lines in a sector of 120° in front of the robot. The grid is restricted to a maximum distance of 4.5 m around the robot since the omni-directional camera system has only a limited field of view with an acceptable resolution. Mapping this grid onto the image with the perspective mapping function given in equation (5.7) results in a set of pixels that cover the relevant parts of the image shown on the right side of Figure 5.7. To extract the angles to the goal and the corner posts that are beyond the limited field of view two special scan lines are introduced into the grid that form two circles near the horizon in the image. Because the goals and corner posts both are higher than the robots, the angles to both landmarks can be extracted from these circles. For a fast access to the coordinates of the grid pixels they are stored in a look-up table (GridLUT). Since parts of the robot chassis are visible in the camera image, the number of processed pixels can be further reduced by removing pixels from the GridLUT that show the robot chassis. This is done automatically by capturing a test image without any obstacles and removing all pixels that are classified as *Black*. The resulting GridLUT is shown in Figure 5.6 and contains 30,000 pixels, representing only 9% of the image pixels. Segmenting these pixels guarantees that every object in the robot's environment is covered with at least two scan lines while keeping the processed pixels at a minimum.

Along the scan lines defined by the GridLUT the image processing algorithm classifies the color values of the grid pixels into color classes according to the ColorLUT. At the same time, sequences of pixels of the same color class (segments) are identified. As these segments are the foundation of the object and landmark extraction algorithm and are used to extract the radius and position of objects, it is crucial that they extend over the complete object from one side to the other. However, sometimes objects are not always uniquely colored or reflection of the environment changes the color of an object (e. g. bright white spots on the shiny orange ball) resulting in gaps in the sequence that are mapped to a different color class. In such situations it is necessary to skip these gaps as noise and continue the segment. Thus, a fault-tolerant segmentation algorithm is needed that on the

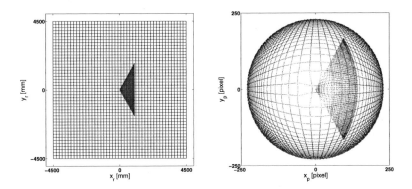

Figure 5.7: A grid of scan lines in I_r covering all relevant parts of the robot's surrounding (left) and the same grid transformed to I_p with the perspective mapping function of equation (5.7) (right).

one hand extends the segments of a color class over small gaps of a different class but on the other hand stops a segment when it reaches the edge of an object or landmark. But how can the algorithm differentiate between gaps in a segment and the edge of an object?

As similar problems are subject to ongoing research in molecular biology, the segmentation algorithm adopts an approach used for local sequence alignment of DNA or amino acid sequences in order to determine similar regions. A well-known algorithm for this approach is the *Smith-Waterman algorithm* for identification of common molecular subsequences [177]. It finds best matching substrings by comparing the nucleotides of two DNA strings one by one, assigning high scores for exact matches and lower or negative scores for unequal pairs or gaps. In the end of this process, the substring with the best score is considered as the best matching substring. This algorithm is fault-tolerant, since it allows a certain number of unequal nucleotides or gaps in the two strings. This number is based on the scores given to the compared nucleotides, which in turn are based on statistical analysis of the mutation rates from one nucleotide to another.

	C	A	T	A	A	C	G
	G	A	T	T	A	C	A
Score:	-1	+2	+2	-1	+2	+2	-3
Total:	-1	+1	+3	+2	+4	+6	+3

Table 5.1: A simplified example of the *Smith-Waterman algorithm*.

In the simplified example of the Smith-Waterman algorithm shown in Table 5.1 the nucleotide sequence *CATAACG* is searched for the best matching substring compared to the sequence *GATTACA*. The third row contains the score of the single comparisons. Obviously a mutation of a C to a G or an A to a T in this example is more likely than a mutation of a G to an A, thus resulting only in a small negative score. Starting at the highest total score given in the forth row, the best matching subsequence is backtracked to the first positive score resulting in the subsequence $ATAAC$ which contains only one non-matching nucleotide which is, however, likely to occur.

Regarding the color transformed scan lines as a DNA string, with the color class of the pixels being an identifier similar to the character of a nucleotide, substrings (segments) of a given color class can be found when comparing the scan line against a string completely filled with this color class. The algorithm assigns positive scores to pixels belonging to the same color class and negative scores to pixels of a different color class. Pixels of a different color class would usually end a segment, without considering the possibility of mappings to such classes that occur due to reflections or noise in the image. Adopting the Smith-Waterman algorithm, however, segments are extended over small gaps of pixels of a different color class.

	Green	White	Yellow	Blue	Orange	Black	Cyan	Magenta	Unknown	Max. Score
White	-3	+2	-3	-3	-3	-3	-3	-3	-1	2
Yellow	-3	-3	+2	-3	-1	-1	-1	-1	-1	30
Blue	-3	-3	-3	+2	-1	-1	-1	-1	-1	30
Orange	-3	-1	-3	-3	+2	-3	-3	-3	-1	11
Black	-3	-3	-3	-3	-3	+2	+2	+2	-1	15

Table 5.2: The scores for the different color classes used in the segmentation step. The color class of the considered segment is given from top to bottom, while the color class of the inspected grid pixel is given from left to right.

While parsing through the scan lines, the algorithm processes the different color classes in parallel. A new segment is started, if there is currently no unfinished segment of the pixel's color class. For all unfinished segments the score for this pixel, which is based on the relation of the pixel's color class and the color class of the segment, is added to a grand total for this segment. The score is +2 for pixels of the same color class, -1 for pixels of a different color class, which is known to occur frequently in segments of that color class, and -3 for pixels of a color class that is unlikely to occur in a segment of that color class. Usually pixels of a different color class get the -3 penalty, whereas the special color class *Unknown* generally gets the -1 penalty. There are some color classes, though, that are likely to occur in segments of another class. The ball in RoboCup for example is so shiny that it is very likely to contain a white spot reflecting the lights. Therefore, *Orange* segments should not end when the white spot is encountered, so only a -1 penalty is assigned to *White* pixels in *Orange* segments. Table 5.2 contains the scores for the segmentation for *White* field markings, the *Yellow* and *Blue* goals, the *Orange* ball and the *Black* robots. Because the *Cyan* and *Magenta* team colors are extracted differently and the *Green* carpet is not segmented, they do not appear in the table. The few exceptions to the general rule mentioned so far are the -1 scores for *Orange*, *Black*, and the team colors

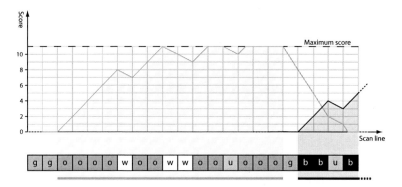

Figure 5.8: Example of a scan line being parsed by the segmentation algorithm for *Orange* (o) and *Black* (b) segments. The extracted segments are marked with a colored bar under the scan line. At the 13th and 15th pixel of the scan line the score of the *Orange* segment is clipped to its maximum score.

when searching for a goal color segment and the score of +2 for the team colors when searching for *Black* robot segments. Robots wearing team colors and the ball frequently appear in front of a goal and thus *Orange*, *Black* and the team colors receive only minor penalties. Since the goals have a width of 2 m, a goal segment can be extended over these larger gaps. When searching for robots, the *Cyan* and *Magenta* pixels of a robot's team color are treated as *Black* pixels, to segment the robot as a whole.

The number of non-matching pixels that can be skipped without finishing a segment depends on the number of matching pixels that occur before and after. Therefore the fault-tolerance would be higher for long segments, probably connecting two long segments which do not belong together. To enforce a common number of pixels that can be skipped, the score is limited to a maximum, which cannot be exceeded. This maximum score depends on the size of the objects and the grid resolution. If the segment never reached the maximum score, it is considered as too small and is dropped. The last column of Table 5.2 contains the maximum scores for the different color classes.

A segment is finished, when its score drops below zero, which is the case after a certain number of non-matching pixels occurred in a row, or when the current scan line is finished. However, the end of the segment is determined as the last position which reached the maximum score in the segment, since this is the point of the highest number of matching pixels and only some small errors in a row. Fig. 5.8 gives an example of a scan line being parsed by the segmentation algorithm.

As often the shirts of spectators or advertising panels outside of the field form perfect regions of a specific color, these segments have to be distinguished from the segments that really represent objects or landmarks on the RoboCup field. Especially for the field

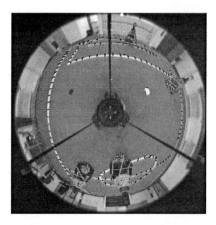

Figure 5.9: The result of the segmentation algorithm applied to the example image shown in Figure 5.1 (left). *White* field marking segments are shown as blue dots, *Black* robot segments and *Orange* ball segments are shown as green dots with red crosses highlighting the segment center points.

markings and the ball this is extremely important, as otherwise the self-localization algorithm presented in Chapter 6 has to cope with phantom field markings which are usually very predominant compared to the small field lines, and the robots could chase phantom balls outside of the field.

The main feature to retrieve the correct segments is the context of the segments. The ball and the robots of a RoboCup match are situated on a *Green* field or in front of a *Blue* or *Yellow* colored goal. Therefore, only segments that are preceded and succeeded by a certain number of *Green*, *Blue*, or *Yellow* pixels are considered as valid segments. The *White* segments are only valid field markings, if they are preceded and succeeded by *Green* pixels, as they have to be surrounded by the green carpet. Only validated segments are used for the following steps of the image processing algorithms. Figure 5.9 displays the result of the segmentation algorithm applied to the example image shown in Figure 5.1 (left).

Object and Landmark Detection

After the color segmentation, the valid segments have to be processed to extract objects and landmarks.

The self-localization algorithm presented in Chapter 6 only needs sample points of the white field markings and angles to the goals or corner posts as input data. Therefore, the pixels of a valid *White* segment are simply transformed to I_r using the inverse perspective mapping of equation (5.2). The *Blue* and *Yellow* segments extracted from the two circles

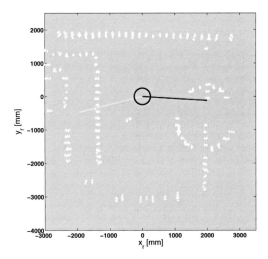

Figure 5.10: The result of the landmark extraction based on the segments shown in Figure 5.9. The *White* pixels of the field marking segments are mapped back to robot centered coordinates in I_r and the extracted angles to the blue and yellow goal are visualized as line directed towards the respective goal.

have to be classified as either a goal segment or a corner post segment. Here, the context of the segment along radial lines towards the image center is inspected. If a change occurs from *Blue* to *Yellow* or vice versa before the *Green* color of the carpet is reached, the segment belongs to one of the alternately colored corner posts. The color class nearest to the *Green* determines if the corner post is colored *Blue-Yellow-Blue* or *Yellow-Blue-Yellow* and thus the side of the field. If only one color appears along the radial line, the segment is considered a goal segment. The angle of the center point of a segment determines the angle to the goal or corner post. Figure 5.10 shows the result of the landmark extraction based on the segments shown in Figure 5.9.

The *Orange* ball segments and *Black* robot segments have to be assigned to different objects first. As the center points of segments belonging to the same object are very near to each other, a clustering algorithm based on the Euclidean distance between the center points is ideal for the assignment.

A very popular clustering approach is the *K-means* algorithm presented by MacQueen [131] that assigns the data points to a fixed number of K clusters. For that, K initial cluster centers are randomly distributed over the search space and the data points are assigned to their nearest cluster based on the Euclidean distance. The cluster centers are then updated as the mean over all data points that were assigned to the cluster and again all data points are assigned to their nearest cluster, now using the updated clusters. These steps are continued until the positions of the cluster centers do not change from one iteration to the next. Although this approach is very popular because of its simplicity, it has several drawbacks concerning the applicability to the segment clustering problem. Firstly, the result of the K-means algorithm is not deterministic, since it is prone to local minima and thus the randomly chosen initial position of the cluster centers influences the clusters that are finally extracted. Secondly, the number of iterations needed to estimate the correct cluster positions depends on the data set, resulting in extremely varying computation times that are undesirable in a system that targets a fixed maximum cycle time of 20 ms. Thirdly, the algorithm always extracts K clusters, whether this number is reasonable for the given data set or not. However, the number of robots on a RoboCup field depends on the size of the robots and not all robots are visible in the camera image at all times. Therefore, it is impossible to define a fixed number of clusters in advance. Although with the *X-means* algorithm Pelleg *et al.* [155] presented an extension to K-means that estimates the number of different clusters, this algorithm is much more time-consuming and the variation in the computation times is even higher than in the K-means approach.

Another simple and popular clustering technique is the *nearest neighbor* approach. Here, the first point forms the initial cluster. If the Euclidean distance of the second point to the first is smaller than a given threshold, the point is assigned to the same cluster. Otherwise, a new cluster is started for the second point. All consecutive data points are assigned to the cluster of their nearest neighbor, if the distance to the nearest neighbor is smaller than the threshold, or new clusters are started. The major drawback of this approach is the runtime that increases quadratically with the number of data points, since for each new data point the distance to all formerly processed data points has to be computed. Furthermore, the selection of the threshold influences the result of the clustering and should thus be handled carefully. Finally, there is no way to restrict the size of a cluster to a reasonable size and thus clusters can be arbitrarily large.

For the clustering of the segments a combination of these two clustering algorithms is used. Instead of computing the distance to all formerly processed data points, for each new data point only the distance to the next cluster is computed. The cluster center for the distance computation is constantly redefined as the mean over the points belonging to a cluster. A new data point is assigned to the nearest cluster, if the distance to the cluster center is below a threshold. Otherwise, a new cluster is started with the data point as center. Because the number of different clusters is small compared to the number of segments and bounded to the number of robots playing a RoboCup match, the number of computed distances is small, too. Concerning that aspect, the combined approach is similar to the K-means clustering. The threshold defining the maximum size of a cluster and thus controlling the number of different clusters, instead, comes from the nearest neighbor approach. However, in the RoboCup domain this parameter is easy to define,

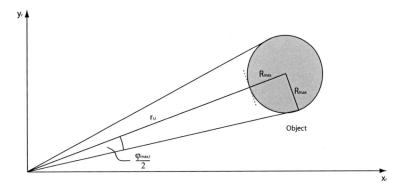

Figure 5.11: The maximum angular range occluded by an object.

because the robots have a maximum size.

With this combined approach, the segments in the image can be efficiently assigned to clusters representing the different objects on the field. However, there is another special aspect of the RoboCup domain that can be exploited to improve the efficiency of the clustering algorithm. As at least the robots of the own team are all of the same height, the mapping of such a robot in the omni-directional camera image always extends to the horizon of the image. Thus, it is impossible to detect any objects that are further away but in the same direction of a closer object.[3] Therefore, it is unnecessary to cluster the segments in the radial direction from the camera center and the clustering is only applied to the angle φ_p of the segment center points. The distance computation of the clustering algorithm is simplified to the calculation of an angular difference and the cluster center is computed as the mean angle of all points of the cluster. The threshold defining the maximum size of cluster i is then given as a maximum angular range $\varphi_{\max,i}$.

The angular range covered by an object and its corresponding cluster in the image, however, depends on the distance of the object to the robot. Objects closer to the robot cover a larger range than objects that are further away. Therefore, the threshold has to be adjusted according to the distance of the represented object to the robot. As shown in Figure 5.11

---

[3]This means that the model of the robot's environment built with the algorithms presented in Chapter 6 will be incomplete in such a situation. Yet, for path planning and collision avoidance, the obstacles further away have only little influence on the robot's movement. Furthermore, the objects are usually not static and the environment model is rebuilt in every cycle of the software system. Since the object tracking algorithms used to built the model are able to estimate the position and movement of an object over a short period of time without incorporating new measurements of the current object position, this does not impose a problem to the system.

it can be computed as

$$\varphi_{\max,i} = 2\,tan^{-1}\left(\frac{R_{\max}}{r_{r,i} + R_{\max}}\right) \qquad (5.10)$$

with $R_{\max}$ being the maximum radius of a RoboCup robot defined as 25 cm and $r_{r,i}$ being the distance to the current object in I_r, which can be computed using the inverse perspective mapping in equation (5.3). Yet, for this, the inverse perspective mapping needs the contact point of the robot to the floor in image coordinates. This is the point nearest to the image center, i.e. the point with the smallest $r_{p,i}$ of each cluster. By sorting the segment center points according to their r_p and clustering the segments starting with the lowest r_p, the threshold $\varphi_{\max,i}$ of a new cluster i is estimated as

$$\varphi_{\max,i} = 2\,tan^{-1}\left(\frac{R_{\max}}{\widehat{f}_r^{-1}(r_{p,i}) + R_{\max}}\right) \qquad (5.11)$$

where $r_{p,i}$ is the distance of the first segment center point of the new cluster to the image center.

The final algorithm can be outlined as follows, with $|\cdot|$ being the absolute value of the smaller angle difference accounting for the 2π period of angles, $\{s_0, \ldots, s_{n_s}\}$ being the set of segments to cluster:

Algorithm 1 Clustering

Returns a set of clusters $\mathbb{C}$

1: $\mathbb{C} = \{\}$; $n_c = 0$;
2: Sort all validated segments ascending according to the r_p of their center points;
3: **for** $i = 0$; $i < n_s$; $i{+}{+}$ **do**
4:      $b = -1$;
5:      **for** $j = 0$; $j < n_c$; $j{+}{+}$ **do**
6:          **if** $|\varphi_{p,i} - \varphi_j| < |\varphi_{p,i} - \varphi_b|$ **then**
7:              $b = j$;
8:          **end if**
9:      **end for**
10:     **if** $(\mathbb{C} = \{\})\ \|\ (b == -1)$ **then**
11:         Initialize a new cluster $c_{n_c} = \{s_i\}$ with $\varphi = \varphi_{p,i}$;
12:         Compute the threshold for this cluster according to equation (5.11);
13:         $\mathbb{C} \cup c$;
14:         $n_c{+}{+}$;
15:     **else**
16:         $c_b \cup s_i$;
17:         Recompute φ_b as mean over all φ_p contained in c_b;
18:     **end if**
19: **end for**

Although the validated ball segments usually all represent the true ball, the clustering step is applied to the *Orange* segments, too. Any additional clusters are treated as additional hypotheses of the ball, if the algorithm really extracts more than one ball cluster. The object tracking algorithm described in Chapter 6 then selects the correct hypothesis for the ball based on the history of the past measurements of the ball's position. Since the ball has only a height of 21 cm the clustering algorithm for ball segments also considers a distance threshold $r_{p,\max}$ when assigning segments to the nearest cluster. Only segments that have a small deviation in r_p to the minimum distance of the cluster compared to $r_{p,\max}$ are assigned to an existing cluster. This also means, that objects behind a ball can be detected as well.

Figures 5.12 and 5.13 visualize a sequence of intermediate steps as well as the final result of the clustering algorithm applied to the segments shown in Figure 5.9.

From the segments of the extracted clusters, the real world position and radius of the represented objects can be computed. Using the inverse perspective mapping the distance of the object to the robot can be computed as

$$r_{r,i} = \widehat{f}_r^{-1}(r_{p,\min,i}) + R_i \tag{5.12}$$

To compute the radius of the object represented by cluster i, equation (5.11) is transformed and solved for the radius

$$R_i = \widehat{f}_r^{-1}(r_{p,\min,i}) \frac{tan(\frac{\varphi_i}{2})}{1 - tan(\frac{\varphi_i}{2})} \tag{5.13}$$

Compared to equation (5.11) where the maximum angular threshold of a cluster was estimated using the segment center points, these equations utilize the correct values for the angular range φ_i covered by the segments in cluster i and the real world distance of the object to the robot using the point in the segments of cluster i with minimal distance $r_{p,\min,i}$ to the image center.

A final verification procedure follows the object generation to remove very small objects and to divide robot objects that are too large compared to the maximum size of a robot. Because there exists not only a maximum size but also a minimum size for the RoboCup robots, objects that are smaller than this minimum size are discarded as noise. Small clusters of *Black* segments are sometimes detected at shadows of the crossbar of the goal or at shadows under the ball. With this verification step such clusters are removed from the list of detected objects. On the other hand, robots are sometimes standing in a group next to each other. The segmentation step then produces large segments extending over more than one robot which are clustered into one big cluster. The objects generated from these clusters can be divided into several smaller objects, approximately representing the objects of the group of robots. As shown in Figure 5.14 such an object is divided into two objects of a radius less than half the radius of the large object. The two smaller objects cover the same angular range and start at the same distance. Using the theorem

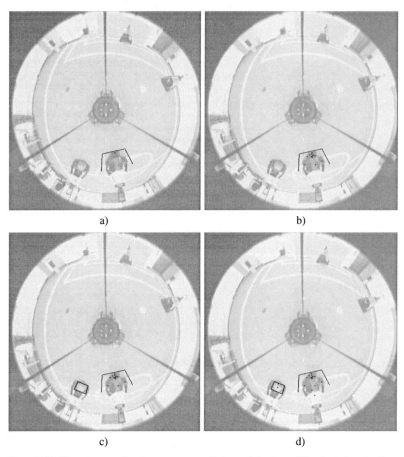

a)   b)

c)   d)

Figure 5.12: These images visualize a sequence of intermediate steps of the clustering algorithm applied to the segment center points extracted by the segmentation algorithm (cf. Figure 5.9). In step a) the first cluster shown as a red bucket with the angular threshold $\varphi_{\max,1}$ defining the outer lines is generated by the first segment center point. This cluster is filled with more points in b) until in step c) a ball cluster is started from the first ball segment and is finally completed in step d). The sequence of intermediate steps is continued in Figure 5.13.

on intersecting lines, the new object radius is computed as

$$R_1 = \frac{r_r R_0}{2r_r + R_0} \qquad (5.14)$$

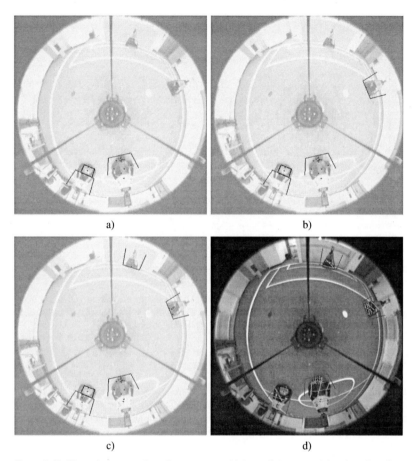

Figure 5.13: These images continue the sequence of intermediate steps of the clustering algorithm applied to the segment center points extracted by the segmentation algorithm (cf. Figure
5.9) started in Figure 5.12. In step a) a new object cluster is opened as the examined segment
center point does not fit into the threshold of the first cluster. In the next steps the clustering
proceeds with the remaining segments. The final result of the clustering is shown in image d).

This subdivision of larger objects is iteratively done until the new object radius R_1 is
smaller than the maximum robot radius.

In the end of the object detection process, the team color of the robot objects is extracted
by starting a radial search for *Cyan* or *Magenta* pixels at each object's position in the

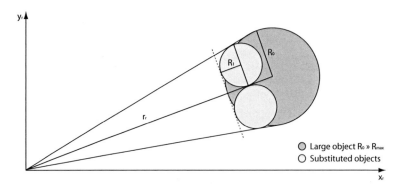

Figure 5.14: Large objects that occur if a group of robots is extracted as one cluster with long segments are divided into two objects of a radius less than half the radius of the large object. The two smaller objects cover the same angular range and start at the same distance. This subdivision is iteratively done until the new object radius is smaller than the maximum robot radius.

image. Figure 5.15 shows the final result of the object extraction process based on the example image shown in Figure 5.1 (left).

The right side of Figure 5.1 shows the landmarks and objects mapped to robot centered world coordinates. Extensive experimental results covering the accuracy and efficiency of the landmark and object detection algorithm are given in Section 5.3.

5.2.2   Automatic Camera Calibration

The results of the presented image processing algorithm depend on the accuracy of the camera calibration in many ways. If the mapping functions from image to robot centered world coordinates and vice versa were inaccurate, the position estimation of the extracted objects in world coordinates would be of low quality. It is even possible that the algorithm completely fails to detect a small object or landmark, since the assumption of covering any object and landmark with at least one scan line would then be unsustainable. An inaccurate color calibration, on the other hand, imposes the problem that the contact point of an object to the floor might not be extracted in the segmentation process, since the pixel is not classified as *Black*, again lowering the quality of the estimated position of the object.

Besides the development of fault tolerant image processing algorithms and probabilistic object tracking and self-localization algorithms the Attempto Tübingen Robot Soccer Team tried to improve the precision of the calibration result by spending a lot of time to the manual calibration of the cameras. However, this not only increased the setup time prior to a RoboCup tournament but also drastically reduced the time spent on the devel-

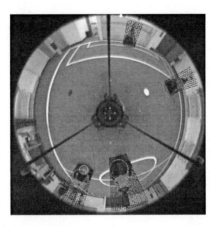

Figure 5.15: The final result of the object extraction process based on the example image shown in Figure 5.1 (left). The circles represent the extracted objects, ball objects are orange, robot objects are cyan or magenta according to the extracted team color. The team color is extracted by inspecting the pixels of radial lines, shown as blue dots, for the team colors. If enough pixels of one team color are found (red dots), the object is classified as robot of the corresponding team.

opment of the robot and software system. Especially at the test field of the team, the illumination was low and constantly changing, which made the color calibration a long and annoying task, trying to separate dark green from dark blue and black. Moreover, it had to be constantly repeated.

Out of this situation the vision of a calibration-free robot arose. The basic idea was to put the robot on the field and exploit knowledge of the well-structured RoboCup environment to let it do the calibration automatically. Two algorithms, developed in the context of a diploma thesis [172], are presented in the following sections that push the software system of the Attempto Tübingen Robot Soccer Team towards this goal. Firstly, an *Evolutionary Algorithm (EA)* [15] is used to estimate the inverse perspective mapping function. For that, the white field markings that are extracted from a camera image taken by the robot at a predefined pose are mapped back to world coordinates and are matched with a model of the field lines. The parameters of the inverse perspective mapping function are changed by the EA until the extracted markings agree with the lines in the model. Since the white markings in the image are identified based on the local difference in contrast, thus without using color information, and the position of the robot is known, this method requires no user input and no special calibration pattern. In a second approach, the same image is used in combination with the newly calibrated mapping function to compute the part of the field to which a pixel corresponds according to the field model. By mapping the color of the pixel to the color class of the corresponding landmark, a ColorLUT can be trained automatically, containing all colors apart from the ball color and the team colors. These colors still have to be trained by hand, however, the calibration time is reduced drastically. Furthermore, the method is able to recalibrate the colors on-line during the game play and thus to react to changes in the illumination.

Automatic Geometry Calibration

In order to automate the geometry calibration method presented in the previous section, the algorithm needs a set of corresponding points in I_p and I_r to fit a function through these data. In contrast to the majority of different calibration methods presented in Section 5.1 the automatic geometry calibration algorithm of the Attempto Tübingen Robot Soccer Team operates without the need for a special calibration pattern. Instead it uses an image of the omni-directional camera system that was taken by the robot while standing at a specific predefined pose on a RoboCup field (shown on the left side of Figure 5.16) to do the calibration. Since the position of the field markings on the RoboCup field and the pose of the robot is known, the algorithm can compute the relative positions of the markings in I_r. By mapping the extracted markings in the image with the inverse perspective mapping function and changing the parameters of the function with an Evolutionary Algorithm until the extracted markings fit onto the computed positions, the mapping function is estimated and thus the DistanceLUT is generated. In this regard, the approach is similar to the calibration method of Egorova *et al.* [48] that was developed for the overhead camera of the RoboCup Small-Size League.

To make sure that the algorithm finds corresponding points at all distances, the robot is placed in the middle of the field 1.5 m away from the center point in the direction of the blue goal with its Y_r-axis pointing towards the middle of the blue goal, away from the center point (cf. left side of Figure 5.16). At this position the markings of the center line and the center circle exhibit enough information in the close-up range, while the touch lines are wide enough to be extracted even at higher distances for information at the limits of the mapping function. All pixels of the image which are in a certain distance to the image center $r_p < r_{p,\max}$ are inspected to find enough markings for a good estimation of the mapping function. The classification of the image pixels as field marking, however, is not done based on color, because there is no ColorLUT at this point in the automatic calibration procedure. Pixels are rather classified as field markings, if they have a high contrast in the R- and B-component of the RGB color space compared to their surrounding

$$R_{x,y} + B_{x,y} > \kappa \sum_{i=x-2}^{x+2} \sum_{j=y-2}^{y+2} R_{i,j} B_{i,j} \qquad (5.15)$$

This turns out to classify best the white markings on the green floor. The necessary conversion to an RGB color value is only used in the off-line calibration and is therefore not critical for the cycle time of the software system.

With these points the calibration algorithm approximates the inverse perspective mapping function as defined in the equations (5.4) to (5.6). In contrast to the polynomial of degree five that was fitted through the corresponding points in the manual calibration method, the automatic calibration method uses a second order polynomial term to model the characteristics of the mapping function in the close-up range, while an exponential term is used to model the infinite slope of the mapping near the horizon

$$\widehat{f}_r^{-1}(\widetilde{r}_p, \mathbf{x}) = (x_0 \exp{(x_1 + x_2\widetilde{r}_p{}^2)} + x_3\widetilde{r}_p{}^2 + x_4\widetilde{r}_p + x_5)x_6 \qquad (5.16)$$

where $\mathbf{x} = \begin{bmatrix} x_0 & \dots & x_8 \end{bmatrix}^T$ is the decision vector of nine parameters of the mapping function. The last two parameters of the vector encode the center point of the mirror $\begin{bmatrix} x_{p,c} & y_{p,c} \end{bmatrix}^T$ used to compute $\widetilde{r}_p$ and $\widetilde{\varphi}_p$ in equations (5.5) and (5.6).

The individuals of the Evolutionary Algorithm represent possible parameter sets or values of the decision vector. To assess the quality of the mapping function described with the parameter set of an individual, the fitness of an individual is computed proportional to the number of field marking points that are mapped to the coordinate of a field line in the model. The EA that performed best on this problem was a *(2,100)-Evolution Strategy* using lazy evaluation and a novel particle mutation operator that performs a local search to identify the most promising direction for the mutation. The details of the algorithm used for the optimization of the mapping function, however, are beyond the scope of this thesis. Figure 5.16 and Section 5.3 merely contain the experimental results influencing the performance of the robotic system. For more information on the optimization algorithm, the interested reader is directed to a publication containing a comparison of different Evolutionary Algorithms applied to this optimization task, the presentation of the novel mutation operator and several experiments on the parameterization of the algorithm [86]. Further information can be found in the master thesis on the automatic calibration algorithms of the team [172].

Automatic Color Calibration

For the automatic color calibration, the same reference pose was used as for the calibration of the camera geometry (shown on the left side of Figure 5.16). The color calibration algorithm compiles a ColorLUT using the known pose of the robot, the automatically calibrated DistanceLUT, and a model of the RoboCup field to compute the expected color class for the pixels. The expected color class for a pixel replaces the ground truth given by a human during the manual calibration. As there will obviously be errors in the computation of the expected color class, e. g. black robots on the field where the static model expects green floor, the algorithm does not make a direct mapping from color values to the computed color classes. Instead, the algorithm models clusters of the color classes in the color space with a mean value and standard deviation, to filter out such errors. Only colors of pixels that fit into an ellipsoid defined by a three-dimensional Gaussian in the color space are added to the look-up table. In addition, colors of pixels that correspond to coordinates outside of the playable field are removed from the look-up table. These pixels do not correspond to any part of the RoboCup field and would thus decrease the accuracy of the following algorithms if mapped to one of the color classes. The removal is only

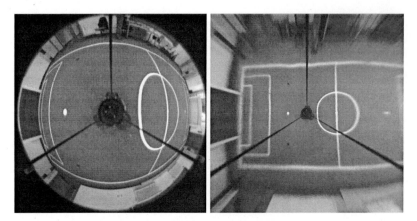

Figure 5.16: An example image taken at the specified pose at the center circle (left) and the same image mapped to world coordinates with the inverse perspective mapping function that results from the automatic geometry calibration method applied to this image (right).

done for color values outside of another ellipsoid, to keep a minimum configuration for each color class. The center of the two ellipsoids of color class k is defined as the mean value of the colors that should belong to the color class $\boldsymbol{\mu}_k = \begin{bmatrix} \mu_{x,k} & \mu_{y,k} & \mu_{z,k} \end{bmatrix}^T$, while the equatorial radii of the ellipsoids are defined as a multiple of the respective standard deviations $\boldsymbol{\sigma}_k = \begin{bmatrix} \sigma_{x,k} & \sigma_{y,k} & \sigma_{z,k} \end{bmatrix}^T$ along the axis of the color space

$$E_{add,k} : \frac{(x - \mu_{x,k})^2}{(\zeta \sigma_{x,k})^2} + \frac{(y - \mu_{y,k})^2}{(\zeta \sigma_{y,k})^2} + \frac{(z - \mu_{z,k})^2}{(\zeta \sigma_{z,k})^2} = 1 \qquad (5.17)$$

$$E_{rem,k} : \frac{(x - \mu_{x,k})^2}{(\xi \sigma_{x,k})^2} + \frac{(y - \mu_{y,k})^2}{(\xi \sigma_{y,k})^2} + \frac{(z - \mu_{z,k})^2}{(\xi \sigma_{z,k})^2} = 1 \qquad (5.18)$$

To generate a ColorLUT for the image taken at the reference pose it would be possible to classify each pixel according to the model and to compute the mean and standard deviations of each color class. Based on the ellipsoids, the ColorLUT could be generated by adding colors inside the first ellipsoid and removing unwanted colors from outside the field that lie outside the second. This would be similar to the approach presented by Sridharan and Stone [183]. However, to make the algorithm adaptive and thus the image processing algorithm robust to changing illuminations, the color calibration needs to be done on-line in each cycle of the software system to adapt the parameters of the color clusters. Therefore, only a subset of the image pixels is examined to estimate the new mean and standard deviation of the color values of a color class in the current image. For the addition and the removal of color mappings different subsets are chosen. This speeds up the algorithm to perform the adaptation of an existing ColorLUT within the 20 ms cycle. After an initial ColorLUT was trained with this algorithm, using the image taken at the reference pose, it is then possible to use the self-localization algorithm presented in Chapter 6 to estimate the pose of the robot. In turn, this pose is used by the color calibration algorithm to compute the expected color class for a pixel even for a moving robot.

However, the use of self-localization for the automatic color training results in a mutual dependency, since there can be no self-localization without the extraction of color coded landmarks and there will be no color-based landmark detection without a pose estimation of the self-localization. Yet, the extraction of the green and the white color class is robust enough to cope with a sudden change in illumination as shown in the worst case experiments in Section 5.3. This enables the robust self-localization to keep track of the correct pose of the robot until the other color classes are adapted.

A cycle of the automatic color calibration algorithm contains the following steps:

1. Obtain a new image and a new robot pose estimation

2. Select a subset of image pixels to adapt the cluster for each color class

3. Select a different subset of pixels to add colors to the look-up table

4. Select a different subset of pixels to remove colors from the look-up table

For the initial ColorLUT, the robot is simply put on the reference pose and several cycles of the algorithm are performed until the parameters of the color clusters are settled. Compared to an examination of the complete pixels of an image from the reference pose, this approach has the advantage that the pixel noise of the CCD camera is taken into account.

The computation of the expected color classes using the estimated pose of the robot and the DistanceLUT works fine for the floor and the lines, because the mapping is trained for the field plane. Every pixel that corresponds to coordinates inside of the field is either classified as white field line or green floor, according to the field model. Since green is the predominant color in an image of a RoboCup field, situations where the static model computes a different color class for a green pixel are very uncommon, even if the pose estimation from the self-localization is not accurate. Therefore, the mapping of colors that are already marked as green cannot be changed. White, however, is very rare in the image but has the main influence on the landmark-based self-localization. Small deviations in the position and the orientation of the pose estimation may already result in a completely wrong mapping from colors to this class. Therefore, a special treatment is used for pixels that are mapped to the white class according to the model. According to the constraint that was already defined in equation (5.15) only those pixels that have a higher intensity than their surrounding are ultimately used to train white.

Objects and landmarks like the two goals extend into the third dimension and thus only the contact points of these objects to the floor can be mapped correctly. Starting with these pixels, however, there is usually a clearly defined region of the image that displays the rest of the object, depending on the camera system used. In case of an omni-directional camera system this region would be a trapezoid for the goals. Only pixels inside this area are mapped to one of the goal color classes, yellow and blue. Because the other robots on the field are not static, the black color class is trained using only pixels that correspond to the black chassis of the robot itself. The ball color, though, is a problem for a completely automatic algorithm, since the ball is not static, too, and there is no way of training the ball color without some previous knowledge about the color or position of the ball. One possibility to overcome this problem would be to have a special color marker of the ball color on the robot itself. But since RoboCup robots are not allowed to expose the ball color, this marker must be hidden such that other robots will not get distracted, but at the same time be illuminated enough to reproduce the real ball color. The other possibility would be to define a base color which represents the real ball color good enough to initially locate the ball on the field. From this point onwards, the predicted ball position could be used to retrain the ball color similar to the color of the goals or the robots, as done e. g. in Gönner *et al.* [69].

Finally, all pixels that are mapped to a position outside of the field are assigned to the special color class *Unknown*.

For each color class k, the algorithm tracks a cluster in the color space with a mean value μ_k and a standard deviation σ_k resulting from the previous cycles. For color values

$$\mathbf{c} = \begin{bmatrix} x_c & y_c & z_c \end{bmatrix}^T \in [0, C_{max}]^3, \tag{5.19}$$

the parameters of the different clusters are initialized as

$$\mu_{k,0} = \frac{1}{2} \begin{bmatrix} C_{max} & C_{max} & C_{max} \end{bmatrix}^T \tag{5.20}$$

$$\sigma_{k,0} = \frac{\sqrt{3}}{2} \begin{bmatrix} C_{max} & C_{max} & C_{max} \end{bmatrix}^T \tag{5.21}$$

for $t = 0$ and are updated in each cycle as follows.

A random set of pixels of the image is taken to update the clusters. To save computation time, the algorithm uses a fixed pattern of every 400th pixel, starting at a random pixel. According to the estimated pose of the robot and the static field model the expected color class of all these pixels is computed considering the special treatments of green and white. Given the set of colors $X_{k,t} = \{\mathbf{c}_1, \ldots, \mathbf{c}_m\}$ at cycle t of all pixels that are expected to belong to color class k the new values are computed as

$$\mu_{k,t} = \frac{1}{\eta + 1} \left(\eta \, \mu_{k,t-1} + \frac{1}{m} \sum_{i=1}^{m} \mathbf{c}_i \right) \tag{5.22}$$

$$\sigma_{k,t} = \frac{1}{\eta + 1} \left(\eta \, \sigma_{k,t-1} + \sqrt{\frac{1}{m-1} \sum_{i=1}^{m} \left(\mathbf{c}_i - \frac{1}{m} \sum_{i=1}^{m} \mathbf{c}_i \right)^2} \right) \tag{5.23}$$

The choice of η determines the responsiveness of the color look-up table update. A value of $\eta = 4$ was empirically determined as optimal, enabling the algorithm to extremely reduce the number of examined pixels. Values of $\eta < 4$ for the filtering result in quicker adaptation of the table but also in a very noisy estimation of the cluster parameters. In order to avoid the cluster from collapsing, a lower bound σ_{min} for the standard deviations along the three axes of the color space is introduced, ensuring a minimum cluster size. If sudden changes in illumination occur, it is possible that the cluster is too small to include the new color values. In such cases the set of color values for a color class is empty, and the standard deviation is doubled

$$\mu_{k,t} = \mu_{k,t-1} \tag{5.24}$$
$$\sigma_{k,t} = 2\,\sigma_{k,t-1} \tag{5.25}$$

to increase the size of the cluster until it includes the new color values. The resulting clusters do not specify the colors that are finally stored in the color look-up table for the associated color class. They are rather a hint, where the color values of the color class might be located in the color space, however, they can be arbitrarily distributed around the cluster center and part of the cluster may belong to another color class.

To find out which color values are finally mapped to the different color classes, again a subset of every 400th image pixel is selected, starting at a different random pixel. After the calculation of the expected color classes, each color value is compared to the mean value of the corresponding color class. Given a color value $\mathbf{c} = \begin{bmatrix} x_c & y_c & z_c \end{bmatrix}^T$ that is computed to belong to color class k, the mapping from $\mathbf{c}$ to k is only added to the look-up table if

$$\frac{(x_c - \mu_{x,k})^2}{\sigma_{x,k}^2} + \frac{(y_c - \mu_{y,k})^2}{\sigma_{y,k}^2} + \frac{(z_c - \mu_{z,k})^2}{\sigma_{z,k}^2} < \zeta^2, \text{ with } \zeta > 1 \tag{5.26}$$

with ζ being a threshold controlling the ratio between higher adaptability of the color look-up table and a higher false positive rate. The influence of this parameter is investigated through experiments in Section 5.3. Similar to the manual training of the look-up table not only the color value itself is added into the table but also a small set of colors around $\mathbf{c}$.

Sometimes the manual or automatic addition of such a set of color values is too much, resulting for example in many occurrences of the white color class outside of the field. Therefore, after the addition of the color mappings to the look-up table, colors that are mapped to the special *Unknown* class are removed from the table. Once again a different subset of pixels is selected to do this. To process a large number of pixels outside of the field, every 20th pixel is used, starting from a random pixel. The higher number of processed pixels is also necessary to completely remove unwanted color mappings, as only the color value itself is removed from the color look-up table. A color value $\mathbf{c}$ that is expected to belong to the *Unknown* class in this step but that is already mapped to color

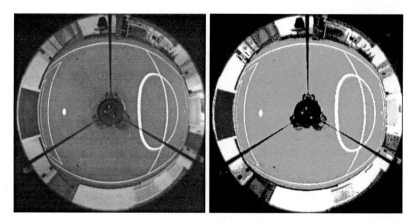

Figure 5.17: The example image of Figure 5.16 (left) classified with an automatically calibrated ColorLUT (right).

class k is removed from the table, if

$$\frac{(x_c - \mu_{x,k})^2}{\sigma_{x,k}^2} + \frac{(y_c - \mu_{y,k})^2}{\sigma_{y,k}^2} + \frac{(z_c - \mu_{z,k})^2}{\sigma_{z,k}^2} > \xi^2, \quad \text{with } \xi > 1 \qquad (5.27)$$

with ξ being a threshold controlling the ratio between a lower false positive rate and lower true positive rate. The influence of ξ is investigated in Section 5.3 which also contains experimental results concerning the influence of the algorithm on the performance of the robotic system. Figure 5.17 again shows the calibration image of Figure 5.16 (left) and the same image classified with an automatically calibrated ColorLUT (right).

5.3   Results

This section contains the experimental results for the image processing algorithms. First of all, the landmark and object extraction result of the basic image processing algorithm applied to the example image shown on the left side in Figure 5.1 are examined concerning the accuracy and the processing speed. Additional experiments investigate the overall performance of the image processing algorithm concerning the object detection by estimating the mean error and the standard deviation. The applicability of the automatic camera calibration techniques presented in Section 5.2.2 is shown in a second series of experiments. Finally, the results of the object extraction using different combinations of automatic and manual calibration methods are compared.

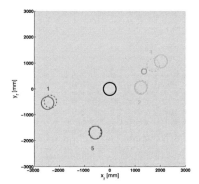

Figure 5.18: A comparison of the real object positions for the scene shown in Figure 5.1 (left) and the object data extracted by the image processing algorithm.

5.3.1 Results of the Basic Algorithm

Figure 5.18 shows the objects extracted from the example image shown on the left side in Figure 5.1 mapped back to robot centered world coordinates in I_r and compared to the real object positions. Full circles represent the position estimations of the image processing algorithm, while dashed circles represent the real positions. The circle colors show the extracted and the real object type (ball, robot of the cyan/magenta team). According to Table 5.5, the two nearest objects (number 2 cyan and number 5 magenta) are estimated with a position error of only 25-50 mm, measured as the Euclidean distance between the real and the estimated object position. The estimated ball even has a position error of only 13 mm. For the most distant object, the goalkeeper (number 1 magenta) with a distance of 2.71 m to the robot, the position error increases to 124 mm for two reasons. Firstly, the estimation error increases with the distance to the robot. One reason for this is, that the DistanceLUT is only an approximation of the real inverse perspective mapping function of the camera system with an approximation error that rises towards the horizon of the mapping, where the infinite slope of the real mapping function cannot be modeled. However, this results in an underestimation of the distance to the robot, whereas the goalkeeper's distance is overestimated. In this case there is second reason for the estimation error that outweighs the first. The shovel-shaped aluminum sheet that is used as a kicker on the goal keeper reflects the ceiling lights and is therefore not classified as *Black*. Thus, the segmentation of the *Black* robot is started above the kicker and the contact point of the object to the floor plane is not correctly identified, resulting in a higher estimated distance as shown for point B in Figure 5.2. Finally, the distance to the object keeping the ball (number 4 cyan) is overestimated, too, for the same reason. The ball is occluding the

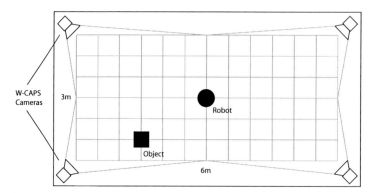

Figure 5.19: The experimental setup for estimating the accuracy of the object detection algorithm using the W-CAPS system [125] to generate the ground truth data. The sensing robot was located at the center of the detection area and a second robot was placed as an object at different positions that approximately formed a grid. More than 100 measurements were taken with the W-CAPS and the robot vision system at each position.

contact point of the robot which is thus mapped to a distance more than 340 mm too far. However, with a mean error of 110.77 mm per object in this example, the object detection algorithm is suitable for the RoboCup scenario. The extracted object coordinates and the exact corresponding measurement errors are listed in Table 5.5 and are compared to the results obtained using different combinations of manually and automatically calibrated look-up tables at the end of Section 5.3.2.

Although the error increasing with the distance to the robot is outweighed by the error resulting from an erroneous detection of the contact point, the first error is systematic and thus mainly influences the accuracy of the landmark and object detection system. Therefore, the magnitude of this error is investigated in a second experiment, where the position estimations of the image processing algorithm were compared to a ground truth generated by the absolute positioning system W-CAPS [125]. For this, one robot was placed at the center of the detection area of the W-CAPS system and a second robot was placed as an object at different positions that approximately formed a grid (cf. Figure 5.19). More than 100 measurements were taken with the W-CAPS and the robot vision system at each position. The position estimates from the W-CAPS were averaged to serve as the ground truth and the algorithm's estimates were compared to this value resulting in an estimation error according to the Euclidean distance. The mean estimation error at the different positions linearly interpolated over the whole area is shown in the error surface in Figure 5.20. The average of the mean errors over all positions is 82 mm, with values ranging from 7 mm to 600 mm. It is thus even lower than the mean estimation error for the example image in the previous experiment. As can be seen, the system is very accurate

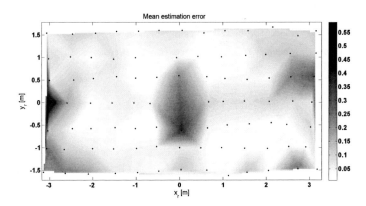

Figure 5.20: The experimental results concerning the accuracy of the object detection algorithm according to the setup shown in Figure 5.19. The error surface shows the linearly interpolated mean estimation error at the different ground truth positions marked as black dots.

in all directions in a range of 0.7m to 3m around the robot showing that the rotational symmetry constraint is fulfilled, whereas for distances of more than 3m the estimation error rises. The high estimation errors near the robot again result from occlusion, because the contact point between the object and the floor was concealed by the robot's body. The maximum estimation errors at the border positions, however, stem from a combination of the high estimation error of the algorithm at higher distances and problems of the W-CAPS system to locate the robot with at least two cameras, resulting in a low quality ground truth.

Besides the approximation error of the DistanceLUT towards the horizon, there is another reason for the increasing error. Although the GridLUT generated with the perspective mapping defined in equation (5.7) was designed to cover each object in the image with the same number of grid points, this is not possible for more distant objects. For the outer regions of the omni-directional camera image, the spatial resolution of the ground plane is lower than for the image center. Several grid points of the equally spaced grid in I_r are therefore mapped back to the same pixel in I_p, extremely reducing the resolution of the grid and thus raising the estimation error. This effect is demonstrated with another experiment regarding the variance of the position estimations. Here, the target object was measured in a distance of 0.65 m to 5.0 m along the X_r-axis in steps of 50 mm. Each position was measured 1000 times to give a sound result for the estimation variance. Figure 5.21 shows the results of the experiment. At distances over 3 m points of the grid are mapped to the same image pixels because of the reduced spatial resolution of the image. Accordingly, the variance of the distance estimation shows several irregular peaks that diverge from a smooth variance curve, starting at 3 m. The irregular peaks are due to interference between the discrete regular grid and the discrete sampling of the image, since only at distinct distances several grid points are mapped to the same image pixel.

Figure 5.21 contains another result concerning the accuracy of the segmentation algorithm that is responsible for the correct detection of the main object parameters. The green dashed line in this figure shows the variance curve of the distance estimation for a hypothetic standard deviation of $3\sigma_p = 1.5$ pixel over the whole measurement range. For that, the standard deviation σ_r in I_r was computed as

$$3\sigma_r(r_r) = \frac{f_r^{-1}(f_r(r_r) + 3\sigma_p) - f_r^{-1}(f_r(r_r) - 3\sigma_p)}{2} \tag{5.28}$$

This curve is a very good approximation of the real variance, even at distances greater than 3 m if the additional peaks of the low image resolution error are neglected. Obviously, the contact point of the object to the ground that is used for the calculation of the object distance r_r is detected with a very low and constant maximum error of only 1.5 pixel in 99.7 % of the measurements (three sigma interval). The red dashed line in Figure 5.21 is a good approximation for the peaks in the variance at distances greater than 3 m. It corresponds to a hypothetic standard deviation of $3\sigma_p = 2.5$ pixel, showing that at positions where two grid points are mapped to the same pixel, the additional estimation error is only 1 pixel.

In addition to the high accuracy of the object and landmark detection, the algorithm should be very fast in terms of the computation time, since the whole software system is synchronized to the cycle time of the image processing algorithm. Since the omni-directional camera system is the only sensor of the new robots, a computation time of up to 10 ms on the on-board computer, i. e. 50 % of the target cycle time of 20 ms, would be acceptable for the extraction of the relevant data from an image. Table 5.3 contains the mean cycle time for the different steps of the image processing algorithm applied to the example image of Figure 5.1, averaged over 1000 cycles on an Intel Pentium 4 computer with 3 GHz and 512 MB RAM[4]. It shows, that for this example image, the time constraints are maintained with a wide margin left. However, what happens if the look-up tables change, the image is different and there are more objects on the field?

Color Segmentation	Clustering	Size Constraints	Total
3.72 ms	1.02 ms	0.61 ms	5.35 ms

Table 5.3: The mean cycle time for the different steps of the image processing algorithm. The first step includes the classification and segmentation of the complete grid. The second step contains the clustering of the segments and the third step covers the application of the size constraints and the mapping to I_r. The last column presents the total cycle time including the data transfer to the shared memory.

---

[4]Such off-line experiments could not be done on the on-board computer of the robots with their extremely reduced operating system. Therefore, a desktop computer with comparable processing power was used.

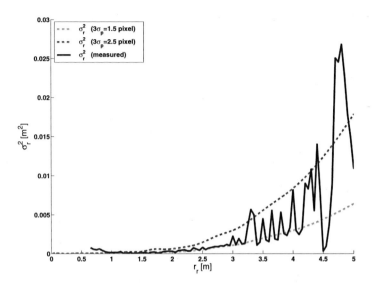

Figure 5.21: The variance of the position estimation of the object detection algorithm. The green and the red dashed line correspond to a hypothetic standard deviation of $3\sigma_p = 1.5$ pixel and $3\sigma_p = 2.5$ pixel, respectively.

To answer this question the *big-O notation* [19] offers a good solution. Here, the big-O notation is used to estimate the maximum processing time of the image processing algorithms, depending on the problem size n, where $O(n)$ means that the processing time is maximally rising linearly with the problem size. Concerning the steps of the image processing algorithm this notation helps to estimate the change of processing time for different scenarios and thus to assess the compliance to the required maximum runtime. The color segmentation of the image includes the classification and segmentation of the complete grid and is the most expensive step of the basic image processing algorithm. The cycle time of this step can be estimated as $O(n_g)$ where n_g is the number of grid points that only depends on the DistanceLUT used to generate the grid and is about the same for all kinds of different mappings. The clustering step includes two subtasks, the sorting of all segments and the clustering itself. For the sorting of the segments the *introsort* algorithm for lists from the *C++ Standard Template Library* is used which has a runtime of $O(n_s\log n_s)$, where n_s is the number of extracted *Black* and *Orange* segments. The clustering itself has a linear runtime $O(n_s)$, as already derived in section 5.2.1. In total, the runtime estimation of the clustering step is therefore $O(n_s\log n_s)$ and depends on the number of extracted *Black* and *Orange* segments. This number, however, can change from image to image. The worst case scenario for the runtime of the clustering step would be an alternating pattern of *Black* or *Orange* and *Green* areas in the image. This could happen, if the robot is surrounded by lots of other robots and the ball. The maximum number of segments is therefore limited to a multiple of the maximum number of segments for one robot, because the number of players on a RoboCup field is limited, too. Furthermore, the number of segments per robot should be more or less the same over the whole image, because of the regular grid. It is thus assumed, that the worst-case number of segments is three times higher than that for the example image containing four robots and the ball, given a maximum number of 12 robots on a RoboCup field. Assuming that the number of segments extracted from the example image was N_s, the maximum runtime of the clustering step could be estimated as

$$3N_s\log(3N_s) = 3(N_s\log3 + N_s\log N_s) < 6N_s\log N_s, \forall N_s > 3 \qquad (5.29)$$

and accordingly the maximum runtime is estimated as 6.12 ms. The last step containing the application of the size constraints to the object clusters and the mapping to world coordinates depends on the number of clusters n_c. The runtime for this step rises linearly with n_c, as the recursive subdivision of the objects is bound to a maximum given by the maximum robot radius $R_{\max}$. The worst-case runtime for this step is thus three times higher than the measured runtime for the example image, i.e. 1.83 ms, since there are maximally three times more robots on a RoboCup field. For the subdivision of large objects, the worst-case scenario is one big object cluster formed by the maximum number of 12 robots standing next to each other. Such a cluster has to be subdivided into at least 12 smaller clusters resulting in 15 subdivisions for a total of 16 object clusters, because of the binary subdivision. Although the objects in the example image were separated and no subdivision occurred, it is still possible to estimate the runtime for this worst-case, because the most time-consuming part of the subdivision is the calculation of the object radius, which was done once for each of the four objects in the example image to check the size constraint. During the subdivision of the large object, the radius of 31 intermediate objects has to be calculated, resulting in a maximum runtime four times higher than the measured runtime for the example image, i.e. 2.44 ms. However, for this worst-case, the number of segments for the clustering step would be much lower than calculated for the clustering worst-case, reducing the runtime for the clustering step. Summing up the worst-case runtime for all steps, the image processing algorithm is estimated to stay below a maximum runtime of 12 ms. This would be slightly more than the target maximum runtime of 10 ms. However, the average runtime should be far below the target runtime, since usually only half of the maximum number of robots are visible in an image. Furthermore the 10 ms are only an artificial runtime limit that could be exceeded in exceptional cases like a worst-case scenario without influencing the system cycle time of 20 ms.

5.3.2 Results of the Automatic Camera Calibration

This section analyzes the influence of the automatic camera calibration algorithms on the image processing system. Firstly, further experimental results show the fundamental applicability of the algorithms to different RoboCup scenarios including the example image shown on the left side of Figure 5.1. Secondly, the results of the image processing algorithm using the different combinations of manually and automatically calibrated look-up tables are compared.

Automatic Geometry Calibration Results

Figure 5.16 presents the successful application of the automatic geometry calibration method to an example image that was generated with the omni-directional camera system of the new omni-directional robots on the 5x11 m² test field of the Attempto Tübingen Robot Soccer Team. In addition, Figures 5.22 and 5.23 show that the algorithm is also suitable for different field sizes and camera systems. The image shown on the left side of Figure 5.22 was taken by the PAL camera system of an old Pioneer2 robot on a 8x12 m² field at the RoboCup 2004 in Lisbon. Instead of the PAL camera system of the Pioneer2 robots that used the same mirror geometry, the image shown on the left side of Figure 5.23 was taken with a completely different camera system mounted on top of a robot of the *Mostly Harmless* RoboCup MSL team of Graz on their very small test field of 5x6 m² size. Although the parameters of the cameras and the lenses were extremely diverse throughout the experiments, the algorithm was still able to calibrate an adequate DistanceLUT, as the right sides of the Figures demonstrate. However, for higher distances, the automatically trained DistanceLUT seems to have problems to approximate the infinite slope of the real mapping function, resulting in an underestimation of the distance that is observable at the smaller right side of the field.

This effect is also visible in a comparison of the automatically and the manually generated DistanceLUT for the example image shown on the left side in Figure 5.16. Figure 5.24 shows the two look-up tables as function of the distance to the image center r_p. First of all, the two mapping functions differ in their mathematical structure. While the automatically generated function is a smooth curve resulting from the combination of a second-degree polynomial and an exponential function, the manually generated function is the output of an interpolation with a polynomial of degree five that has several inflection points. As long as the mirror and the camera are flawless and without dents, this high number of inflection points results from inaccuracies during the manual collection of correspondences between image pixels and coordinates in I_r. On the right side of Figure 5.25, the lack of smoothness of the manually calibrated mapping function can be observed at the slightly winding left touch line. However, this function is able to better handle the infinite slope of the mapping function near the horizon (here: $r_p > 230$) resulting in a better mapping at higher distances that is observable at the lower part of the right touch line. Furthermore, the overall result of the manually calibrated inverse perspective mapping function shown in Figure 5.25 is slightly better than that of the automatically calibrated one. Accord-

Figure 5.22: An example image taken by the PAL camera system of an old Pioneer2 robot on a 8x12 m^2 field at the RoboCup 2004 in Lisbon (left) and the same image mapped to world coordinates with the inverse perspective mapping function that results from the automatic geometry calibration method applied to this image (right).

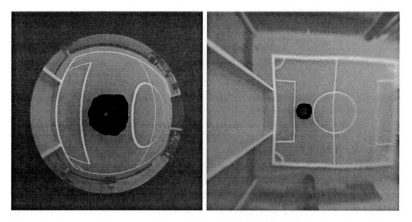

Figure 5.23: An example image taken by a robot of the *Mostly Harmless* RoboCup MSL team of Graz on their very small test field of 5x6 m^2 size (left) and the same image mapped to world coordinates with the inverse perspective mapping function that results from the automatic geometry calibration method applied to this image (right).

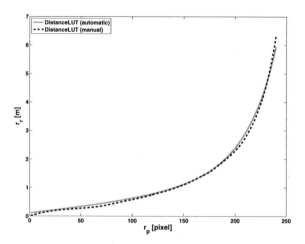

Figure 5.24: A comparison of the automatically and the manually generated DistanceLUT.

ingly, the mean estimation error of 179.70 mm per object for the object extraction using the automatically calibrated DistanceLUT and the manually calibrated ColorLUT is 60 % higher than for solely using the manually calibrated look-up tables. Again, the extracted object coordinates and the exact corresponding measurement errors are listed in Table 5.5.

The time needed to automatically generate a DistanceLUT for the previous examples was below 30 s on a Pentium 4 computer with 3 GHz and 512 MB RAM, compared to a minimum of five minutes it took to calibrate the camera geometry manually. The geometric calibration of a robot camera system is thus no longer a source of delay when testing and working with multi-robot systems in the RoboCup domain. Moreover, the automatic calibration also works on images of a field crowded with other people and robots, which often happens during the setup at the RoboCup tournaments, as long as there are still enough parts of the field lines visible.

Automatic Color Calibration Results

The first result regarding the automatic color calibration is the correct selection of the two thresholds for addition and removal of color values ζ and ξ. These parameters have to be chosen such, that there is a hysteresis for a stable optimization of the color look-up table. The major influence of the parameters ζ and ξ onto a correct classification result using an automatically generated ColorLUT is shown in Figures 5.26 and 5.27. Depending on the selection of the two thresholds, the classification of the *Green* color class applied to the image shown on the left side of Figure 5.22 is extremely diverse. For the experiments

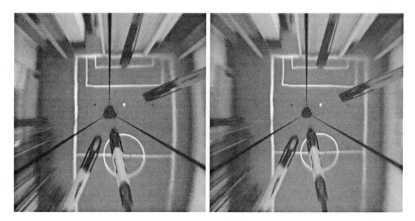

Figure 5.25: The example image of Figure 5.1 mapped to world coordinates with the inverse perspective mapping function generated automatically (left) and manually (right).

presented in this thesis, values of $\zeta = 6.25$ and $\xi = 2.0$ were used, since these values turned out to be optimal for a variety of images taken under different lighting conditions [85].

The following experiments review some of these images and present the classification results using the parameters for the automatic color calibration. The left side of Figure 5.28 again shows the example image taken by a robot of the *Mostly Harmless* RoboCup MSL team of Graz, while the right side shows the classification result of the image using the ColorLUT that was trained by the automatic color calibration method. Although the image has a very different color temperature, the parameters used for adding and removing color mappings from the look-up table are still applicable to this image. However, the surrounding of the field contains colors that are very similar to the field color or the blue goal color. It is thus difficult to separate these colors and remove them from the table resulting in many classified pixels in those areas.

The next experiment demonstrates the real-time adaptability of the ColorLUT to sudden changes of the lighting conditions when using the automatic on-line color calibration. In Figure 5.29 the upper left image again shows an example image taken by an old Pioneer2 robot in Lisbon. The upper right image shows classification result using the automatically trained ColorLUT. The lower left image simulates a change of the lighting conditions by reducing the brightness and the contrast of the upper left image by 50 %. Using a static ColorLUT would result in a misclassification of the image that is surely not suitable as a basis for intelligent robot behavior, as can be observed in the lower right image that shows the classification result of the darker image using the ColorLUT trained for the brighter image. With the presented on-line adaptive approach to generate the ColorLUT, however,

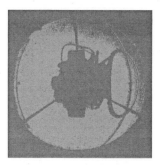 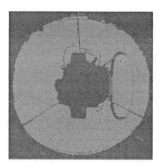

Figure 5.26: The influence of the parameter ζ on the automatic calibration of the *Green* color class applied to the image shown on the left side of Figure 5.22. If ζ is too small (left), too many color values lie outside the ellipsoid defined by equation (5.17) and are thus not added to the look-up table. Thus, large parts of the field are not correctly classified. If ζ is too large (right), too many color values lie inside the ellipsoid and are thus incorrectly added to the table resulting in a misclassification of the field lines.

 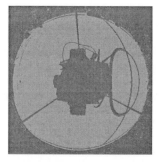

Figure 5.27: The influence of the parameter ξ on the automatic calibration of the *Green* color class applied to the image shown on the left side of Figure 5.22. If ξ is too small (left), too many color values lie outside the ellipsoid defined by equation (5.18) and are thus incorrectly removed from the look-up table. Thus, some parts of the field are not correctly classified. If ξ is too large (right), too many color values remain inside the ellipsoid and are thus prohibited from a removal resulting in many incorrectly classified pixels outside of the field.

the good quality of the classification that was achieved with the bright image is restored after only 12 cycles of adaptation to the darker image (cf. Figure 5.30). The important classification of the green field and the white lines needed for the self-localization of the robot is at an acceptable level even after 8 cycles of adaptation. The experiments concerning the computation time for the image processing algorithms at the end of this section show that even with the automatic on-line adaption of the ColorLUT all algorithms fit into

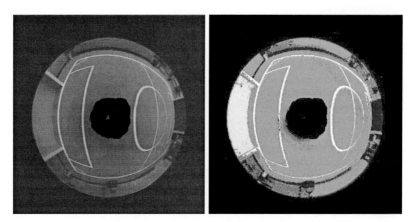

Figure 5.28: An example image taken by a robot of the *Mostly Harmless* RoboCup MSL team of Graz on their very small test field of 5x6 m^2 size (left) and the same image classified with the ColorLUT that was trained by the automatic color calibration method applied to this image (right).

the target cycle time of 20 ms for the whole system. Therefore, the on-line adaptation of the ColorLUT to the simulated change in lighting conditions shown in Figures 5.29 and 5.30 lasted only 240 ms.

Finally, Figure 5.31 shows experimental results of the automatic color calibration applied to images of a worst-case scenario. Although there is some direct illumination through the windows resulting in bright spots on the blue PVC floor in the upper left image, the overall illumination on the field is rather low. Thus, instead of spreading into the full range of the color space, the color values of the different color classes are all situated in a small part making the separation of the classes very difficult. In the lower left image the windows were covered with a blind resulting in even lower illumination. Nevertheless, even for this worst-case scenario the classification result using the automatically adapted ColorLUT shown on the right side is acceptable, although large sections of the walls outside the field are classified as green, which is mainly due to the low dynamic range of the image and reflection of the floor color in the walls.

To compare the results of the automatic color calibration algorithm to the results using a manually trained ColorLUT, Figure 5.32 opposes the classification results of the two methods applied to the example image of Figure 5.1. It is observable that the manually trained ColorLUT yields a more complete and uniform classification result that is particularly fitted for the example image. The automatic color calibration algorithm, in contrast, has to be applicable to a wide variety of different images and is therefore not necessarily optimal for the given example. Thus, the shadows in the yellow goal that can be easily added to the ColorLUT for this image during manual calibration are not included in the

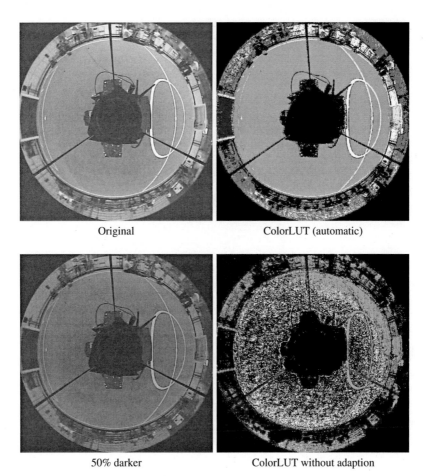

| Original | ColorLUT (automatic) |
| 50% darker | ColorLUT without adaption |

Figure 5.29: An experiment demonstrating the real-time adaptability of the ColorLUT to sudden changes of the lighting conditions when using the automatic on-line color calibration.

automatic calibration result. Similarly, the automatic calibration has difficulties to separate the very bright cyan team colors from the white of the field lines, because in this case even the contrast constraint of equation (5.15) does not apply, as the cyan team colors are also surrounded by green floor. Therefore, the team color of one of the objects is not detected correctly and the object is classified as having no team color. Nevertheless, the

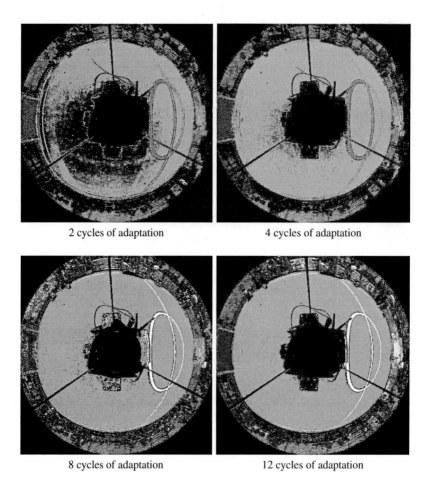

2 cycles of adaptation   4 cycles of adaptation

8 cycles of adaptation   12 cycles of adaptation

Figure 5.30: Continuation of the experiment demonstrating the real-time adaptability of the Color-LUT to sudden changes of the lighting conditions when using the automatic on-line color calibration.

automatically calibrated ColorLUT also has some advantages in this image. The colors of the shovel-shaped kicker of the goalkeeper are correctly classified as *Black*, reducing the error in the distance estimation of the object. Likewise, the color classification of the object behind the ball seems to be more complete, since the contact point of the object to the floor was detected at one of the robot parts that are visible at both sides of the ball,

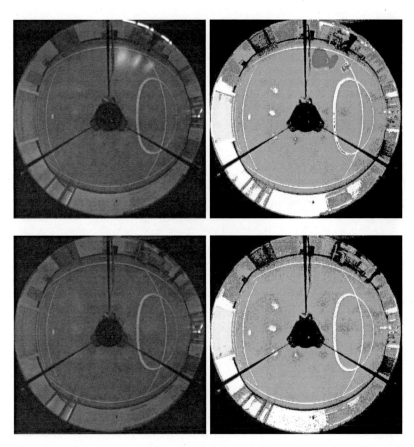

Figure 5.31: The performance of the automatic color calibration applied to images of a worst-case scenario. The images on the left were taken by a new field player on the 5x10 m² test field without the green carpet. Nevertheless, the classification result using the automatically adapted ColorLUT shown on the right side is acceptable for this worst-case scenario.

reducing the estimation error of this object as well. Again, the exact results of the object detection algorithm using the automatically generated ColorLUT are presented in Table 5.5.

As shown in Table 5.4 the cycle time of the image processing algorithm using the automatic adaptation of the ColorLUT changes significantly. Although the cycle times of the steps of the basic algorithm remained constant, the total cycle time of the image process-

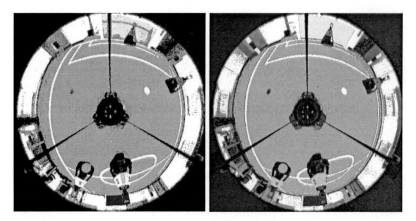

Figure 5.32: The example image of Figure 5.1 classified using the ColorLUT generated automatically (left) and manually (right).

Autom. Color Calibration	Color Segmentation	Clustering	Size Constraints	Total
2.27 ms	3.88 ms	1.09 ms	0.72 ms	7.96 ms

Table 5.4: The mean cycle time for the different steps of the image processing algorithm using the automatic color calibration. Here, the first step contains the automatic adaptation of the ColorLUT. The second step includes the classification and segmentation of the complete grid. The third step contains the clustering of the segments and the fourth step covers the application of the size constraints and the mapping to I_r. The last column presents the total cycle time including the data transfer to the shared memory.

ing algorithm was raised by 2.27 ms to an amount of 7.96 ms. However, the total cycle time is still keeping the 10 ms constraint. Furthermore, the cycle time of the automatic color calibration can be estimated as $O(n_p)$, where n_p is the number of pixels used for the color calibration which remains constant.

Comparison of Manual and Automatic Camera Calibration

This section compares the results of the image processing algorithm applied to the example image of Figure 5.1, using different combinations of manually and automatically calibrated look-up tables. Table 5.5 contains the results of the object detection for these combinations and their accuracy compared to the real object positions. The completely manually calibrated versions of the look-up tables produce good results. The mean estimation error over all objects is of an acceptable magnitude with a value of 110.77 mm. The inaccuracy is mainly due to the overestimation of the distance to objects because of a wrongly detected contact point to the floor. This happens if the contact point is hidden behind another object, e. g. the ball, or if the color classification of the black robot is imperfect. Because of the latter, the mean estimation error nearly halves to an amount of 58.45 mm, when using the automatically generated ColorLUT in combination with the manually calibrated DistanceLUT. Here, the color classification of the robots is more complete and thus the overestimation of the objects is reduced. However, the more extensive representation of *Black* in the automatically generated ColorLUT has some disadvantages, too, because some phantom objects were detected at the darker regions outside of the field. Furthermore, since the cyan color of the team markers of and the white color of the field lines was not perfectly separated by the automatic calibration, the team color of object 4 could not be detected. Combining the automatically trained DistanceLUT with the manually calibrated ColorLUT seems to be the worst decision, as the mean estimation error rises to 179.70 mm. This is due to some small errors in the approximation of the inverse perspective mapping just at those distances, where the objects reside (cf. Figure 5.24). With the manual ColorLUT, the overestimation of the object distance for the goalkeeper and the robot behind the ball is also included in the mean estimation error. Using both automatically calibrated versions of the look-up tables, the lower quality of the DistanceLUT and the good detection of the object's contact points to the floor compensate to a mean estimation error of 139.76 mm. Although this is still higher than the mean estimation error using manually trained look-up tables, it is an acceptable result for the automatic camera calibration technique compared to the advantages this method has, concerning the massively reduced setup time and the adaptability to changing lighting and even a small amount of daylight.

5.4   User Interface

The `ImageServer` and the `ImageProcessor` are each accessed through two different interfaces. The interfaces used to get data are called `ImageServerDataClient` and `ImageProcessorDataClient`. The command interfaces are only used by the GUI during calibration to send commands to the related process, e. g. to read in a newly generated ColorLUT for immediate visualization of the calibration result. They are called `ImageServerCommandClient` and `ImageProcessorCommandClient`.

ImageServerDataClient
To get data from an `ImageServer`, other processes have to create an instance of the `ImageServerDataClient`, giving a device name as a parameter. This parameter is necessary in systems with more than one camera system, e. g. the old Pioneer robot system with a perspective and an omni-directional camera, to select the `ImageServer` that delivers data from the desired camera, which is identified based on the device it is connected to. Besides the pixel data, the available data includes the time stamp taken at the moment the image was acquired, the size of the image, the pixel format (RGB24, YUV4:2:2, etc.), and the type of camera (perspective or omni-directional) that is connected, to let the `ImageProcessor` select the appropriate algorithms. Furthermore,

DistanceLUT	ColorLUT	Object 1 magenta	Object 5 magenta	Object 2 cyan	Object 4 cyan	Ball
Object positions [m]						
Real		-2.61,-0.74	-0.84,-1.94	1.01,-0.17	1.47,0.67	1.26,0.58
manual	manual	-2.72,-0.80	-0.81,-1.94	0.98,-0.20	1.78,0.82	1.25,0.57
manual	auto[a]	-2.67,-0.77	-0.82,-1.95	0.97,-0.19	1.44,0.78[b]	1.21,0.55
auto	manual	-2.81,-0.85	-0.82,-2.01	1.05,-0.23	1.89,0.91	1.29,0.55
auto	auto[a]	-2.64,-0.80	-0.80,-1.97	1.03,-0.22	1.81,0.89	1.38,0.59

Estimation error [mm]						
manual	manual	123.88	27.19	46.87	343.31	12.62
manual	auto[a]	64.93	25.85	45.46	112.56[b]	43.45
auto	manual	228.15	72.06	72.91	481.93	43.45
auto	auto[a]	67.69	52.59	53.47	403.45	121.58

[a]The automatically calibrated ColorLUT was manually extended to include the ball and team colors.

[b]The team color of this object was not detected, since the cyan color on this object was classified as *White*.

Table 5.5: Comparative results of the object detection algorithm using different combinations of manually and automatically calibrated look-up tables.

the set of current camera parameters (shutter time, white balance, etc.) can be read from the client, if a FireWire camera was selected.

ImageServerCommandClient

The graphical user interface creates an instance of the `ImageServerCommandClient` to command the `ImageServer` to read a new camera configuration from a file and send the given parameters to the FireWire camera. Thus, a user can control the camera parameters to adapt to a new illumination or a new environment and immediately receives images reflecting the changes without restarting the `ImageServer`. Using this mechanism it would be possible to implement a real-time version the algorithm of Grillo *et al.* [70] to adjust the parameters of a FireWire camera to optimize the camera image for a good color classification.

ImageProcessorDataClient

Through the creation of an instance of the `ImageProcessorDataClient`, processes get access to the processed image data of the `ImageProcessor`. Again, a specific camera and the related `ImageProcessor` is selected by giving the appropriate device name. In addition to the basic parameters of the processed image like size, camera type, and time stamp, the client provides the angles to the goals and the corner posts, a list of the extracted line points and objects, and the position of the ball. All landmark and object data are given in robot centered world coordinates in I_r. If the GUI is used to calibrate the robot, it makes the `ImageProcessor` write additional data into the shared memory buffer. Then, the client also provides access to the segmented image data.

ImageProcessorCommandClient

For a real-time visualization of the calibration results, the GUI creates an instance of the `ImageProcessorCommandClient` to send commands to the `ImageProcessor`. Besides the commands to read a new DistanceLUT, ColorLUT, or GridLUT from file to reflect the calibration changes, the client can also command the `ImageProcessor` to write the segmented image data into the shared memory for a better visualization of the color calibration result. As the process of writing the segmented image data to the shared memory is very time consuming, this is only done during the calibration.

5.5 Implementation

ImageServer

To start the `ImageServer`, the user has to specify a configuration file that contains all parameters controlling the functionality of the `ImageServer`. In the initialization phase, the process tries to establish a connection to the camera connected to the device given in the configuration file. If the connection is established and the device is a FireWire camera, the set of camera parameters given in the configuration file is sent to the camera. After the initialization the process enters the main loop that grabs new images as fast as possible and delivers them to the shared memory.[5] Since both, the BT848 frame grabber of the PAL cameras and the FireWire drivers of the new cameras deliver their data through a DMA access to the memory, independently from the process, the main processing time of the `ImageServer` is used to copy the image data to the shared memory. Unfortunately, it was not possible to combine the internal ring buffer of the FireWire drivers with the ring buffer of the shared memory to write the image data directly to the shared memory to even save the time for copying the data. At the end of the loop, the time stamp and all other data is written into the shared memory and the buffer is released for access by a client. At the beginning of each cycle of the main loop, the `ImageServer` furthermore checks if there is a client connected to the command shared memory. During a game no client is attached and the operation is fast enough not to interfere with the desired cycle time. However, if there is a client connected and a new command is given, the `ImageServer` reacts to the command by reading a new set of camera parameters from file and sending them to the camera.

---

[5]As all other processes in the software system of the Attempto Tübingen Robot Soccer Team are directly (`ImageProcessor`) or indirectly (`EnvironmentModel`, `Tactics`, etc.) depending on the image data, the frame rate of the camera or rather the `ImageServer` controls the update rate of the whole system.

ImageProcessor

A different configuration file is used to start the `ImageProcessor` that contains not only the device of the desired camera but also the filenames of the look-up tables. In the initialization phase, it creates an instance of the `ImageServerDataClient` to access the image data of the camera connected to the device given in the configuration file. It also reads and stores the DistanceLUT, ColorLUT, and GridLUT in the process memory for further use. After the initialization phase, the main loop is entered, that retrieves a new data buffer from the related `ImageServer` using the client. Here, the client is configured to try to retrieve the newest data buffer and waits, if there is currently no new data buffer available. Thus, no image is computed twice and the `ImageProcessor` is completely synchronized to the related `ImageServer` or rather the camera. According to a flag given in the configuration file, the next step is the application of the automatic on-line color calibration algorithm presented in Section 5.2.2 to the image. This algorithm then generates an appropriate version of the ColorLUT that is used in the following steps. Based on the look-up tables, the basic image processing algorithm presented in Section 5.2.1 is applied to the image starting with the color segmentation, followed by the landmark and object detection. Finally, all extracted data is written to a free shared memory buffer which is then released for access by a client. Again, at the beginning of each cycle of the main loop, the `ImageProcessor` checks for a command client connection. If a client is connected and a new command is given, the `ImageProcessor` reacts to the command and reads a new look-up table from a file or writes the complete segmented image data into the shared memory in the next cycle.

Chapter 6

Environment Modeling

At the next stage of the software system of the Attempto Tübingen Robot Soccer Team, the landmarks and objects extracted from the images of the omni-directional camera system are transformed from the local robot centered coordinate system I_r to a global coordinate system I to build a two-dimensional model of the RoboCup field. For this, the robot's pose on the field has to be estimated using the self-localization algorithms presented in Section 6.3. If the position and the orientation of the robot in I is known, all extracted landmarks and objects are inserted at the correct position of an *environment model*. Although this model of the robot's environment is rebuild in every cycle of the software system, the information from the current sensor readings is combined with the model of the last cycle to consider the history of the past measurements. Thus, using filtering techniques for tracking objects or the robot's pose the noise in the state estimation is reduced over time or at least kept at a low level, misreadings and failures in the detection of objects are bypassed, and also information on the velocity of the objects is extracted. The object tracking algorithms used in the `EnvironmentModel` process are presented in Section 6.4. Finally, the information in the environment model is communicated to the teammates over the WLAN connection of the robots. That way, robots can amend their model with information on the RoboCup field they cannot acquire themselves because of the limited view of the omni-directional camera system. The amount of data sent to the other robots depends on the available bandwidth and ranges from a minimum, i.e. the own pose and the ball position, to a maximum, which is sending all object information that is needed for an accurate sensor data fusion. Section 6.5 presents the communication techniques used by the Attempto Tübingen Robot Soccer Team. First of all, however, the next two sections present an overview of the related work on self-localization and object tracking in RoboCup and introduce *Bayesian Filtering* as the basic theory for both, the localization and the object tracking techniques that are used to build the environment model.

6.1   Related Work

The type of environment model used in a mobile robot depends to a great extent on the
high-level control algorithm that utilizes the sensor data for making decisions on the
movement of the robot. Therefore, the different approaches to control a mobile robot
existing in the literature affect the characteristics and even the presence of an environment model. To illustrate the motivation for the various characteristics of environment
models used in the RoboCup MSL, the three main robot control approaches are briefly
introduced in the following.

In [135] Mataric identified three main architectures for robot control in the literature, the
Behavior-Based Architecture, the *Sense-Model-Plan-Act Architecture*, and hybrid architectures that mix features of the first two. The main characteristic of a Behavior-Based
Architecture is the close coupling of inputs to outputs. It consists of a set of concur-
rent behaviors that generate an output based on preprogrammed condition-action rules.
Thus, the system reacts very quickly to changes in the robot's environment. Yet, a modeling of this environment is often not necessary and too time consuming to fit into the
highly reactive architecture. Translated to RoboCup this means that the reactive systems
of some teams do not incorporate an environment model at all. A robot dribbling the ball
for example could simply drive into the direction of the opponent's goal color, locally
avoiding obstacles (black regions) and finally shoot the ball towards the goal without
ever knowing its exact position. Teams that use a basic model and self-localization in
their reactive architecture have to be able to cope with substantial errors in the simple
model to keep the computation time as low as possible. Accordingly, the survey on the
self-localization methods used at the RoboCup 2005 at Osaka [181] lists a localization
error of up to 100 cm for those teams[1]. However, for team play like passing the ball to
a well-positioned teammate or playing in a special formation as well as for exchanging
information on positions and movements of objects on the field, an accurate environment
model in a global coordinate system is needed. In fact, passing to a teammate is also sup-
posable using the direct sensor information relative to the robot. However, the detection
of a good passing situation is much easier using a model of the robot's environment that
includes information on the exact position of the pass receiver as well as objects in its
vicinity and their movements. Finally, it might be desirable to inform the pass receiver
of the incoming pass or even to arbitrate the idea of passing the ball between the two
participating robots. This form of team cooperation can only be done based on an environment model with a common global coordinate system, an accurate self-localization of
the robot, and communication between the robots. This is the kind of environment model
the Sense-Model-Plan-Act Architecture needs, built from the sensed data of one or more
robots. Using the data of this model, a planner identifies a sequence of actions that lead to
the desired goal and that are executed on the robot. The more accurate the self-localization
is, and the more information is communicated between the robots of a team, the more ac-

---

[1]This is comparable to a human player who usually has only a vague notion of his position on the field.

curate and consistent the environment model of each robot gets. The better the quality of the model, the better the chances for a successful execution of the plan. However, the time needed to build and communicate a consistent environment model over a team of robots and to plan and possibly coordinate a sequence of actions per robot is too high for the dynamic environment of a RoboCup match. Therefore, the pure deliberative approach of the Sense-Model-Plan-Act Architecture is not used in RoboCup at all. Instead, several approaches exist to combine the advantages of the reactive Behavior-Based Architecture and the deliberative Sense-Model-Plan-Act Architecture and the majority of high-level control systems applied to the RoboCup MSL are such combinations. Likewise, the environment modeling process of the Attempto Tübingen Robot Soccer Team presented in this chapter was designed to build a model as accurately as possible to perform path planning and team play, while consuming as few computational resources as possible to keep the cycle rate of 20 ms.

The remainder of this section deals with the related work on the self-localization and object tracking algorithms used to compute the environment model.

Self-Localization

Pose tracking is the simplest version of self-localization, where the pose of a robot is tracked, starting at a known pose and using information on the relative movement of the robot from one cycle to the next. This information can for example be extracted from the internal wheel encoders of a wheeled robot (cf. equations (4.22) and (4.27) in Chapter 4) or by locally matching features of a camera image to a model starting at the pose from the last cycle [96, 92]. Although this dead reckoning approach is usually very fast, errors in the estimation of the ego-motion of the robot accumulate to a large error in the pose estimation over time. Therefore, these methods are only applicable to bridge short periods where no other localization method is available and have to be reset from time to time by a *global localization* that is able to estimate the pose of the robot without previous knowledge. The most challenging form of the self-localization problem, however, is the so called *kidnapped-robot problem* [53]. Here, the robot is taken to a different pose, while the localization algorithm might firmly believe that the robot is still positioned at the old pose. Nevertheless, it should be able to localize the robot at the new position. An algorithm able to handle the kidnapped-robot problem is thus also supposed to be able to recover from severe localization failures. A more detailed survey on different self-localization techniques can be found in [23].

Independent of the type of sensor data used as input, nearly all of the global self-localization methods presented in the literature are based on the relative distance and angle of landmarks to the robot. By comparing this geometric data to an *a priori* model of the landmarks, a self-localization algorithm estimates the pose of the sensing robot. In RoboCup, the various approaches to self-localization can be differentiated by the type of data they match to the model. Some methods use raw data like angles to the goals, goal posts and corner posts or individual points on the field markings, others use lines that were extracted from samples of the field markings in a preprocessing step. Furthermore, methods that directly generate a position estimation from the sensor data can be distinguished from probabilistic methods that calculate probabilities for several position estimates. The different methods are presented in the following paragraphs.

In the beginning of RoboCup walls still surrounded the RoboCup field and the Attempto Tübingen team used line segments extracted from the distance data of a laser range finder for a very fast and accurate localization. It was based on a line matching algorithm that relates the extracted lines with the lines in a model of the RoboCup field [73, 157]. However, as soon as the walls were removed, the laser sensors became nearly useless for self-localization.[2] Nevertheless, the idea of extracting lines from distance data to match them to a simple geometric model found its way into several other approaches that now use distances to field markings extracted from images. Iocchi *et al.* [96], Marques *et al.* [133, 134, 126], and Jong *et al.* [104] presented very similar algorithms where the lines are extracted from detected points of the field markings using the Hough Transform [45]. Exploiting the rectangular layout of the field lines, the orientation of the extracted lines can be aligned to the model first. The angular correction needed to fit the main direction of the extracted lines with that of the model lines is a measure of the orientation of the robot. Finally, the displacement of the extracted lines to the model lines after the correction of the orientation is used to estimate the position of the robot. Instead of matching lines extracted with the Hough Transform to a model of the field lines, Utz *et al.* [197] computed the distances of these lines to the model at given positions, to exploit the advantages of *Monte-Carlo Localization (MCL)* [59].

Although it is obvious to use lines as landmarks in a mostly polygonal environment like RoboCup, the line extraction of most of these algorithms is too slow even to process the full 25fps of typical PAL camera systems, which would be necessary to compete in such a highly dynamic environment. Furthermore, the extraction of straight lines can be hampered if not made impossible due to a distorted inverse perspective mapping of the line points when using poorly calibrated camera systems. To improve the self-localization accuracy and robustness of such systems, Hundelshausen *et al.* [90] proposed a method that extracts special shape features like corners (U-features), T-junctions and parallelism from the line points. These features are then related to the same features extracted from a geometric model of the field lines to estimate the robot's pose. Instead of the white line markings, the algorithm presented by Sekimori *et al.* [173] extracts points on the boundary of the green field and computes features like the center of gravity and the principal axes of the set of points. Translating the points relative to the center of gravity and rotating it by the angle of the main principal axes results in a first pose estimation. This estimation is improved by calculating the distances of the points to a model of the boundaries and finding small translational and rotational deviations from the first estimation that minimize the distances.

---

[2]Currently, only a single RoboCup MSL team still uses laser scanners for self-localization [187].

To avoid the time-consuming line feature extraction process that is needed even for the approaches of Hundelshausen *et al.* and Sekimori *et al.*, algorithms were developed, that were able to handle the angle and line point features. Using the angles to the goals, goal posts and corner posts, Plagge *et al.* [158], Menegatti *et al.* [141], and Buchheim *et al.* [29] directly estimate the pose of the robot through geometric triangulation. Yet, probabilistic approaches like Monte-Carlo Localization, that use sensor data only to assess given position samples became the most popular localization methods in RoboCup because of their multi-modality and their robustness to erroneous sensor measurements. Enderle *et al.* [51, 52, 1] presented an MCL approach using the angle to goal posts and corner posts extracted from perspective camera images. Hundelshausen *et al.* [92], Lauer *et al.* [122], Menegatti *et al.* [142, 143, 144], Merke *et al.* [145], Röfer *et al.* [163, 164], and Wolf *et al.* [207] instead use points of the field markings. These versions of MCL mainly differ in the efficiency of the assessment of position estimates and the number of samples needed for an accurate localization. The computation of the angles where the goal and corner posts are to be expected at a given position is very simple. Therefore, the method of Enderle *et al.* is very efficient in assessing a given position by comparing the extracted and the expected angles. Furthermore, the number of 150 samples used for the pose estimation is moderate. However, as the field gets larger and the corner posts get smaller in relation to the field size to resemble a real soccer field, occlusion of the posts and problems with detecting the posts at higher distances will increase. Thus, localization using these sparse features becomes difficult. Other approaches transform the line points to the inspected pose and evaluate the estimation by calculating their distance to the model lines. If the total distance of all points to the model is low, the pose estimation has a high likelihood for representing the correct pose. Depending on the number of line points, the computation of the distances can be very expensive. Therefore, the approaches of Hundelshausen *et al.*, Röfer *et al.*, and Menegatti *et al.* adopted an idea of Fox *et al.* [61] to store the precomputed distances in a look-up table for fast access. The number of samples used to estimate the pose of the robot ranges from 100 in the algorithm of Röfer *et al.* to 1000 in the algorithm of Menegatti *et al.*.

Apart from the methods that use landmarks to precisely localize the robot, there also exist localization methods originating in systems for topological navigation. Here, a set of sensor measurements (usually camera images) is collected at several key positions on the RoboCup field and is stored in a database. During a game, the robot compares its current sensor readings with the previously collected data and identifies the key position with the best matching sensor data as current position. The algorithm of Neto *et al.* [150] is based on images from a perspective camera, while that of Steinbauer *et al.* [185] uses the images of an omni-directional camera. Yet, both methods use *Principal Component Analysis (PCA)* to reduce the amount of data stored in the database and to define a robust similarity measure needed for the retrieval of the best matching key position. The resolution of these approaches depends on the number of key positions stored in the database and is usually very low. However, the presented algorithms can be used in reactive control systems that often do not depend on an exact pose estimation.

Object Tracking

Object tracking is the process of incorporating a series of past and present measurements of an object's position into a model of its movement. This model should contain information on the current velocity to predict the object's movement over a short period of time. The object tracking method used in this thesis tracks the movement of the ball and other objects on the RoboCup field using the object data from the image processing algorithm.

There are two main tracking methods, the Kalman filter [107], which is the most popular method, and the particle filter [43], which can be advantageous for non-linear system dynamics and multiple objects. In RoboCup, both methods are applied.

The first approaches to track objects in RoboCup were the simple low-pass filters of Gutmann *et al.* [72] and Nakagawa *et al.* [148] that use the mean change of the object's position over the last measurements to compute the objects movement. Later on, the methods evolved over a simplified Kalman filtering approach presented by Brusey *et al.* [28] towards the true Kalman filter approaches of Weigel *et al.* [203], Dietl *et al.* [42], and Ruiz-del-Solar *et al.* [178], whereas the approach of Dietl *et al.* is also able to integrate measurements of teammates observing the same object. Kurihara *et al.* [118] used an extended Kalman filter to track the ball, as the dynamics is non-linear when tracking in polar coordinates. Instead of modeling a constant velocity for the objects that is done in most Kalman filter applications, Karol *et al.* [110] used a non-linear model of the ball's velocity incorporating the retardation of the ball on the carpet and therefore also uses an extended Kalman filter approach. Schmitt *et al.* presented a multi object tracking method using a multi-hypothesis algorithm that tracks the objects with several single Kalman filters [169, 168, 170]. In contrast to the Kalman filter based approaches, Nisticò *et al.* [151] presented a particle filter method for ball tracking. Besides these implicit sensor integration approaches, Lauer *et al.* [121] presented an approach that calculates the motion of the ball from the latest observations by optimizing the parameters of the motion model to minimize the least-squares error between predicted and observed positions of the ball.

6.2   Bayesian Filtering

This section briefly introduces Bayesian Filtering as a basic principle to a probabilistic estimation of the state of a dynamic system, e. g. the pose of a moving robot, by incorporating the uncertainty of the sensor measurements. In their survey on Bayesian Filter techniques, Fox *et al.* [62, 63, 58] state that:

> Bayesian Filter techniques provide a powerful tool to help manage measurement uncertainty and perform multi-sensor fusion. Their statistical nature makes Bayesian Filters applicable to arbitrary sensor types and representations of environments.

Given the n-dimensional state of a discrete dynamic system at time t as $\mathbf{x}_t \in \mathbb{R}^n$ a Bayesian Filter represents the uncertainty of the state estimation by a *probability density function (PDF)* over the state space based on all prior sensor measurements $\mathbf{z}$ and all prior control inputs $\mathbf{u}$ as

$$Bel\left(\mathbf{x}_t\right) = P\left(\mathbf{x}_t | \mathbf{z}_t, \mathbf{u}_{t-1}, \mathbf{z}_{t-1}, \ldots, \mathbf{u}_0, \mathbf{z}_0\right) \tag{6.1}$$

assuming that we have one sensor measurement per control input. This PDF is called *belief function* and models the probability for the real state being $\mathbf{x}_t$. The belief function can model multi-modal distributions and is thus able to represent more than one state hypothesis. According to the Bayes' theorem, equation (6.1) can be rewritten as

$$Bel\left(\mathbf{x}_t\right) = \frac{P\left(\mathbf{z}_t | \mathbf{x}_t, \mathbf{u}_{t-1}, \mathbf{z}_{t-1}, \ldots, \mathbf{u}_0, \mathbf{z}_0\right) P\left(\mathbf{x}_t | \mathbf{u}_{t-1}, \mathbf{z}_{t-1}, \ldots, \mathbf{u}_0, \mathbf{z}_0\right)}{P\left(\mathbf{z}_t | \mathbf{u}_{t-1}, \mathbf{z}_{t-1}, \ldots, \mathbf{u}_0, \mathbf{z}_0\right)} \tag{6.2}$$

To avoid storing and reprocessing all past measurements in every cycle, the dynamic process is assumed to be Markov [57], meaning that a sensor measurement $\mathbf{z}_t$ only depends on the current state $\mathbf{x}_t$ which contains all relevant information. With the Markov assumption, equation (6.2) can be simplified as

$$Bel\left(\mathbf{x}_t\right) = \frac{P\left(\mathbf{z}_t | \mathbf{x}_t\right) P\left(\mathbf{x}_t | \mathbf{u}_{t-1}, \mathbf{z}_{t-1}, \ldots, \mathbf{u}_0, \mathbf{z}_0\right)}{P\left(\mathbf{z}_t | \mathbf{u}_{t-1}, \mathbf{z}_{t-1}, \ldots, \mathbf{u}_0, \mathbf{z}_0\right)} \tag{6.3}$$

and finally results in the recursive Bayesian Filter

$$Bel\left(\mathbf{x}_t\right) = \alpha_t\, P\left(\mathbf{z}_t | \mathbf{x}_t\right) \int P\left(\mathbf{x}_t | \mathbf{x}_{t-1}, \mathbf{u}_{t-1}\right) P\left(\mathbf{x}_{t-1} | \mathbf{z}_{t-1}, \mathbf{u}_{t-2}, \mathbf{z}_{t-2}, \ldots, \mathbf{u}_0, \mathbf{z}_0\right) d\mathbf{x}_{t-1}$$

$$= \alpha_t\, P\left(\mathbf{z}_t | \mathbf{x}_t\right) \int P\left(\mathbf{x}_t | \mathbf{x}_{t-1}, \mathbf{u}_{t-1}\right) Bel\left(\mathbf{x}_{t-1}\right) d\mathbf{x}_{t-1} \tag{6.4}$$

where α_t is a normalization factor ensuring

$$\int Bel\left(\mathbf{x}_t\right) d\mathbf{x}_t = 1 \tag{6.5}$$

and $P\left(\mathbf{x}_t | \mathbf{x}_{t-1}, \mathbf{u}_{t-1}\right)$ denotes the system dynamics, i.e. the probability for the dynamic system to change its state from $\mathbf{x}_{t-1}$ to $\mathbf{x}_t$ in one time step considering the control input $\mathbf{u}_{t-1}$. Thus, the state estimation problem is recursively defined depending on the estimation of the previous time step. $Bel\left(\mathbf{x}_0\right)$ can be modeled to represent any prior knowledge of the initial state or simply constitutes a uniform distribution over the state space.

The recursive Bayesian Filter is usually updated in two steps, the *prediction* step and the *correction* step. In the prediction step, the belief function is computed *a priori* as

$$Bel^-\left(\mathbf{x}_t\right) = \int P\left(\mathbf{x}_t | \mathbf{x}_{t-1}, \mathbf{u}_{t-1}\right) Bel\left(\mathbf{x}_{t-1}\right) d\mathbf{x}_{t-1} \tag{6.6}$$

$Bel^-(\mathbf{x}_t)$ represents the PDF predicted at time t by applying the system dynamics to the PDF at time $t - 1$. In the correction step, the *a posteriori* PDF that includes the new sensor information is computed by multiplying with the probability to receive sensor measurement $\mathbf{z}_t$ under the condition that the current state is $\mathbf{x}_t$ and then normalizing to fulfill the constraint of equation (6.5)

$$Bel(\mathbf{x}_t) = \alpha_t \, P(\mathbf{z}_t|\mathbf{x}_t) Bel^-(\mathbf{x}_t) \qquad (6.7)$$

For tracking the position of an object, the state is usually comprised of the position and velocity of the object or robot in the global reference frame I

$$\mathbf{x} = \begin{bmatrix} x & y & v_x & v_y \end{bmatrix}^T \qquad (6.8)$$

For the tracking the pose of the robot, this state is extended to include the orientation and the change in orientation of the robot

$$\mathbf{x} = \begin{bmatrix} x & y & \theta & v_x & v_y & v_\theta \end{bmatrix}^T \qquad (6.9)$$

In this context the term $P(\mathbf{x}_t|\mathbf{x}_{t-1}, \mathbf{u}_{t-1})$ is called *motion model*, while $P(\mathbf{z}_t|\mathbf{x}_t)$ is called *sensor model*. The property of the belief function to be able to model multi-modal distributions provides a perfect basis for global localization. In case of ambiguous sensor readings, the belief function has several peaks at different possible poses (i. e. several pose hypotheses) until the update with a sequence of sensor data provides a definite result with one of the peaks being significantly more possible than the others.

In their survey Fox *et al.* [62, 63, 58] identify several possibilities to approximate the belief function. Kalman filters [107, 138, 180, 205] use a Gaussian representation of the PDF by modeling the first and second moments, i. e. the mean and a covariance matrix. By modeling only a Gaussian with mean and covariance, the Kalman filter is computationally highly efficient, as all operations for prediction and correction are simple matrix multiplications. However, the system dynamics is assumed to be linear with Gaussian noise. Furthermore, the Kalman filter also assumes the sensor model to only introduce Gaussian noise and the initial state uncertainty to be unimodal. Although it can be shown that the Kalman filter is optimal under these assumptions [138], the majority of real systems does not fulfill these assumptions. Nevertheless, Kalman filters are the most widely used variant of Bayesian Filters [58], as there are extensions to the original Kalman filter that overcome the restrictive assumptions. To handle non-linear system dynamics the *extended Kalman filter (EKF)* linearizes the system dynamics at the current state with a first-order Taylor series [205]. However, the *unscented Kalman filter (UKF)* [106] has been shown to yield better results than the EKF [202]. The UKF selects characteristic samples (sigma-points) of the Gaussian state of the previous time step and processes them with the non-linear system dynamics. The resulting samples are then fitted with a Gaussian to represent the *a priori* belief of equation (6.6). Finally, there also exist approaches that model a multi-modal belief function with a mixture of Gaussians, where each of the Gaussians is tracked with a single Kalman filter. In mobile robot localization, these *multi-hypothesis approaches* are able to handle the global localization problem, in contrast to the single Gaussian Kalman filter that assumes a unimodal belief function and Gaussian sensor noise. A very detailed survey of Kalman filter approaches was published by Blackman *et al.* [20].

The Kalman filter based approaches model the belief function with one or more continuous Gaussian functions. However, there also exist discrete methods that approximate the belief function as a piecewise constant function or by sampling the belief function only at distinct positions in the state space. Several grid-based methods were proposed for approximating the continuous belief function with a grid of piecewise constant patches [32, 31, 57, 61]. However, there is a trade-off between the accuracy of the state estimation and the computational costs depending on the *a priori* defined resolution of the grid. Yet, there exist algorithms that use adaptive, tree-based representations to increase the accuracy by locally increasing the resolution without raising the computational costs too much [31]. In contrast to the grid-based methods, *particle filters* [43] use an efficient sample-based approximation of the belief function using a *sampling/importance resampling (SIR)* approach that assigns the majority of samples to states of high probability. Besides the standard approaches using a fixed number of samples, there also exist algorithms that adapt the number of samples used according to the current state to further increase the efficiency [59, 58]. Thus, for estimating a robot's pose, more samples are used to cover the state space during global localization or when the pose estimation is inaccurate, whereas during tracking a few samples suffice. The efficiency of the particle filter method is due to the assignment of computational resources to where or when they are needed. In mobile robot localization particle filters are applied with great success (e. g. [59, 41, 60, 58] and the RoboCup related methods presented in Section 6.1) and are known as *Monte-Carlo Localization (MCL)* [59].

As the object tracking and self-localization algorithms of the Attempto Tübingen Robot Soccer team are based on Kalman filters and particle filters, both methods are briefly introduced in the following sections.

6.2.1 Kalman Filters

The basic version of the Kalman filter is able to estimate the state of a linear process

$$\mathbf{x}_t = \mathbf{A}\mathbf{x}_{t-1} + \mathbf{B}\mathbf{u}_{t-1} + \mathbf{w}_{t-1} \qquad (6.10)$$

with $\mathbf{A}$ being a $(n \times n)$ matrix relating the state at time $t - 1$ to the state at time t, called *process matrix*, $\mathbf{B}$ being a $(n \times l)$ matrix relating the l-dimensional control input $\mathbf{u}_{t-1}$ to a change in the state, and $\mathbf{w}_{t-1}$ being an additional noise resulting from inaccurate modeling of the process, called *process noise*. Kalman filters assume the process noise to be a mean-free Gaussian noise

$$p(\mathbf{w}) \sim N(0, \mathbf{Q}) \qquad (6.11)$$

where $\mathbf{Q}$ is a $(n \times n)$ covariance matrix. Usually, there is no control input or the control input is not modeled. In the latter case, the influence of the control inputs on the system is included in a higher process noise. The m-dimensional sensor measurement vector $\mathbf{z}$ of the system state is modeled as

$$\mathbf{z}_t = \mathbf{Hx}_t + \mathbf{v}_t \tag{6.12}$$

where $\mathbf{H}$ is a $(m \times n)$ matrix that determines the measurement of the current state $\mathbf{x}_t$, which a perfect sensor would generate, and $\mathbf{v}_t$ is the *measurement noise* that compensates for the imperfectness of the real sensor. Again, Kalman filters assume the measurement noise to be a mean-free Gaussian noise

$$p(\mathbf{v}) \sim N(0, \mathbf{R}) \tag{6.13}$$

where $\mathbf{R}$ is a $(m \times m)$ covariance matrix. The process noise and the measurement noise as well as the matrices $\mathbf{A}$, $\mathbf{B}$, and $\mathbf{H}$ can be different at each time step. In this thesis, however, and in fact in most Kalman filter applications, these matrices are assumed to be constant.

As long as the requirements for the process and measurement noise (equations (6.11) and (6.13)) are met, the state estimation of the Kalman filter is also Gaussian with

$$\widehat{Bel}\,(\mathbf{x}_t) = N(\widehat{\mathbf{x}}_t, \mathbf{P}_t) \tag{6.14}$$

where $\widehat{\mathbf{x}}_t$ is the estimation of the n-dimensional state and

$$\mathbf{P}_t = E\left[\mathbf{e}_t\,\mathbf{e}_t{}^T\right] \tag{6.15}$$

is the corresponding error covariance matrix for the *a posteriori* estimation error

$$\mathbf{e}_t = \mathbf{x}_t - \widehat{\mathbf{x}}_t \tag{6.16}$$

As a recursive Bayesian Filter, the Kalman filter is updated in two steps. The prediction step generates an *a priori* estimation for the state $\widehat{\mathbf{x}}_t^-$ and the error covariance

$$\mathbf{P}_t^- = E\left[\mathbf{e}_t^-\,\mathbf{e}_t^{-T}\right] \tag{6.17}$$

with

$$\mathbf{e}_t^- = \mathbf{x}_t - \widehat{\mathbf{x}}_t^- \tag{6.18}$$

from the previous state and the control input

$$\begin{aligned}
\widehat{\mathbf{x}}_t^- &= \mathbf{A}\widehat{\mathbf{x}}_{t-1} + \mathbf{B}\mathbf{u}_{t-1} \\
\mathbf{P}_t^- &= \mathbf{A}\mathbf{P}_{t-1}\mathbf{A}^T + \mathbf{Q}
\end{aligned} \tag{6.19}$$

The correction step corrects the *a priori* estimation and results in an *a posteriori* estimation by adding a fraction of the *residual* $\left(\mathbf{z}_t - \mathbf{H}\widehat{\mathbf{x}}_t^-\right)$, representing the difference between the real and the expected measurement, to the *a priori* state estimation

$$\widehat{\mathbf{x}}_t = \widehat{\mathbf{x}}_t^- + \mathbf{K}_t\left(\mathbf{z}_t - \mathbf{H}\widehat{\mathbf{x}}_t^-\right) \tag{6.20}$$
$$\mathbf{P}_t = \left(\mathbf{I} - \mathbf{K}_t\mathbf{H}\right)\mathbf{P}_t$$

with

$$\mathbf{K}_t = \frac{\mathbf{P}_t^- \mathbf{H}^T}{\mathbf{H}\mathbf{P}_t^- \mathbf{H}^T + \mathbf{R}} \tag{6.21}$$

being a $(n \times m)$ matrix that minimizes the *a posteriori* covariance $\mathbf{P}_t$.[3]

A non-linear process

$$\mathbf{x}_t = f\left(\mathbf{x}_{t-1}, \mathbf{u}_{t-1}, \mathbf{w}_{t-1}\right)$$
$$\mathbf{z}_t = h\left(\mathbf{x}_t, \mathbf{v}_t\right) \tag{6.22}$$

with the non-linear, but differentiable functions f and h can be handled either by the extended Kalman filter that linearizes these functions around the current state estimation using a Taylor series approximation or by the unscented Kalman filter that processes several samples with the non-linear functions and fits the outcome with a Gaussian.

6.2.2 Particle Filters

In particle filters the belief function from equation (6.1) is approximated by a set of samples $S_t = \{\mathbf{s}_{t,i} | \mathbf{s}_{t,i} = (\widehat{\mathbf{x}}_{t,i}, w_{t,i}), i = 1, \ldots, N_t\}$, where each sample $\mathbf{s}_{t,i}$ contains a state estimation $\widehat{\mathbf{x}}_{t,i}$ and a weight $w_{t,i}$ that represents $Bel\left(\mathbf{x}_t\right)$.

The prediction step of a particle filter is an importance resampling of the *a posteriori* sample set S_{t-1} according to the motion model, resulting in an *a priori* set of samples S_t^- for the next time step. A sample $\mathbf{s}_{t-1,i}$ is chosen with a probability equal to $w_{t-1,i}$ and a new sample $\mathbf{s}_{t,j}^-$ is generated by drawing a random sample from $P\left(\widehat{\mathbf{x}}_t^- | \widehat{\mathbf{x}}_{t-1}, \mathbf{u}_{t-1}\right)$. In the correction step, the weights of all samples are updated according to the sensor model

$$w_{t,j} = \alpha_t P\left(\mathbf{s}_{t,j}^- | \widehat{\mathbf{x}}_t^-\right) \tag{6.23}$$

with α_t such that

$$\sum_j w_{t,j} = 1 \tag{6.24}$$

Finally, the *a posteriori* state estimation $\widehat{\mathbf{x}}_t$ is calculated as the weighted mean over the best n samples. The advantage of the sample-based approximation is that through the

---

[3]A complete derivation of the *Kalman gain* $\mathbf{K}_t$ can be found in [138].

importance resampling only those samples with a high probability of representing the correct state are used as an input for the next steps. Thus, only few samples are needed to approximate the belief function at the local maxima with a high accuracy and major parts of the belief function with a low probability are not sampled at all, saving computational resources. The number of samples used for the approximation of the belief function can be chosen as a fixed number or can be adapted according to the quality of the state estimation after each cycle to save even more resources [59, 58, 109].

6.3   Self-Localization

The self-localization algorithm used in the software system of the Attempto Tübingen Robot Soccer Team is similar to the more recent algorithms presented in Section 6.1. It is based on the line points and the angles to the two goals provided by the image processing algorithm and uses Monte-Carlo Localization to represent the belief function of the robot pose. Furthermore, the quality of a candidate pose (a sample) is assessed using a precomputed look-up table for the distances of the line points to the model. In contrast to the other approaches, however, this algorithm exploits the idea of adapting the size of the sample set according to the quality of the pose estimation. In the initialization phase, in cases of low quality sensor data, or when kidnapping the robot (e. g. when exchanging players during a game) the robot has to perform a global localization and the quality of the estimation is low as the samples are equally distributed over the multi-modal belief function. After the global localization, however, the samples are condensed around the pose with the highest quality, i. e. the maximum of the belief function, and the quality of the pose estimation is high. By executing the localization algorithm in every cycle of the system, i. e. 50 times a second, the pose of the robot changes only slightly from one cycle to the other, and it is sufficient to track the current maximum of the belief function after the global localization. Thus, instead of using a fixed number of samples, this algorithm uses a maximum number of samples in cases of a global localization phase, when it needs to examine the multi-modal belief function, and gradually reduces the number of samples in cases of a good pose estimation. However, as the number of samples influences the approximation quality of the peak in the belief function, a minimum number of samples is needed for an acceptable pose estimation. To further reduce this minimum number of samples, the presented algorithm improves the pose estimation of the particle filter by a local optimization strategy. Using this optimization, the minimum number of samples needed can be reduced to a single sample without reducing the quality of the pose estimation. As shown in Section 6.3.3, the maximum number of samples used for the presented algorithm is in the magnitude of the related algorithms using a fixed but low number of samples, while the mean number of samples used in the experiments is far below this number, as the algorithm remains in the efficient single sample *tracking mode* during more than 90% of the cycles. Nevertheless, the method is still able to cope with the kidnapped-robot problem. Thus, the presented self-localization algorithm is a

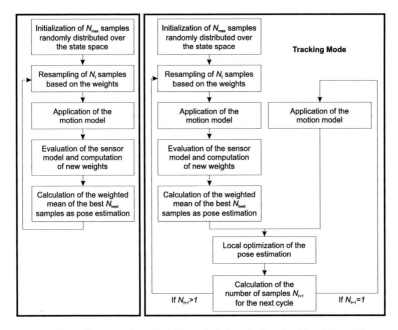

Figure 6.1: The major steps of a typical Monte-Carlo Localization algorithm (left) and the combined Monte-Carlo Localization and tracking algorithm (right).

sophisticated combination of Monte-Carlo Localization and pose tracking.

6.3.1 Basic Algorithm

The major steps of the self-localization algorithm are shown in Fig. 6.1 and are compared to a typical Monte-Carlo Localization algorithm.

Initialization

When the algorithm starts, there is no previous knowledge about the robot's pose, therefore the maximum number of samples N_{max} is generated and uniformly distributed over the state space, which consists of the field plus small parts beyond the touch and goal lines that are used to maneuver. If there is previous knowledge of the pose, e. g. if the robot always starts at the same position, this knowledge can be represented by a different non-random initialization. Before entering the main cycle of the particle filter, all samples are evaluated using the sensor model as explained later, to update their weights.

Resampling

The prediction step of the particle filter is divided into two steps. In the first step, the amount of samples for the current cycle N_t is generated by an importance resampling of the old sample set S_{t-1}. In the first cycle N_1 is set to $N_{\max}$. For all other cycles the number of samples was calculated in the last cycle based on the estimation quality of the last cycle. If $N_t > 1$, samples are chosen for the new sample set S_t with probability $w_{t,i}$ until the number of samples N_t is reached. In this case it is possible to insert a number of R randomly distributed samples to ensure a faster recovery if a localization error should occur. If $N_t = 1$, the pose estimation of the last cycle is used as the only sample in the new sample set S_t and the algorithm enters the tracking mode.

Application of the Motion Model

In the second step, the samples are repositioned according to a motion model. The linear motion model used in this self-localization algorithm assumes a motion with constant velocity, while the changes in the motion of the robot, i. e. any kind of acceleration, are included as a certain amount of prediction error

$$
\widehat{\mathbf{x}}_t^- =
\begin{bmatrix}
\widehat{x}_t^- \\
\widehat{y}_t^- \\
\widehat{\theta}_t^- \\
\widehat{v}_{x,t}^- \\
\widehat{v}_{y,t}^- \\
\widehat{v}_{\theta,t}^-
\end{bmatrix}
=
\begin{bmatrix}
1 & 0 & 0 & \Delta t & 0 & 0 \\
0 & 1 & 0 & 0 & \Delta t & 0 \\
0 & 0 & 1 & 0 & 0 & \Delta t \\
0 & 0 & 0 & 1 & 0 & 0 \\
0 & 0 & 0 & 0 & 1 & 0 \\
0 & 0 & 0 & 0 & 0 & 1
\end{bmatrix}
\begin{bmatrix}
\widehat{x}_{t-1} \\
\widehat{y}_{t-1} \\
\widehat{\theta}_{t-1} \\
\widehat{v}_{x,t-1} \\
\widehat{v}_{y,t-1} \\
\widehat{v}_{\theta,t-1}
\end{bmatrix}
+
\begin{bmatrix}
d_{x,t-1} \\
d_{y,t-1} \\
d_{\theta,t-1} \\
0 \\
0 \\
0
\end{bmatrix}
\qquad (6.25)
$$

with $d_{x,t-1}$, $d_{y,t-1}$, and $d_{\theta,t-1}$ being random mean free position and orientation noise with a standard deviation equal to the amount of position and orientation change $\widehat{v}_{x,t-1}\Delta t$, $\widehat{v}_{y,t-1}\Delta t$, and $\widehat{v}_{\theta,t-1}\Delta t$. However, a minimum noise of $d_{x,t-1} = d_{y,t-1} = 10\,\mathrm{mm}$ and $d_{\theta,t-1} = 0.01\,\mathrm{rad}$ is always added, even if the robot does not move. In the one sample tracking mode, the noise term of equation (6.25) is not added.

Evaluation of the Sensor Model

For a fast and efficient evaluation of the sensor model $P\left(\mathbf{z}_t|\mathbf{x}_t\right)$, several authors presented the idea of transforming the line points to the pose $\mathbf{l}_{t,i}$ that is represented by the sample $\mathbf{s}_{t,i}$, such that the base coordinate system of the line points is located at position $\begin{bmatrix} x_{t,i} & y_{t,i} \end{bmatrix}^T$ and oriented according to $\theta_{t,i}$ as shown in Figure 6.3. Denoting the new location of line point j as $\begin{bmatrix} x_{i,j} & y_{i,j} \end{bmatrix}^T$ and the vector from this point to its nearest model line in the *a priori* known model of the field as

$$
\mathbf{f}_{i,j} = \begin{bmatrix} x_{m,j} \\ y_{m,j} \end{bmatrix} - \begin{bmatrix} x_{i,j} \\ y_{i,j} \end{bmatrix}
\qquad (6.26)
$$

an estimated position error $\widehat{e}_{L,i}$ per sample can be calculated by summing over the squared distances of the line points to the model as

$$\widehat{e}_{L,i} = \frac{1}{j} \sum_j \|\mathbf{f}_{i,j}\|^2 \tag{6.27}$$

In contrast to the original methods the proposed algorithm uses the squared distances to let line points with a higher distance to the next model line have an even greater influence than line points that are almost perfectly matched. Recently, Lauer *et al.* [122] proposed to calculate $\widehat{e}_{L,i}$ using a Maximum-Likelihood-Estimator

$$\widehat{e}_{L,i} = \frac{1}{j} \sum_j 1 - \frac{c^2}{c^2 + \|\mathbf{f}_{i,j}\|} , \quad c \in \mathbb{R} \, [m] \tag{6.28}$$

that is similar to the function of equation (6.27) for distances $\|\mathbf{f}_{i,j}\| \leq c$ but is bounded for higher values of $\|\mathbf{f}_{i,j}\|$ to reduce the influence of outliers in the set of extracted line points. Section 6.3.3 contains a comparison of the two functions using squared distances and using the Maximum-Likelihood-Estimator with $c = 0.8 \, \text{m}$. As the distances $\|\mathbf{f}_{i,j}\|$ only depend on the position $\begin{bmatrix} x_{i,j} & y_{i,j} \end{bmatrix}^T$ on the field they can be precomputed on a discrete grid (here a resolution of 5 cm was used) and easily stored in a two-dimensional look-up table called *Distance Matrix* , which is shown for the squared distances in Figure 6.2 as a height map. As $\widehat{e}_{L,i}$ is only based on the symmetric marking lines on a RoboCup soccer field, it would be the same for at least two poses on the field. Thus, to resolve the symmetry, the angle to the two differently colored goals was introduced as a supplemental feature for the evaluation of the sensor model. From the image processing algorithm the angles $\widetilde{\varphi}_B$ and $\widetilde{\varphi}_Y$ to the blue and yellow goal are extracted. The comparison of these angles with the expected angles to the goals at the pose of a sample $\varphi_{B,i}$ and $\varphi_{Y,i}$ results in an estimated orientation error

$$\widehat{e}_{G,i} = \left(|\widetilde{\varphi}_B - \varphi_{B,i}| + |\widetilde{\varphi}_Y - \varphi_{Y,i}| \right)^2 \tag{6.29}$$

where $|\cdot|$ is the absolute value of the smaller angle difference accounting for the 2π period of angles. Again the error is squared to let higher angular differences have a greater influence. The total estimated pose error is computed by a linear combination as

$$\widehat{e}_i = (1 - \lambda)\widehat{e}_{L,i} + \lambda\widehat{e}_{G,i} \tag{6.30}$$

with $\lambda \in [0, 1]$ representing the balance of the two error terms, and finally, the weights are updated as

$$w_{t,i} = \alpha_t \frac{1}{\widehat{e}_i} \tag{6.31}$$

with α_t being the normalization factor from equation (6.23). The weighted mean over the best N_{best} samples is calculated as the initial pose estimation for the local optimization

$$\widehat{\mathbf{l}}_t^- = \sum_{i=1}^{N_{\text{best}}} w_{t,i} \begin{bmatrix} x_{t,i} \\ y_{t,i} \\ \theta_{t,i} \end{bmatrix} \tag{6.32}$$

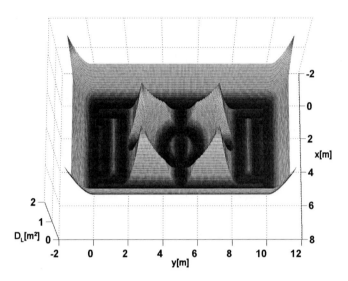

Figure 6.2: The Distance Matrix. The height map visualizes the squared distance of each position on the field to the next field marking line.

To save the computational costs for sorting the samples according to their weight, $N_{best} = N_t$ is chosen for the rest of the thesis. In the tracking mode $\widehat{l}_t^-$ is the pose of the single sample.

Local Optimization of the Pose Estimation

Hundelshausen *et al.* [92] had the idea to extend the quality measure based on the distance of the line points to the model to forces exerted by the model lines trying to pull the line points into the correct position. With these forces the estimated pose can be locally improved. Again, the forces can be precomputed and stored in a look-up table called *Force Matrix* . This idea was adopted in this algorithm that uses a Force Matrix precomputed on a regular grid with 5 cm resolution to improve the pose estimation $\widehat{l}_t^-$ in a number of iterations k. In contrast to Hundelshausen *et al.*, however, who used their ideas only for dead-reckoning after an initial global localization, the algorithm presented here integrates the local optimization in a combined Monte-Carlo localization and tracking algorithm that gradually switches from global localization to a fast tracking of the robot's pose and backwards.

The two-dimensional vectors from equation (6.26) can be interpreted as a force which is exerted onto a line point by the nearest model line proportional to the distance to the model line. A mean force acting on the pose estimation $\widehat{\mathbf{l}}_{t,k}^-$ can be computed as

$$\mathbf{F}_k = \frac{1}{j} \sum_j \mathbf{f}_{a,j} \qquad (6.33)$$

with $\begin{bmatrix} x_{a,j} & y_{a,j} \end{bmatrix}^T$ in the term $\mathbf{f}_{a,j}$ being the position of the line point j transposed to the pose estimation $\widehat{\mathbf{l}}_{t,k}^-$. A fraction of this force is added to the pose estimation $\widehat{\mathbf{l}}_{t,k}^-$ in each iteration k to improve it regarding the position. To improve the orientation of the pose estimation, a mean torque according to the base coordinate system of the set of points is computed by summing over the single torques as

$$\mathbf{M}_k = \frac{1}{j} \sum_j \begin{bmatrix} x_{a,j} \\ y_{a,j} \end{bmatrix} \times \mathbf{f}_{a,j} \qquad (6.34)$$

Again, a fraction of this torque is added to the pose estimation $\widehat{\mathbf{l}}_{t,k}^-$ in each iteration to improve it regarding the orientation. Thus, in each iteration k a new pose estimation $\widehat{\mathbf{l}}_{t,k}^-$ is generated

$$\begin{aligned} \begin{bmatrix} \widehat{x}_{t,k}^- \\ \widehat{y}_{t,k}^- \end{bmatrix} &= \begin{bmatrix} \widehat{x}_{t,k-1}^- \\ \widehat{y}_{t,k-1}^- \end{bmatrix} + \mu \mathbf{F}_{k-1} \\ \widehat{\theta}_{t,k}^- &= \widehat{\theta}_{t,k-1}^- + \nu \mathbf{M}_{k-1} \end{aligned} \qquad (6.35)$$

The iterations can be seen as steps of a controller that minimizes $\mathbf{F}$ and $\mathbf{M}$. Therefore, if the control parameters μ and ν are set too high, the pose estimation oscillates around the optimum or diverges. The iterations are continued until a maximum number of iterations $K_{\max}$ is reached or the improvement between the iterations was too low. The final pose estimation after the local optimization $\widehat{\mathbf{l}}_t$ is the pose resulting from the last iteration. Figure 6.3 shows an example of a set of line points transformed to the initial pose estimation (left) and the optimized final pose estimation (right).

Lauer *et al.* [122] proposed a different method called *RPROP* [165] for the local optimization. RPROP is a gradient descent method that was originally designed as a learning rule for multi-layer perceptrons. Starting with an initial step width $\delta_{1,0}$, $\delta_{2,0}$, and $\delta_{3,0}$ for translation and rotation, in each iteration k the new pose estimation is reached by going one step in the direction of the negative gradient of the estimated error function

$$\begin{aligned} \begin{bmatrix} \widehat{x}_{t,k}^- \\ \widehat{y}_{t,k}^- \end{bmatrix} &= \begin{bmatrix} \widehat{x}_{t,k-1}^- \\ \widehat{y}_{t,k-1}^- \end{bmatrix} - \begin{bmatrix} \delta_{1,k-1} \, g_{1,k-1} \\ \delta_{2,k-1} \, g_{2,k-1} \end{bmatrix} \\ \widehat{\theta}_{t,k}^- &= \widehat{\theta}_{t,k-1}^- - \delta_{3,k-1} \, g_{3,k-1} \end{aligned} \qquad (6.36)$$

with

$$\begin{bmatrix} g_{1,k-1} \\ g_{2,k-1} \\ g_{3,k-1} \end{bmatrix} = \nabla \widehat{e}(\widehat{x}_{t,k-1}^-, \widehat{y}_{t,k-1}^-, \widehat{\theta}_{t,k-1}^-) \qquad (6.37)$$

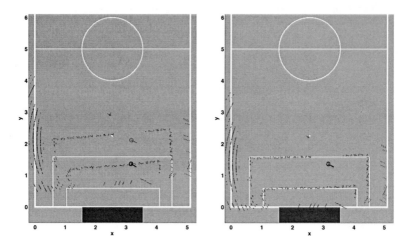

Figure 6.3: A set of line points (blue dots) extracted from the omni-directional camera system transformed to the corresponding pose estimation before the local optimization $\hat{\mathbf{l}}^-$, visualized as red circle (left). The same line points transformed to the final pose estimation after the local optimization $\hat{\mathbf{l}}$ which is nearly identical with the true pose shown as black circle (right).

In each iteration, the step width is updated as

$$
\delta_{i,k} = \begin{cases} 1.2\,\delta_{i,k-1} & \text{if} \quad \text{sign}(g_{i,k}) = \text{sign}(g_{i,k-1}) \\ 0.5\,\delta_{i,k-1} & \text{if} \quad \text{sign}(g_{i,k}) \neq \text{sign}(g_{i,k-1}) \,, \quad \forall i \in \{1,2,3\} \\ 0.0 & \text{if} \qquad g_{i,k} = g_{i,k-1} \end{cases} \tag{6.38}
$$

The iterations are continued until a maximum number of iterations $K_{\max}$ is reached. Again, the final pose estimation $\hat{\mathbf{l}}_t$ is the pose resulting from the last iteration. Similar to Hundelshausen *et al.*, Lauer *et al.* use the local optimization only for tracking. However, in contrast to Hundelshausen *et al.* several pose hypotheses are tracked over time, selecting the hypothesis with the best quality as final pose estimation. Section 6.3.3 contains comparative results concerning the two optimization strategies.

It is important to note that apart from inserting the final pose estimation after the local optimization $\hat{\mathbf{l}}_t$ into the sample set S_{t+1} the stochastic process of the Monte-Carlo Localization is not influenced by the local optimization at all. The optimization can be seen as a local search for a maximum in the belief function which stabilizes the pose estimation by removing the noise from the weighted mean when $N > 1$ and reducing the tracking errors when $N = 1$.

Calculation of the Number of Samples

The number of samples N_{t+1} needed for the next cycle is calculated depending on the estimated error $\widehat{e}$ of the final pose estimation $\widehat{l}_t$ as

$$N_{t+1} = \begin{cases} N_{\max} & : \quad \text{if } N_{\max} \leq \gamma\widehat{e} + \eta \\ \gamma\widehat{e} + \eta & : \quad \text{if } 1 < \gamma\widehat{e} + \eta < N_{\max} \\ 1 & : \quad \text{if } \gamma\widehat{e} + \eta \leq 1 \end{cases} \tag{6.39}$$

where γ and η are the parameters for a linear function that controls how fast the number of samples N is reduced to a single sample.

6.3.2 Improvements

While the basic self-localization algorithm presented in the last section was published in [80, 81, 82], this section contains unpublished improvements made to the basic algorithm to further improve the quality of the pose estimation. Comparative results concerning the quality of the pose estimation using these improvements are given in Section 6.3.3.

Evaluation of the Sensor Model

The linear combination of the two estimated errors in equation (6.30) is very hard to parameterize. It is not obvious how much the estimated position error should influence the total estimated error compared to the estimated orientation error, especially as the unit of the two is different (m^2 and rad^2). Therefore, two different approaches for the evaluation of the quality of the samples are presented that are solely based on the estimated position error, i. e. equation (6.30) is replaced by

$$\widehat{e}_i = \widehat{e}_{L,i} \tag{6.40}$$

To solve the symmetry problem, the first approach separates the set of samples into two subsets along a symmetry line through the center of the field. A fixed subdivision along the center line of the field would produce erroneous results if the correct pose was near the center line and the cloud of samples representing the same pose was subdivided. Therefore, the symmetry line is defined depending on the final pose estimation of the last cycle to result in the best possible subdivision of the sample set

$$sl(x, y, d = 0) : \left\langle \begin{bmatrix} x \\ y \end{bmatrix} - \begin{bmatrix} x_c \\ y_c \end{bmatrix}, \frac{\mathbf{n}}{\|\mathbf{n}\|} \right\rangle = d \tag{6.41}$$

with $\langle , \rangle$ being the scalar product, $\begin{bmatrix} x_c & y_c \end{bmatrix}^T$ being the center point of the field, and $\mathbf{n}$ being the vector from the center point to the final pose estimation of the last cycle. Figure 6.4 shows an example of the symmetry line. The new subsets are defined as

$$\begin{aligned} S_{s1,t} &= \{\mathbf{s}_{t,i} | \mathbf{s}_{t,i} \in S_t \wedge sl(x, y, d \leq 0)\} \\ S_{s2,t} &= \{\mathbf{s}_{t,i} | \mathbf{s}_{t,i} \in S_t \wedge sl(x, y, d > 0)\} \end{aligned} \tag{6.42}$$

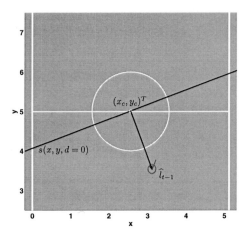

Figure 6.4: An Example of a symmetry line for subdividing the sample set.

For both subsets the weighted mean of the samples is calculated as pose hypothesis and the estimated orientation error is computed for both. The hypothesis with the lower estimated orientation error is finally used as pose estimation.

In the second approach, the best sample in the set is retrieved and is used as pose hypothesis along with its symmetric pose gained by rotating the pose 180° around the center of the field. Again, the estimated orientation error is computed for both and the hypothesis with the lower estimated orientation error is finally used as pose estimation. Although a search for the best sample is needed, the computation time for this approach is comparable to that of the other method, as the state space now only includes one half field and the number of samples needed for a given quality of the pose estimation as well as the Distance Matrix and the Force Matrix can be halved.

Additional Kalman Filtering

As the basic self-localization algorithm merely fits the pose as well as possible to the current sensor readings, the noise of the sensor readings is yet unconsidered and still reduces the estimation quality. Thus, similar to Lauer *et al.* [122], the stability of the pose estimation is improved by using the final pose estimation of the basic algorithm as a measurement input for a Kalman filter tracking the pose of the robot to reduce this noise. Although the basic self-localization algorithm already contains a pose tracking, the additional Kalman filter does not impose higher inertia.

As shown in equation (6.25) for this Kalman filter the motion model contained in the matrix $\mathbf{A}$ used in equation (6.19) is defined as

$$
\mathbf{A} = \begin{bmatrix}
1 & 0 & 0 & \Delta t & 0 & 0 \\
0 & 1 & 0 & 0 & \Delta t & 0 \\
0 & 0 & 1 & 0 & 0 & \Delta t \\
0 & 0 & 0 & 1 & 0 & 0 \\
0 & 0 & 0 & 0 & 1 & 0 \\
0 & 0 & 0 & 0 & 0 & 1
\end{bmatrix}
\tag{6.43}
$$

and no control input is used. The matrix $\mathbf{H}$ used in equation (6.20) is defined as

$$
\mathbf{H} = \begin{bmatrix}
1 & 0 & 0 & 0 & 0 & 0 \\
0 & 1 & 0 & 0 & 0 & 0 \\
0 & 0 & 1 & 0 & 0 & 0
\end{bmatrix}
\tag{6.44}
$$

relating the predicted state $\widehat{\mathbf{x}}_t^-$ to the measurement $\mathbf{z}_t = \widehat{\mathbf{l}}_t = \begin{bmatrix} \widehat{x}_t & \widehat{y}_t & \widehat{\theta}_t \end{bmatrix}^T$. The elements of the process noise and the measurement noise covariance matrices $\mathbf{Q}$ and $\mathbf{R}$ of equation (6.11) and (6.13) are zero except from constant diagonal elements. However, the measurement noise covariance matrix can also be defined based on the current sensor measurement according to one of the methods presented in [74].

Application of the Motion Model

The experimental results presented in Section 6.3.3 show that the basic self-localization algorithm including the improvements described in the previous paragraphs raises the accuracy of the pose estimation for a moving robot compared to a standard MCL algorithm while extremely reducing the necessary computational resources. However, the fast reduction of the number of samples used in the particle filter step of the algorithm makes the algorithm prone to premature convergence to local optima in the belief function. In combination with a process noise that is modeled proportional to the movement of the robot, the algorithm has difficulties to handle the kidnapped-robot problem, i. e. to recover from a wrong pose estimation. Especially in case of a non-moving robot, the additional noise is minimal and the algorithm needs many cycles to spread the samples until the correct pose can be found, independent of the estimated pose error, which could already indicate that the current pose estimation is of low quality. The final improvement to the basic self-localization algorithm thus redefines the variance of the noise terms $d_{x,t-1}$, $d_{y,t-1}$, and $d_{\theta,t-1}$ of equation (6.25) proportional to the estimated pose error of time step $t-1$. This enables the algorithm to immediately perform a broad search for a new optimum by spreading the samples if the estimation of the last cycle was of low quality. As the experimental results show, this improves the ability for a fast recovering out of a local minimum without reducing the overall accuracy of the algorithm.

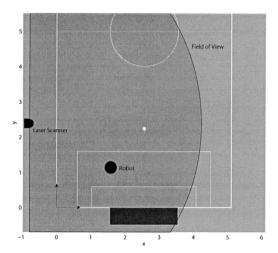

Figure 6.5: The experimental setup for the self-localization experiments. A robot moves around the RoboCup field trying to localize while a laser scanner placed outside the field observes the robot. An object detection algorithm using the distance data of the laser scanner provides ground truth data for the robot's position. The field of view of the laser scanner is limited as the effective radius of the robot is rather small and the limited angular resolution of the laser scanner results in an insufficient sampling rate at higher distances to the scanner.

6.3.3   Self-Localization Results

This section describes the experiments carried out on the new omni-directional robots to investigate the performance of the basic self-localization algorithm and its different improvements. A robot running the self-localization is statically positioned on the field or is manually controlled to move around the field and tries to localize itself. To acquire results concerning the accuracy of the pose estimation the true position of the robot was measured using a laser scanner and an accurate object detection algorithm that was used on the old Pioneer robots [157]. However, the laser scanner based object detection needs a certain amount of single rays that hit the robot for a reliable detection and thus the detection radius is rather small for the low effective diameter of the robot. The experimental setup is shown in Figure 6.5.

To identify the different versions of the self-localization algorithm compared in this section, each version was given a special name.

- The basic unaltered self-localization algorithm explained in Section 6.3.1 is referred to as *Basic* algorithm.

- The Basic algorithm with the exchanged method for evaluating the sensor model using the symmetry line is referred to as *Improved1* algorithm.

- The Basic algorithm with the exchanged method for evaluating the sensor model using the best sample is referred to as *Improved2* algorithm.

- The experiments show that the Improved2 algorithm is outperforming the others, therefore algorithm *Improved3* is based on the Improved2 algorithm but uses the Maximum-Likelihood-Estimator and the RPROP optimization technique.

- To further improve the results of the Improved3 algorithm, algorithm *Improved4* exploits the additional Kalman filtering step.

- Finally, the *Improved5* algorithm changes the motion model of algorithm Improved4 to adding noise proportional to the quality of the last pose estimation.

- To compare the performance of the self-localization algorithms to a standard Monte-Carlo localization algorithm, the Improved4 algorithm was forced to use a fixed number of 200 samples and no local optimization ($K_{max} = 0$) was used, resulting in the *MCL Reference* algorithm.

The parameterization for these algorithms used in all following experiments is given in Table 6.1.

N_{max}	R	N_{best}	λ	μ	ν	c	$\delta_{1,0}, \delta_{2,0}$	$\delta_{3,0}$	K_{max}	γ	η
200	$0.1 N_t$	N_t	0.01	0.2	$0.5 \cdot 10^{-6}$	0.8 m	10 mm	0.01 rad	20	$1.5 \cdot 10^{-3}$	-30

Table 6.1: The parameter set used for the self-localization experiments.

The first experiment that was carried out was a qualitative comparison between the Basic self-localization algorithm and a dead reckoning method for tracking the robot from a known pose using the odometry information of the wheel encoders. The robot was standing on the field and was accelerated to full speed moving 4 m and than stopped with full negative acceleration. The results shown in Figure 6.6 prove the necessity of using an external sensor for localization, as the odometry overestimates the movement of the robot because of slippage in the acceleration phases. Even with less acceleration the dead reckoning approach would fail to correctly estimate the pose of the robot after a few meters.

Then, a series of experiments with a moving robot was carried out to compare the different versions of the self-localization algorithm. The robot was manually controlled randomly around the field at two different speeds of 1 ᵐ/s and 2 ᵐ/s. Furthermore, the orientation of the robot was controlled in two different ways to simulate a differential drive, i. e. the orientation was constantly changing to be tangential to the moved path, and an omni-directional drive, i. e. the orientation was constant throughout the run. Table 6.2 lists the results of the different algorithms for the different runs, where e is the mean position error

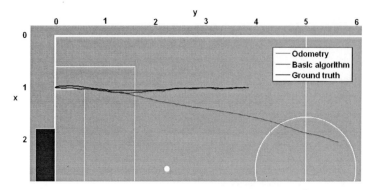

Figure 6.6: A comparison between self-localization algorithms using odometry and the omni-directional camera as external sensor for a robot moving 4 m. The odometry overestimates the movement of the robot because of slippage in the acceleration phase.

over all cycles of the run excluding the initialization phase and e^+ is the mean position error over all cycles, which is obviously worse because of the high estimation error for the initial global localization.[4] Furthermore, the mean number of samples used over all cycles N_{mean} and the percentage of cycles the algorithm used the tracking mode are shown in the table. Finally, the table lists the mean computation time per cycle for the particle filter T_{MCL}, the optimization T_{opt}, the additional Kalman filtering T_{Kafi}, and for the complete self-localization T_{tot}. The times were taken offline on a desktop computer with an Intel Pentium-4 processor with 3 GHz and 512 MB RAM which has comparable computation power to the Pentium-M computer on the robots. Graphical versions of the different results are presented in Appendix B.

Test Runs with v = 1 $^{m}\!/\!_{s}$

Obviously, the Basic algorithm and its two improved versions Improved1 and Improved2 already performed very well on the different 1 $^{m}\!/\!_{s}$ runs. With estimation errors of 10 cm to 13 cm excluding the initialization, the performance of the combined MCL and tracking algorithm was comparable to the MCL Reference algorithm. Yet, the mean number of samples used to achieve that accuracy was only 5-10% of the 200 samples of the MCL Reference algorithm, enabling the presented self-localization algorithm to perform in real-time and fit into the global 20 ms cycle of the software system. The introduction of the RPROP optimization technique using the Maximum-Likelihood-Estimator in the Improved3 algorithm further improved the self-localization algorithm. Both, the mean position error and the mean number of samples used to compute the estimation are lower. However, as the RPROP optimization technique has no termination condition other than the maximum

---

[4]The mean error excluding the initialization phase cycles was separately listed to allow for a better comparability as the length of the initialization phase and thus the magnitude of e^+ mainly depends on the initial distribution of the samples, which is random.

Algorithm	e^+ [cm]	e [cm]	N_{mean}	% Tracking	T_{MCL} [ms]	T_{opt} [ms]	T_{Kafi} [ms]	T_{tot} [ms]
Differential drive 1 m/s								
Basic	40.29	12.17	23.84	84.43	1.70	0.59	0.00	2.31
Improved1	14.66	10.89	6.31	97.17	0.36	0.38	0.00	0.77
Improved2	13.00	10.87	3.20	92.92	0.16	0.37	0.00	0.55
Improved3	9.65	9.66	2.02	99.06	0.07	1.54	0.00	1.63
Improved4	8.66	8.58	1.94	99.53	0.06	1.52	3.09	4.70
Improved5	8.93	8.77	2.08	98.58	0.07	1.56	3.14	4.81
MCL Reference	19.09	13.79	200.00	0.00	14.16	0.09	3.78	18.06
Omni-directional drive 1 m/s								
Basic	20.72	13.37	10.16	92.75	0.65	0.51	0.00	1.21
Improved1	32.94	12.50	9.84	92.31	0.65	0.43	0.00	1.10
Improved2	47.97	12.85	9.30	89.86	0.57	0.39	0.00	0.99
Improved3	29.61	11.00	3.79	94.20	0.20	1.58	0.00	1.81
Improved4	8.01	7.93	1.94	99.53	0.06	1.61	3.11	4.80
Improved5	7.88	7.88	1.96	99.52	0.06	1.62	2.95	4.66
MCL Reference	14.42	10.84	200.00	0.00	14.22	0.10	3.84	18.19
Differential drive 2 m/s								
Improved4	14.83	13.02	2.76	97.50	0.12	1.62	3.14	4.90
Improved5	16.02	13.29	2.61	97.50	0.11	1.57	3.10	4.80
MCL Reference	27.05	25.62	200.00	0.00	14.25	0.12	3.71	18.14
Omni-directional drive 2 m/s								
Improved4	25.98	22.91	10.30	83.91	0.63	1.60	3.10	5.37
Improved5	15.61	15.66	5.61	91.23	0.33	1.56	3.21	5.15
MCL Reference	36.77	33.16	200.00	0.00	13.94	0.13	3.93	18.03

Table 6.2: The experimental results of the self-localization algorithm.

number of iterations, the mean computation time increased by 1 ms compared to the Improved2 algorithm that used the optimization based on forces, which terminated when a given estimation quality was reached. Finally, the best performing algorithm on the 1 m/s runs was the Improved4 algorithm that extends the Improved3 algorithm by an additional Kalman filtering of the pose estimation. This filtering of the estimation particularly improved the results of the run with the omni-directional moving robot significantly. The mean estimation error excluding the initialization dropped to 8 cm using a mean of less than 2 samples, which is due to a very high percentage of more than 99% of the cycles where the pose was tracked with only a single sample. The additional Kalman filtering step, however, raised the mean computation time by 3 ms. Yet, an optimization of the Kalman filtering code, especially a change of the generic matrix classes to matrices that are optimized for the given problem, would reduce the computation time significantly. Nevertheless, a mean total computation time of less than 5 ms still perfectly fits into the global 20 ms cycle of the software system.

Test Runs with $v = 2$ m/s

As the best performing algorithm for the 1 m/s runs, the Improved4 algorithm was also tested for a robot running at 2 m/s. For comparison, the MCL Reference algorithm was also applied to these runs. As expected, the performance was not as good as for the 1 m/s runs, as the sensor data of the omni-directional vision system contains more noise for a fast moving robot resulting in more vibrations and even some tilting of the robot in very sharp turns. Furthermore, the relative movement from one cycle to the next is doubled. Nevertheless, the performance of the Improved4 algorithm was acceptable with a mean estimation error of 13 cm and a mean number of less than 3 samples for the differential-drive run. Unfortunately, the robot left the maximum detection range of the laser scanner for this run, as can be seen in the figures in Appendix B, resulting in a wrong ground truth and thus a high estimation error for the loop on the right side of the penalty area, which the laser did not detect.[5] In the omni-directional run with 2 m/s and constant orientation the self-localization algorithms even failed to track the position of the robot in one of the cycles where the robot was tilted by some degrees because of a sharp turn taken at the high speed, resulting in an estimation error of 23 cm for the Improved4 algorithm and 33 cm for the MCL Reference algorithm. The problem to keep track of the robot in that cycle is due to a wrong mapping of the line points from camera to world coordinates as the assumption that the main axis of the camera and the mirror is perpendicular to the floor plane does not hold for the tilted robot. However, although both algorithms simultaneously converged to the correct position of the robot after a few cycles, the Improved4 algorithm still outperformed the MCL Reference algorithm concerning the overall performance.

---

[5]The laser measurements were taken at a lower sample rate and were then interpolated to serve as the ground truth for the specific time when the images were taken on the robot. During the differential drive 2 m/s run there was a detection gap on the right side of the penalty area where the robot left the maximum detection range of the laser scanner which was interpolated as straight line resulting in a wrong ground truth for these cycles.

Kidnapped Robot Tests

The omni-directional run with 2 ᵐ/s clearly showed that a fast recovery from localization errors is an important property of a good self-localization algorithm. To estimate the performance of the different algorithms concerning the recovery from errors, a kidnapped-robot experiment was carried out. Two series of 50 images each were taken by the robot at two different poses and combined to one test sequence simulating a kidnapped-robot. The Improved4 and the MCL Reference algorithm both computed the pose estimations for the sequence in 10 different runs. The results per cycle were averaged and are shown in Figure 6.7. While the MCL Reference algorithm steadily decreased the estimation error over the first 20-30 cycles in the initialization phase and after the kidnapping, representing a stable localization of the true pose throughout all runs, the Improved4 algorithm had problems to reliably localize the robot in less than 50 cycles, especially after the kidnapping. This is due to the non-moving robot that represents a worst-case scenario for this algorithm, as the motion model of the Improved4 algorithm distributes the samples proportional to the robot's movement. To better handle the recovery from severe estimation errors, the Improved5 algorithm uses the altered motion model that spreads the samples proportional to the quality of the pose estimation. As Figure 6.7 shows, the application of this algorithm to the kidnapped-robot problem improved the performance of the combined MCL and tracking method. Although the MCL Reference algorithm still had a smaller estimation error from cycle 10 to 37, the Improved5 algorithm converges to a much better pose estimation in the long run and even handled the kidnapping better than the Reference algorithm. Nevertheless, the performance of the Improved5 algorithm for the tracking experiments was comparable to the Improved4 algorithm. For the omni-directional run with 2 ᵐ/s the results were even significantly better for the Improved5 algorithm, as the recovery from the localization error was much faster. The results for the Improved5 algorithm are also given in Table 6.2 and in the figures in Appendix B.

Finally, the Improved5 algorithm was chosen as self-localization algorithm for the software system of the Attempto Tübingen Robot Soccer Team, as it combines a very high accuracy of the pose estimation with a fast recovery from severe errors in the pose estimation. This algorithm also outperforms a standard Monte-Carlo Localization with a fixed number of samples both in accuracy and computation time and fits perfectly into the global 20 ms cycle of the software system.

6.4 Object Tracking

To let the robot move at high speeds in its dynamic environment without colliding with other objects implies not only a good pose estimation and an accurate object detection but also an object tracking approach that is able to give qualitative estimations of an object's position even if the object is temporarily out of the sensor's field of view. Furthermore, information on the velocity of an object and thus its predicted movement is important for

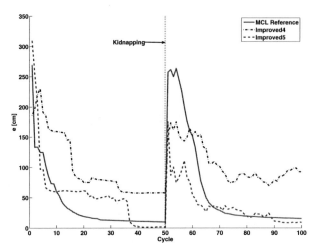

Figure 6.7: The results of the kidnapped-robot problem.

avoiding the highly dynamic objects in RoboCup. Especially, for the more sophisticated actions like passing and intercepting the ball, the estimation and incorporation of the movement of objects is essential. Therefore, the environment modeling process of the Attempto Tübingen Robot Soccer Team includes a Kalman filter based object tracking.

In contrast to the self-localization algorithm, the state vector of a tracked object includes only two-dimensional position and velocity information, as the ball has no orientation and the orientation of other robots is hard to detect

$$\mathbf{x}_t = \begin{bmatrix} x & y & v_x & v_y \end{bmatrix}^T \tag{6.45}$$

As most of the robots in RoboCup are equipped with omni-directional drives, this does not impose a problem to the tracking, as the orientation of an omni-directional robot does not give any information on the direction of movement. Similar to the self-localization algorithm, the motion model assumes an object movement with constant velocity which is applicable to the low acceleration of a robot

$$\mathbf{A} = \begin{bmatrix} 1 & 0 & \Delta t & 0 \\ 0 & 1 & 0 & \Delta t \\ 0 & 0 & 1 & 0 \\ 0 & 0 & 0 & 1 \end{bmatrix} \tag{6.46}$$

However, the ball sometimes collides with other objects or changes its velocity rather quickly when being kicked by a robot. Such accelerations are not designed in the motion model and reduce the quality of the tracking. There are several ways to handle such situations. Firstly, the process noise could be increased to include the expected inaccuracies of the model. This would raise the influence of the measurement and could improve the tracking in such situations. However, this would also increase the overall variance of the estimation, as the measurement has more influence. Secondly, the ball could be tracked by a separate filter with a more sophisticated motion model or even with a bank of filters using different motion models as done in the *IMM-Filter* approach [21]. Thirdly, an efficient management of object hypotheses can be used to start new object tracks if the ball abruptly changes its direction of movement and therefore the current measurement does not match any existing hypothesis. The latter approach is used in the environment model of the Attempto Tübingen Robot Soccer Team. The probabilistic methods for assigning measurements to existing object hypotheses and for the creation and deletion of new hypotheses presented in [74] in combination with the very high update rate of the system result in an acceptable tracking accuracy even for the ball.

As the image processing can not give any information on the velocity of the objects it is estimated as a hidden state in the Kalman filter and the matrix $\mathbf{H}$ is

$$\mathbf{H} = \begin{bmatrix} 1 & 0 & 0 & 0 \\ 0 & 1 & 0 & 0 \end{bmatrix} \tag{6.47}$$

For obvious reasons, the control input vector of equation (6.19) is neglected in the object tracking filter algorithm.

6.5 Inter-Robot Communication

There are three reasons for a communication from a control computer to the robots and between the robots of a team. Firstly, the control computer is used to remotely start the robots prior to a match and to stop their motion in case of an emergency. Furthermore, the game flow messages and the commands of the Referee Box have to be sent to the robots. Secondly, the communication of the robot's pose and the tracked objects enables the teammates to enhance the field of view of their own environment model by integrating the information. Thirdly, some teams use the communication to negotiate high-level decisions like passing or role assignment.

As explained in Chapter 7, the inter-robot communication used in the software system of the Attempto Tübingen Robot Soccer Team follows the paradigm of distributed control, where each robot takes its high-level decisions based only on the information in its environment model. Therefore, there is no communication or negotiation of high-level decisions between the robots. However, the robots communicate a certain amount of the information contained in their environment model to enhance the limited field of view of the single robot and enable the robot to decide on a broader basis. Instead of a simple insertion of remote objects that lie outside of the own field of view into the own environment model, the Kalman filter based object tracking algorithm is able to do a matching of the remote object hypotheses to its own object hypotheses in cases where an object is seen by more than one robot of a team. For that, the algorithm uses the covariance matrices of the remote object hypotheses for an intelligent object matching. After the matching process, the object hypotheses from other robots can be integrated just like any other measurement of the object state. This not only enhances the field of view of the robots, but also improves the estimation accuracy [74]. However, the probabilistic object fusion algorithm needs to communicate the complete covariance matrix of the objects which results in a higher amount of data transmitted between the robots. As the organizers of the RoboCup championships recommend a rather low bandwidth of 1 Mbit/s per team and the bandwidth needed for this type of communication is nearly twice as high, this object fusion technique was never used in the tournaments. Instead, the robots only communicated their own position and that of the ball which was included in the models of the teammates, keeping the bandwidth at a minimum.

6.6   User Interface

The EnvironmentModel process provides access to its data through an interface called EnvironmentModelClient. A process trying to read the environment model data thus creates an instance of the client interface and can use the provided methods to get the current pose of the robot, the object data including the team color of the object, the current home field color and all other robot and environment related data. In contrast to the clients presented in the previous chapters no device has to be specified as only one instance of the EnvironmentModel exists per robot.

The interface to the CommServer process handling the inter-robot communication is split into two clients. To access the current status of the game flow as sent by the Referee Box or the graphical user interface, other processes create an instance of the CommServerRemoteCommandClient. To access the remote data of the teammates, processes create an instance of the CommServerRemoteDataClient.

6.7   Implementation

Upon startup, the EnvironmentModel reads the configuration information from a file that specifies the device names of the sensors that provide data of the environment. The amount of sensors ranges from two cameras, a laser scanner, and the wheel encoders of the old Pioneer robots to only one camera and the wheel encoders of the new robots. The main loop of the process starts with the collection of the data from the sensors. Here, only the client for the sensor with the lowest update rate is configured to wait for new data, as all other sensors queried later are expected to have new data anyway. That means, that the environment modeling process and thus the high-level control, which is depending on the environment model data, is synchronized to the cycle time of the slowest sensor. For the old Pioneer robots this resulted in the 100 ms cycle time of the laser sensor, while for the new robots a cycle time of 20 ms could be achieved with the new camera system. The collection of the sensor data also includes the retrieval of remote data from the teammates using the client to the `CommServer` data. The next step in the loop is one complete cycle of the pose estimation process generating a new pose estimation for the current sensor data followed by a Kalman filtering step resulting in the final pose estimation which is written into the shared memory buffer. Afterwards, all object hypotheses are predicted, matched, and updated with the object data of the own sensors or, if specified, of the remote robots. For that, a synchronization of the clocks of the robots is needed to compare the time stamps included with the remote data and to predict the object hypotheses to the time of the sensor snapshot. Therefore, each robot has a network time protocol daemon running that synchronizes the clocks of the robot computers with that of the control computer.

The `CommServer` process is split up into two independent threads. The first thread collects the environment model data and sends it to the teammates. For this type of communication UDP broadcast messages are used to keep the network traffic as low as possible by sending the information to all computers in the team's subnet with only one message. The second thread collects the broadcast data received from the teammates and the Referee Box and stores the data in internal buffers for each remote robot. Thus, the internal buffers always represent the status quo of the asynchronously sent data from the remote robots. In a fixed interval of 20 ms this thread fills the data from the internal buffers into a shared memory buffer and releases it to be read by the `EnvironmentModel`.

Chapter 7

High-Level Control

This chapter presents the final module of the software system of the Attempto Tübingen Robot Soccer Team. The high-level control process analyzes the data contained in the environment model and computes driving and kicking commands that are sent to the motor controller to successfully play a game of robot soccer in cooperation with its teammates. The amount of preprocessed data used from the environment model, however, differs between the goalkeeper and the field players, as they are controlled by two different systems. The goalkeeper software was essentially designed as a reactive behavior-based system with simple condition-action rules. Although the goalkeeper has a behavior that exploits the velocity information of the ball given by the environment model, the majority of behaviors simply reacts directly to the ball's position. The field players, on the other hand, are built as a hybrid control system that also includes some simple behaviors, e. g. for dribbling and shooting the ball, but furthermore uses different roles based on the current game situation and a path planner algorithm to plan an efficient collision-free path to a given target point. To classify and to compare the high-level control systems of the goalkeeper and the field players with other systems presented in the literature, the next section resumes the review of the different control architectures that has been touched on in Chapter 6, followed by a survey on the approaches used by other RoboCup teams. The subsequent sections cover the control systems of the goalkeeper and the field players, followed by a review of the cooperative elements in the high-level control of the Attempto Tübingen Robot Soccer Team. Finally, the last section contains a detailed presentation of the path planning algorithm used in the field player software.

Experimental results that evaluate the high-level control architecture are very hard to carry out, since it has to be tested in a real RoboCup match, and there are many uncontrollable influences, to which the control system reacts, which makes a sound comparison of different approaches impossible. Yet, Chapter 8 presents a review of the overall team performance at the past RoboCup tournaments which contains some hints on the impact of several design issues, including the high-level control software, on the team's performance.

7.1   Related Work

> To quickly react against the ball and move around the field, the use of sub-
> sumption architecture (Brooks 1986), or another reactive approach, might be
> effective. However, soccer players need to have global strategy as well as
> local tactics, which cannot be accomplished by mere reactive systems.
>
>   Hiroaki Kitano *et al.* [114]

This statement of Kitano *et al.* precisely characterizes one of the main research topics especially in RoboCup but also for a huge number of real world robotics applications. Robo-
Cup was initially designed as a standard challenge for artificial intelligence and robotics
that reveals how inadequate the Omniscient Fortune Teller Assumptions model the real
world (cf. Chapter 1). Therefore, the pure deliberative Sense-Model-Plan-Act architecture presented in Chapter 6 that is based on these assumptions of a complete and definite
knowledge is not applicable to RoboCup. In their statement, however, Kitano *et al.* also
note that the other extreme, the mere reactive approach, might be effective for quick re-
sponses to the dynamically changing environment, but not powerful enough to cope with
the strategic demands of playing soccer.

In his book on behavior-based robotics [8] Arkin depicts a spectrum of robot control
strategies comparing the deliberative and the reactive architectures. While the speed of
the system response to changes in its environment increases with the amount of reactiveness of a system, the capabilities of a system to predict the results of its actions and
thus the ability to take strategic decisions rises with the amount of deliberation. Furthermore, the dependence on accurate and complete world models increases towards the
deliberative systems. As an example for the pure deliberative approach Arkin indicates
the hierarchical architecture presented by Albus [4], whereas the leading proponent of the
mere reactive approach is Brooks with the subsumption architecture [26] that was also
mentioned in the statement of Kitano *et al.*. Obviously, both architectures provide solu-
tions for different requirements and there is a trade-off between the advantages of the two
methods. Although there exist hybrid approaches trying to integrate reactive and deliberative aspects in a single system, current robotics research tries to find the most promising
balance of the two philosophies. The book of Hannebauer *et al.* [77] contains an overview
of recent proposals.

In the RoboCup research it seems that the number of architectures used to control the
robots is as high as the number of competing teams and the balance between reactive
and deliberative aspects of the systems varies greatly. A large amount of approaches from
different leagues of the RoboCup is based on a set of reactive behaviors. However, to gain
a certain amount of tactical and strategic qualities, different behavioral architectures were
proposed. Lenser *et al.* [124] and Behnke *et al.* [17] presented a hierarchy of behaviors.
In the system of Lenser *et al.* the behaviors of the higher levels define goals for those

of the lower levels, thus refining a given abstract task to concrete actions taken by the robot. The system of Behnke *et al.* is based on the *Dual Dynamics* approach of Jaeger *et al.* [98] where the lower level behaviors establish the high speed basic skills while the higher level behaviors are responsible for the low speed tactical and strategic skills. Each behavior not only computes commands for the robot but also an activation value that controls the amount of influence the behavior has on the robot. According to the system design, higher level behaviors can influence the activation of lower level behaviors to change the overall dynamics of the basic skills. A different way to generate an overall team performance from simple behaviors that is able to fulfill the strategic demands of RoboCup is to apply optimization algorithms. In their first approach, Uchibe *et al.* [194] used genetic programming techniques to learn simple if-then rules from a set of predicates and actions as optimal behaviors. In a second approach, they extended their learning algorithm to an optimal switching strategy between behaviors [195]. Takahashi *et al.* [188] proposed a method for learning the best combination of different player types, each with a fixed set of behaviors, as a team strategy according to the observed strategy of the opponent team. The basic assumption of the last two approaches is that, depending on its current environment and the specific game situation, different sets of behaviors are optimal for a robot. These behavior sets are also called *roles*. In many architectures each robot in a team is assigned a specific role that may also dynamically change [156, 72, 17, 30, 123]. A common role is that of an attacker, which is usually the role of the robot that is in possession of the ball. It is obvious that this role is comprised of a completely different set of behaviors than the role of a defender. In contrast to Uchibe *et al.*, the system of Behnke *et al.* [17] uses a manually developed, dynamic assignment of the roles. Each role has a certain home position that defines the center of an area of the field where it is reasonable to take this role and the role assignment depends on the dynamic position of the robot relative to the home positions of the roles. Instead of externally computing and assigning the roles to the robots, in the system of Buck *et al.* [30] each robot locally computes a global role assignment and selects its assigned role. A good overview of different role assignment techniques is given in [66].

Although nearly all architectures include some sort of low-level reactive component that tries to cope with the game dynamics, many groups try to enhance the tactical and strategic abilities of their systems through a certain amount of planning. In its simplest case, this includes only the planning of a collision-free path towards a target with moderate computational costs in order to stay reactive [72]. Other approaches try to keep the resources needed for planning at a low level by mixing reactive and deliberative components such that the reactive components are traversed at a higher rate and the deliberative component is given more time to plan [190, 37]. In order to use behaviors for planning and reasoning, Shen *et al.* [174] proposed the concept of *purposeful behaviors* where the purpose of a behavior is a prediction of the state after the action of the behavior was taken. This prediction enables the system to do backward planning from a specified target state. Finally, the architectures of Burkhard *et al.* [33], Vecht *et al.* [199], and Fraser *et al.* [65] include the extensive use of deliberation through case based reasoning, arrangements and commitments made between two players, and planning with plan invariants, respectively. Especially for multi-robot tactics and team strategy using the commitments mechanism of the system of Vecht *et al.*, the robot team needs some kind of explicit communication. A pass commitment, for example, is negotiated between the passing and the receiving robot with special request and accept messages. This is similar to the passing procedure proposed in [94]. Other forms of explicit communication include team strategy agreement between the robots of a team [127], role assignment [72], and even requests and orders sent to other robots [208, 2]. Although Iocchi *et al.* classify only systems using strong coordination through a coordination protocol as deliberative in their multi-robot systems classification [97], the use of explicit communication and coordination is not necessary for high-level cooperative team behavior. Several publications demonstrated a certain level of cooperation without communication [153, 38, 17]. These systems cooperate through observation of the environment and by anticipating the behaviors of others, especially teammates, resulting in successful passing between two robots.

7.2 Goalkeeper Control

The Attempto Tübingen Robot Soccer Team always had a separate hardware configuration for the goalkeeper, i. e. a special goalkeeper robot, and thus never changed the role of the goalkeeper dynamically with other robots. The extra rules for the goal area that no other robot is allowed to enter and the exceptional size constraints of goalkeepers further support the use of a dedicated goalkeeper robot. Therefore, the tactical system of the goalkeeper of the team is completely self-sufficient and different from that of the field players.[1] Without the need of team coordination, the goalkeeper high-level control was thus entirely designed as a reactive behavior-based system. Even obstacle avoidance skills that are necessary for all other players can be neglected if the goalkeeper stays in its goal area.

Figure 7.1 shows the behavioral system designed for the goalkeeper. There are two general types of behaviors, *drive behaviors* and *kick behaviors*, as the RobotServer can either process a drive or a kicking command per cycle.[2] While there is only a simple kick behavior, which kicks the ball at full strength, if the robot is in possession of the ball, a collection of different drive behaviors is contained in the system. Obviously, the majority of the drive behaviors tries to move the goalkeeper to a position were it can effectively prevent the ball from entering the goal. If the ball is not visible for more than two seconds, the HomeDefense behavior positions the goalkeeper at its home position

---

[1]In case of a hardware failure, though, it is still possible to run the high-level control software of the goalkeeper on a field player robot, since the hardware abstraction layer provides a common interface for all hardware including the different kicking devices.

[2]Nevertheless, the robot does not stop when a kicking command is executed, as it keeps the wheel speeds of the last driving command until a new driving command is issued.

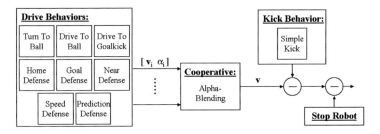

Figure 7.1: The behavior-based high-level control system of the goalkeeper.

in the middle of the goal area. The GoalDefense behavior follows the paradigm to minimize the angular range for a successful kick into the goal. To prevent complex angular calculations the bisecting line of the goal's opening angle is approximated by the line from the ball to the middle of the goal as shown in the top left panel of Figure 7.2. In conclusion, the goalkeeper is positioned on this line in a distance to the goal line equal to that of its home position. However, if the ball is near the goal, especially near one of the goal posts, this position is inappropriate, as it does not defend the short corner. Therefore, the NearDefense behavior was introduced that moves the goalkeeper in a line between the ball and the goal line, perpendicular to the goal line as shown in the top right panel of Figure 7.2. Furthermore, there are two more sophisticated behaviors that react to the ball's velocity or try to guess the direction of a future kick. If the SpeedDefense behavior detects that the ball moves towards the goal, it tries to intercept the ball by moving perpendicular into the ball's trajectory as shown in the lower left panel of Figure 7.2. The PredictionDefense, instead, tries to effectively position the goalkeeper before the ball is kicked by moving the robot onto the line through the ball and the opponent robot that is in possession of the ball. Since most RoboCup robots are only able to shoot the ball radially away from their center this line is a good prediction of the ball's trajectory after a kick. These defensive behaviors are very similar to those presented by Weigel *et al.* [203] and Menegatti *et al.* [141].

In addition to the defensive drive behaviors, there are three special drive behaviors. The TurnToBall behavior rotates the robot front with the kicker towards the ball. To kick the ball away from the goal, the DriveToBall behavior moves the goalkeeper to the ball. Finally, if there is a goal kick, the DriveToGoalkick behavior moves the robot to the appropriate restart point.

Since none of these behaviors is exclusively optimal, except from the DriveToGoalkick behavior, the drive behaviors in this system can all be active at the same time. Thus, a special behavior selection and switching mechanism as used in many approaches presented in Section 7.1 is not needed. Yet, to save computational resources for behaviors that do complex calculations, all behaviors initially decide on their activation based on simple

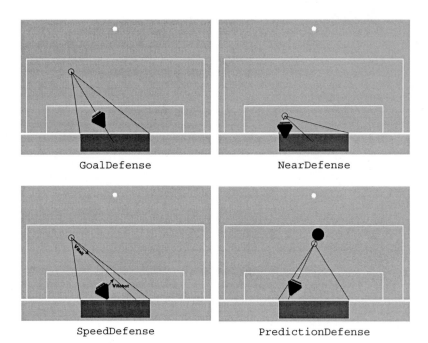

GoalDefense   NearDefense

SpeedDefense   PredictionDefense

Figure 7.2: The defensive drive behaviors of the goalkeeper.

preconditions, like being in possession of the ball (`SimpleKick` behavior) or seeing the ball. All active drive behaviors then compute a driving command $\mathbf{v}_i$ and a weight $\alpha_i \in \mathbb{R}^+$ that expresses the suitability of the behavior to defend the goal in the current game situation. The different driving commands of the active behaviors are finally averaged by normalizing the weights and computing the weighted mean of the single commands

$$\mathbf{v} = \frac{1}{\sum_i \alpha_i} \sum_i \alpha_i \mathbf{v}_i \qquad (7.1)$$

As a fallback behavior, the `HomeDefense` behavior is always active but has a very low weight to prevent interference with other behaviors if the ball is visible. Similar, the `TurnToBall` behavior is always active, since it is the only drive behavior that sets a rotational speed. Furthermore, it is obvious, that the `DriveToGoalkick` behavior is only active in the special game situation of a goal kick. All other drive behaviors, however, cooperatively control the robot to defend the goal. Although it is not possible to present exact results on the performance of this behavioral system, the defensive records of the Attempto Tübingen Robot Soccer Team addressed in Chapter 8 exhibit a strong improvement with the introduction of the new goalkeeper system in 2004.

7.3   Field Player Control

In contrast to the goalkeeper that has a clearly specified task and workspace, the field players have a more distinctive mission ranging from defensive to offensive tasks and also have to cope with competing and cooperating robots. The behavioral system of the field players is thus more complex and is designed as a hybrid control system that also includes some basic behaviors but furthermore contains a set of tactical roles that specify a target point and a path planner that plans a collision-free path to this target. Figure 7.3 gives an overview of the field player high-level control architecture.

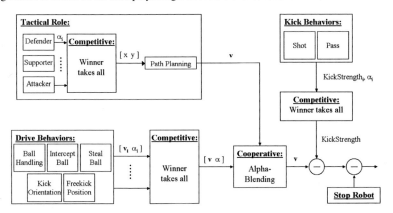

Figure 7.3: The hybrid high-level control system of the field players.

Tactical Roles

There are three different tactical roles, `Attacker`, `Supporter`, and `Defender`, of which the `Attacker` is the most elaborate role.

Generally, the `Attacker` tries to obtain control over the ball, then drive to the opponent goal and score a goal. As long as the robot is not in possession of the ball, the target of the `Attacker` is the ball and is thus constantly changing. Once the robot has the ball, its new target depends on its relative position to the goal. If the `Attacker` is inside a special trapezoid area in front of the goal, called *shot zone*, it is allowed to move directly to the free corner of the goal and try to score. This shot zone is defined by two points on the field and is usually as wide as the penalty area and extends to the penalty point (cf.

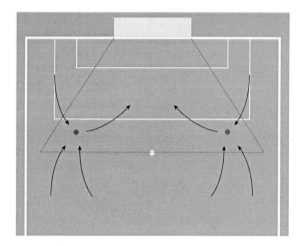

Figure 7.4: The fixpoints and the shot zone for the `Attacker` role.

the red trapezoid shown in Figure 7.4). If the robot is not inside the shot zone, however, instead of moving directly towards the goal, the `Attacker` first heads to one of two special points near the goal, called *fixpoints*, that usually are defined in the corners of the trapezoid shot zone (cf. red circles in Figure 7.4). Upon entering the shot zone, the robot can directly move to the goal. The detour to the fixpoint has a positive effect on the game play of the `Attacker`. If the ball was captured in a corner of the field, heading directly towards the goal will most likely fail, since the opponent goalkeeper will stand close to the short corner of the goal. By first moving away from the goal line, the shooting angle towards the goal and thus the possibility to score increases. The same applies to situations where the `Attacker` obtains the ball in the middle of the field. It is a common practice in soccer to move with the ball towards one side of the field to attract the goalkeeper to the short corner. This enables the `Attacker` to shoot into the far corner of the goal or to play a pass to a teammate on the other side of the field.

For the latter case, the `Supporter` moves to the second fixpoint that is on the other side of the field and awaits a pass from the `Attacker`. As the `Supporter` is moving towards the fixpoint as soon as the `Attacker` captures the ball, it can also receive clearance passes from the own half of the field.

Finally, a `Defender` tries to cover one of the corners of the own goal in the same way as the goalkeeper does but taking only one of the goal posts and the position of the goalkeeper to define the opening angle. As there are usually two robots with the `Defender` role, each `Defender` covers the corner that it is closer to in relation to the other `Defender`.

The inter-robot communication used in the software system of the Attempto Tübingen Robot Soccer Team follows the paradigm of distributed control, i. e. each robot takes its high-level decisions based only on the information in its environment model. Therefore, no communication or negotiation of high-level decisions between the robots is designed in the system. The assignment of the tactical roles to the robots is thus made autonomously on each robot according to a simple geometric rule, similar to the system of Buck *et al.* [30]. The robot that is nearest to the ball is assigned the `Attacker` role. From the remaining robots, the one that is nearest to the opponent goal becomes the `Supporter` and the two remaining robots are assigned the `Defender` role. As this assignment rule is identical for all robots, the roles assigned should be identical, too, provided that the environment model of the robots includes the same information on the position of the ball and the teammates. This is already achieved with the minimum communication described in Chapter 6 that includes only the positions of the ball and the sending robot. However, even in case of a communication failure this assignment rule is robust, as all robots that do not see the ball for more than two seconds become defenders until they see the ball. Likewise, if two robots only see the ball and both select the role of the `Attacker` they will adjust their role assignment as soon as they are both close enough to the ball and detect each other with their object detection. Although this is not an optimal behavior, it appeared to be quite effective in many official RoboCup games where communication failures were a common problem.

To keep the set of tactical roles modular and scalable, each tactical role computes an activation value between zero and one and a successive competitive arbitration unit then selects the tactical role with the highest activation. If no tactical role computed an activation value greater than zero, a default role, i. e. the `Defender`, becomes active. Thus, the set of tactical roles can be easily extended. With the simple geometric rule for role assignment described above, the roles either select full activation or none and are completely disjunct. However, the activation values could also be used to implement a temporal hysteresis in role assignment.

While the tactical roles only define a target point for the robot, the path planning module takes the position and the movement of the other robots into account to plan a collision-free path towards the target. Using this path, the desired velocity of the robot is determined by multiplying a normalized tangential vector to the path with the maximum speed of the robot. The path planner thus always controls the robot at full speed. However, the maximum speed of the robot can be lowered in the vicinity of other robots to reduce the risk of a collision. As the path planning approach is a research topic of its own, the algorithm is explained in full detail in Section 7.5.

Drive Behaviors

The resulting velocity from the tactical system is used as input to the drive behaviors which compute a modulation to this globally optimal movement according to local influences. Again, the behaviors supply an activation value specifying the importance of their local deviation and only the behavior with the highest activation is allowed to modulate the global movement. The movement computed by the behavior and the movement computed by the tactical role are finally combined in a cooperative arbitration unit using alpha blending with the activation value. The higher the activation of the behavior, the higher its influence on the resulting movement. This is similar to the behavior selection by behavior specified activation values presented in [124].

The need for local deviations from the global path is most evident for an attacking robot, which is in control of the ball. Since the robot has no active device to keep the ball under control, its movement is constrained. Sharp turns with the ball, for example, cannot be achieved without reducing the robot's speed and adding a rotational component. In such situations the `BallHandling` behavior therefore slightly changes the movement of the robot. The stronger the desired movement of the tactical role differs from the current movement of the robot, the higher the activation value of the `BallHandling` behavior and the higher the influence of the local deviation from the global path to keep the ball under control. In the current system, the `BallHandling` behavior only competes with the `KickOrientation` behavior that also tries to rotate the robot around the moving ball to reach a good orientation to kick the ball, either shooting it into the goal or passing it to a teammate. As a kick without the control over the ball is useless, the `BallHandling` behavior generally computes a higher activation value to allow a change of the orientation by `KickOrientation` only if the ball is completely under control.

Another pair of competing behaviors is active, if the attacking robot is not in possession of the ball. Then, the `StealBall` behavior is active, if the ball is under control by an opponent player, and the `InterceptBall` behavior is active, if the ball is freely moving. The `StealBall` behavior gradually slows down the movement in the vicinity of the ball, not to risk a foul when bumping into the opponent. Furthermore, it rotates the robot around its center after reaching the ball to be able to steal the ball from the opponent without touching the robot. However, if the ball is freely moving around the field, the `InterceptBall` behavior tries to intercept the ball and obtain control over it. Besides the `BallHandling` behavior, that uses a model predictive controller to rotate the robot to keep the ball in possession, the `InterceptBall` is the most elaborate behavior. In an intercept scenario, the `Attacker` role computes a target position where the robot is able to intercept the ball by extrapolating the current velocity of the ball. It then tries to control the robot at full speed to this position. However, if the robot stops at the intercept position, the ball will hit the robot and rebound. To effectively gain control over the ball, the robot should face the ball and try to anticipate the movement of the ball, i. e. moving backwards with nearly the same speed to gradually slow down the ball. This is done through the alpha blending with the movement of the `InterceptBall` behavior. The software implementation of this behavior and also some hardware means to decelerate the bouncing ball are published in [12].

Finally, the `FreekickPosition` behavior is responsible for positioning and orienting the robots in a game stop situation, e. g. a throw-in or a goal kick, in order to be able to play a pass. The figures in Appendix C show image sequences of robots controlled by the mentioned behaviors during games of the RoboCup World Cup 2006 in Bremen. If the robot is in a good pose for shooting into the goal or for passing the ball to a teammate, the kick behaviors might suppress the current driving command and release a kicking command instead. However, as this avoids changing the current speed of the robot and the capacitor for the electric kicker needs to reload, a kicking command is only allowed once every second. Again the two kick behaviors $Shot$ and $Pass$ compute an activation value and are arbitrated in a competitive way. While the $Shot$ behavior simply kicks the ball with full strength, if the robot is oriented towards a free part of the goal, the $Pass$ behavior tries to pass the ball, if there is a free corridor towards a teammate. The kicking strength is then lowered accordingly to enable the pass receiver to gain control over the ball.

For safety reasons, the final output can be suppressed by a stop signal, i. e. a special command that immediately stops the robot's movement. In each cycle of the high-level control process, the tactical role is computed, a new path is planned, a behavior is selected and its output is combined with the driving command of the tactical role, and finally, the resulting drive or kicking command is assigned to the $RobotServer$ process. Thus, the control of the robot remains very reactive, as it still keeps the global 20 ms cycle time.

7.4 Cooperation

Besides the cooperation that is already inherent in the role assignment, i. e. the distribution of tasks to the different robots of a team, successfully passing the ball to a teammate out of a disadvantageous situation is probably the most wanted, but also most challenging cooperative team behavior in robot soccer. There are many necessary prerequisites for a successful pass. Firstly, the passing robot must recognize a teammate that is in a good pass receiving position, i. e. in a strategic position free of covering opponent robots. Secondly, it has to assure a free corridor towards the pass receiver throughout the time until the pass reaches the receiving robot, considering the velocity of the opponent robots. And finally, it has to pass the ball at a reasonable speed into the correct direction. On the other hand, the pass receiver has to find a position for receiving a pass, it has to recognize a pass when the ball approaches, and it has to intercept the ball and gain control over it.

Passing the ball to a teammate in standard situations, e. g. a throw-in or a goal kick, is quite easy to accomplish, since the game is stopped, the robots have time to drive to predefined positions, and there is an area with a radius of 2 m around the ball where no opponent player can interfere with the pass. Therefore, a number of teams including the Attempto Tübingen Robot Soccer Team were able to pass in these situations at the RoboCup World Cup 2006 in Bremen (cf. Figures C.2 and C.3 in Appendix C). However, passing in a running game is much more difficult, as the position of the passer and the pass receiver is variable, opponent robots could interfere with the pass, and the pass has to be played into the trajectory of the pass receiver. There are several approaches to handle these difficulties. The first is not to pass at all, as done by many teams, since the identification of a good passing situation is complex in a distributed system and the possibility to loose the ball is often perceived as being higher than the potential benefit of keeping the ball and trying to score. Another approach is to try to lower the possibility of a ball loss by extensive planning and negotiation between the passer and a possible pass receiver as presented in Section 7.1. Since the inter-robot communication used in the software system of the Attempto Tübingen Robot Soccer Team follows the paradigm of distributed control, where each robot takes its high-level decisions based only on its own environment model, there is no communication or negotiation of high-level decisions between the robots. Cooperative team behaviors like passing thus have to emerge from implicit rules that are known by each robot of the team.

A pass in this framework is only done between the Attacker as the passer and the Supporter as the pass receiver. Therefore, to formulate implicit rules to accomplish a passing behavior is not very complex. The Attacker constantly assesses the position of the Supporter in terms of a good pass receiving position. In the simplest case the Supporter is in a good position, if there is no opponent robot in a certain radius around it and no opponent would interfere with a pass, considering its current velocity. In such a situation, a pass can be played by kicking the ball at a speed proportional to the distance to the receiver. Soon after the ball was passed, the Attacker and the Supporter switch their roles, as the ball is now approaching the Supporter and the Attacker is usually the nearest robot to the opponent goal. The pass receiver now automatically tries to intercept the ball as the new Attacker using the InterceptBall behavior. Thus, without specifying a special behavior or negotiating a pass, a passing behavior emerges. With this approach, the Attempto Tübingen Robot Soccer Team was one of a very few teams that performed successful in-game passing at the RoboCup World Cup 2006 in Bremen, as shown in Figures C.7 and C.8 in Appendix C. Although this was not yet done, it is easy to use the algorithm of the Attacker to assess a good receiving position of the Supporter, on the Supporter to specify a good receiving position as target. Furthermore, it is possible to enhance the algorithm to incorporate a good strategic position into the assessment of the receiving position. Finally, with this approach even a double pass is possible, as the Attacker, after passing the ball to the Supporter, becomes Supporter itself and tries to reach a good receiving position, while the pass receiver now becomes the Attacker which might recognize the new Supporter as being in a good receiving position and pass the ball again, thus concluding a double pass.

7.5   Path Planning

Planning collision-free paths is one of the basic skills that is needed by a mobile robot in order to perform a goal-oriented task. Especially in highly dynamic environments there is a need for efficient navigation avoiding the fast moving obstacles. Navigation thus requires real time path planning considering the movement of the obstacles. Although there are publications on path planning in the RoboCup domain (e. g. [13, 204, 40]), the presented approaches do not incorporate the speed of the obstacles into the planned paths. This section presents a path planning algorithm that extends the approach introduced by Weigel *et al.* [204] to a path planner that considers the movement of the obstacles over time. Using this method results in smoother paths and less collisions in several scenarios, that frequently occur in RoboCup.

The method of Weigel *et al.* is one of the most efficient approaches for path planning in the RoboCup domain. It uses a combination of a *potential field* and grid-based path planning to plan out of local minima, which is presented in the next three sections.

Potential Field

The idea of using a potential field for mobile robot movement was first presented by Khatib [111]. The robot is exposed to an attractive potential towards the target and repulsive potentials away from obstacles and field boundaries or walls and moves according to an artificial force computed as the negative gradient of this potential field. The path followed by the robot in such a potential field is comparable to the path an electric particle would follow in a potential field produced by other attractive or repulsive electric charges. The robot is always heading towards the next position with lower potential, thus automatically avoiding the high potential of the obstacles.

The potential field at position $\mathbf{x} = \begin{bmatrix} x & y \end{bmatrix}^T$ is composed of an attractive potential well $p_{att}(\mathbf{x})$ centered at the target $\mathbf{g} = \begin{bmatrix} g_x & g_y \end{bmatrix}^T$ and repulsive potential barriers $p_{obs,i}(\mathbf{x})$ centered at the position of obstacles $\mathbf{o}_i = \begin{bmatrix} o_{x,i} & o_{y,i} \end{bmatrix}^T$ as well as $p_{wall,j}(\mathbf{x})$ at walls $\mathbf{w}_j = \begin{bmatrix} 0 & w_{y,j} \end{bmatrix}^T$ in x-direction and at walls $\mathbf{w}_j = \begin{bmatrix} w_{x,j} & 0 \end{bmatrix}^T$ in y-direction. The attractive potential is modeled as a conic potential well

$$p_{att}(\mathbf{x}) = \rho_{att} \| \mathbf{d}_{att}(\mathbf{x}) \| \tag{7.2}$$

with $\mathbf{d}_{att}(\mathbf{x}) = (\mathbf{x} - \mathbf{g})$ that results in a movement towards the target at constant velocity, as the artificial force

$$f_{att}(\mathbf{x}) = -\nabla p_{att}(\mathbf{x}) = -\frac{\rho_{att}}{\| \mathbf{d}_{att}(\mathbf{x}) \|} \mathbf{d}_{att}(\mathbf{x}) \tag{7.3}$$

linearly decreases towards the target. The repulsive potential barriers are modeled with a potential inversely proportional to the squared distance to the obstacle

$$p_{obs,i}(\mathbf{x}) = \begin{cases} \rho_{obs} & \text{if} & \| \mathbf{d}_{obs,i}(\mathbf{x}) \|^2 \leq {\mu_{obs}}^2 \\ \rho_{obs} \kappa_{obs} \left(\frac{1}{\| \mathbf{d}_{obs,i}(\mathbf{x}) \|^2} - \frac{1}{{M_{obs}}^2} \right) & \text{if} & {\mu_{obs}}^2 < \| \mathbf{d}_{obs,i}(\mathbf{x}) \|^2 < {M_{obs}}^2 \\ 0 & \text{if} & {M_{obs}}^2 \leq \| \mathbf{d}_{obs,i}(\mathbf{x}) \|^2 \end{cases} \tag{7.4}$$

for the obstacles, with vectors $\mathbf{d}_{obs,i}(\mathbf{x}) = (\mathbf{x} - \mathbf{o}_i)$. Here

$$\kappa_{obs} = \frac{M_{obs}{}^2 \mu_{obs}{}^2}{M_{obs}{}^2 - \mu_{obs}{}^2} \tag{7.5}$$

is a normalization factor used to make $p_{obs,i}(\mathbf{x})$ continuous at $\|\mathbf{d}_{obs,i}(\mathbf{x})\|^2 = \mu_{obs}$. As the potential $p_{obs,i}(\mathbf{x})$ would infinitely increase towards the obstacle, a minimum distance μ_{obs} is introduced. For positions that are closer to the obstacle than this distance, the potential is at the maximum possible value for obstacles ρ_{obs}. The obstacles are assumed to be round, which simplifies the computation of the potential field. Thus, the minimum distance is composed of the obstacle radius R_{obs}, the robot's radius R and a security distance ϵ as

$$\mu_{obs} = R_{obs} + R + \epsilon \tag{7.6}$$

Additionally, a maximum distance M_{obs} is used to cut of the influence of obstacles that are far away from the robot and thus should not influence its path. This also reduces the amount of local minima resulting from the superposition of the fields of many obstacles. The artificial force for the obstacles is computed as

$$f_{obs,i}(\mathbf{x}) = \begin{cases} -\nabla p_{obs,i}(\mathbf{x}) & \text{if} & \mu_{obs}{}^2 < \|\mathbf{d}_{obs,i}(\mathbf{x})\|^2 < M_{obs}{}^2 \\ \begin{bmatrix} 0 & 0 \end{bmatrix}^T & \text{if} & \|\mathbf{d}_{obs,i}(\mathbf{x})\|^2 \le \mu_{obs}{}^2 \vee \|\mathbf{d}_{obs,i}(\mathbf{x})\|^2 \ge M_{obs}{}^2 \end{cases} \tag{7.7}$$

with

$$-\nabla p_{obs,i}(\mathbf{x}) = 2 \frac{\rho_{obs}\kappa_{obs}\mu_{obs}{}^2}{\|\mathbf{d}_{obs,i}(\mathbf{x})\|^4} \mathbf{d}_{obs,i}(\mathbf{x}) \tag{7.8}$$

Since in RoboCup and other applications of robotics the space for driving with the robot is limited, walls and artificial limitations of this space are modeled as potential barriers, too. The computation of these is similar to that of the obstacles

$$p_{wall,j}(\mathbf{x}) = \begin{cases} \rho_{wall} & \text{if} & \|\mathbf{d}_{wall,j}(\mathbf{x})\|^2 \le \mu_{wall}{}^2 \\ \rho_{wall}\kappa_{wall}\left(\frac{1}{\|\mathbf{d}_{wall,j}(\mathbf{x})\|^2} - \frac{1}{M_{wall}{}^2}\right) & \text{if} & \mu_{wall}{}^2 < \|\mathbf{d}_{wall,j}(\mathbf{x})\|^2 < M_{wall}{}^2 \\ 0 & \text{if} & M_{wall}{}^2 \le \|\mathbf{d}_{wall,j}(\mathbf{x})\|^2 \end{cases} \tag{7.9}$$

with $\mathbf{d}_{wall,j}(\mathbf{x}) = \begin{bmatrix} 0 & y - w_{y,j} \end{bmatrix}^T$ for walls in x-direction or $\mathbf{d}_{wall,j}(\mathbf{x}) = \begin{bmatrix} x - w_{x,j} & 0 \end{bmatrix}^T$ for walls in y-direction. Again

$$\kappa_{wall} = \frac{M_{wall}{}^2 \mu_{wall}{}^2}{M_{wall}{}^2 - \mu_{wall}{}^2} \tag{7.10}$$

is a normalization factor used to make $p_{wall,j}(\mathbf{x})$ continuous at $\|\mathbf{d}_{wall,i}(\mathbf{x})\|^2 = \mu_{wall}$. Here, the minimum distance μ_{wall} only consists of the robot's radius R and a security distance ϵ. The artificial force for the walls is computed as

$$f_{wall,i}(\mathbf{x}) = \begin{cases} -\nabla p_{wall,i}(\mathbf{x}) & \text{if} & \mu_{wall}{}^2 < \|\mathbf{d}_{wall,i}(\mathbf{x})\|^2 < M_{wall}{}^2 \\ \begin{bmatrix} 0 & 0 \end{bmatrix}^T & \text{if} & \|\mathbf{d}_{wall,i}(\mathbf{x})\|^2 \le \mu_{wall}{}^2 \vee \|\mathbf{d}_{wall,i}(\mathbf{x})\|^2 \ge M_{wall}{}^2 \end{cases} \tag{7.11}$$

with

$$-\nabla p_{wall,i}(\mathbf{x}) = 2\frac{\rho_{wall}\kappa_{wall}\mu_{wall}^2}{\|\mathbf{d}_{wall,i}(\mathbf{x})\|^4}\mathbf{d}_{wall,i}(\mathbf{x}) \tag{7.12}$$

The final potential field that attracts the robot towards the target while keeping it away from the obstacles can be computed as a superposition of the singular potential fields

$$P(\mathbf{x}) = p_{att}(\mathbf{x}) + \sum_i p_{obs,i}(\mathbf{x}) + \sum_j p_{wall,j}(\mathbf{x}) \tag{7.13}$$

and the resulting force is given by

$$\begin{aligned}F(\mathbf{x}) = -\nabla P(\mathbf{x}) &= -\nabla p_{att}(\mathbf{x}) - \sum_i \nabla p_{obs,i}(\mathbf{x}) - \sum_j \nabla p_{wall,j}(\mathbf{x})\\ &= f_{att}(\mathbf{x}) + \sum_i f_{obs,i}(\mathbf{x}) + \sum_j f_{wall,j}(\mathbf{x})\end{aligned} \tag{7.14}$$

Although the potential field of obstacles and walls is not continuously differentiable at the minimum and maximum distances, this does not affect the presented approach, as in the final algorithm the gradient will be approximated. The computation of the potentials uses the norm of the distance vectors only for the attractive potential. For the obstacles and walls the squared norm is used, avoiding the extraction of the root, which is computationally expensive. Especially if many obstacles and walls are present, this results in a large performance benefit.

Grid Step Planner

Since moving directly in the direction of the negative gradient $F(\mathbf{x}) = -\nabla P(\mathbf{x})$ takes the risk of ending up in a local minimum, a mechanism is needed to detect that the robot is trapped and to generate a reasonable movement out of such local minima. Therefore, the state space is subdivided into an equally spaced grid with α being the size of a grid cell and a complete set of way points is planned from the current position of the robot towards the target. When planning the path, the next way point is the next grid cell following the direction of the gradient. The error made in choosing a discrete grid cell in the direction of the gradient is accumulated and affects the grid cell chosen in the next step similarly to Bresenham's line-drawing algorithm [25]. The gradient is approximated by evaluating the potential field locally using the difference quotient, which reduces the computational costs for evaluating the whole potential field

$$\text{grad}(u,v) = \frac{1}{2\alpha}\begin{bmatrix}P(u+1,v) - P(u-1,v) & P(u,v+1) - P(u,v-1)\end{bmatrix}^T \tag{7.15}$$

If the next grid cell is already contained in the path, the algorithm has detected a local minimum. Then, a recursive best-first search is started over the adjacent grid cells that ends if either the target cell is found, or a cell is found with a potential lower than the potential of the cell where the search started. As the set of grid cells generated as a path by the grid step planning algorithm is very square-edged due to the discretization on the grid, the vector of movement followed by the robot is calculated as average over the first m way points. If $\mathbf{w}_1, \ldots, \mathbf{w}_n$ denote the way points of the planned path and $\mathbf{s} = \begin{bmatrix} s_x & s_y \end{bmatrix}^T$ denotes the current position of the robot, the robot moves into the direction

$$\mathbf{v} = \frac{1}{m} \sum_{i=1}^{m} \mathbf{w}_i - \mathbf{s} \qquad (7.16)$$

Backwards Planning

The main advantage of the approach of Weigel *et al.*, however, is the idea to plan the path backwards from the target to the robot to avoid heading directly into an obstacle and then following a curve around it. If the path planning is reversed, the robot directly enters a trajectory that leads around the obstacle. Figure 7.5 shows the potential field for a typical situation. It ranges from a low potential (black) at the target located in the upper middle to a high potential at the location of an obstacle in the middle. Furthermore, a path generated by planning from the start in the lower middle towards the target is shown. The path directly approaches the obstacle and gets very near until it starts to surround the obstacle in a very close curve. After passing the obstacle, the robot moves to the goal in a smooth curve. Although the presented implementation of the path planning algorithm is able to constantly replan the paths in every cycle of the robot control algorithm, the path that the robot finally takes when moving is identical to the path planned in the first cycle, as the potential field does not change. Therefore, the path is planned backwards by changing the target and the start location. In the first cycle shown in Figure 7.6, the planned path seems to be identical to the path planned forwards, taking into account that the start and the target location were exchanged. However, if the robot follows the path in reverse order from its real start location in the lower middle towards the target, it directly enters a smooth curve around the obstacle. The constant replanning of the path in each cycle changes the path to a smooth curve even behind the obstacle as the potential well follows the robot position when moving (cf. the images for cycle 60 and cycle 120 in Figure 7.6).

Time Variant Potential Field

Although the idea of Weigel *et al.* to plan the path backwards from the target to the goal results in very smooth and efficient paths for slowly moving obstacles, there are many situations where the planned path is inefficient because of the unconsidered movement of faster moving obstacles. To overcome this shortcoming of the approach of Weigel *et al.* the improved path planning method presented here extends the algorithm to cope with moving obstacles. For that, the position of the obstacles is no longer assumed to be static for the whole planning process. Instead, whenever the next grid cell is reached in the planning process, the obstacles are moved to a new position

$$\mathbf{o}_i(t + \tau) = \begin{bmatrix} o_{x,i}(t+\tau) & o_{y,i}(t+\tau) \end{bmatrix}^T = \begin{bmatrix} \mathbf{o}_{x,i}(t) + \tau \mathbf{v}_{x,i} & \mathbf{o}_{y,i}(t) + \tau \mathbf{v}_{y,i} \end{bmatrix}^T \qquad (7.17)$$

Cycle 1   Cycle 60   Cycle 120

Figure 7.5: The potential field for a typical situation. Lower potentials are shown in darker
color than higher potentials. The robot is located in the lower half and plans a path (green
way points) towards the target in the upper half
around an obstacle in the middle.

Figure 7.6: The same situation, but the path is
planned backwards from the target to the robot.
By constantly replanning the path after moving
to the next way point the robot finally follows a
smooth trajectory (red points) around the sta-
tionary obstacle.

with $\mathbf{o}_i(0) = \mathbf{o}_i$, $\mathbf{v}_i = \begin{bmatrix} v_{x,i} & v_{y,i} \end{bmatrix}^T$ being the observed velocity of obstacle $\mathbf{o}_i$ at $t = 0$,
and τ being the time the robot needs to reach the next grid cell, which depends on the
maximum speed of the robot $\mathbf{v}_{\max}$ as the robot should always move with this speed. This
process results in a time variant potential field reflecting the changed obstacle situation in
each planning step. Planning in this time variant potential field avoids paths that interfere
with the predicted trajectories of the moving obstacles, while a conventional path planner
based on the approach of Weigel *et al.* fails to plan an efficient path as shown in Figures
7.7 and 7.8. As the original method included backwards planning from the target to the
starting point of the robot and thus also backwards in time, the proposed algorithm must
know the time T the robot needs to reach the target a priori to predict the obstacle positions. However, T depends on the planned path, which is unknown before the planning.
To overcome this mutual dependency two proposals are made and compared. Firstly, the
Euclidean distance estimator uses the Euclidean distance from the start to the target point
to calculate an a priori estimation of the time needed to reach the target

$$\widehat{T}_{e,0}^- = \frac{\|\mathbf{g} - \mathbf{s}\|}{\mathbf{v}_{\max}} \tag{7.18}$$

where $\mathbf{s}$ is the current position of the robot and $\mathbf{g}$ is the target position, as defined earlier.
This time is an underestimation of the time needed to follow the resulting path. Starting
with this a priori estimation, an iterative process is started to estimate T. Denoting the a
priori estimation in iteration k with $\widehat{T}_{e,k}^-$ and the a posteriori estimation as

$$\widehat{T}_{e,k} = \frac{L_{b,k}}{\mathbf{v}_{\max}} \tag{7.19}$$

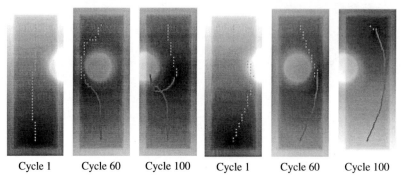

Cycle 1	Cycle 60	Cycle 100	Cycle 1	Cycle 60	Cycle 100

Figure 7.7: Again, the robot is located in the lower middle and plans a path towards the target in the upper middle. In this scenario, a moving obstacle crosses the path from right to left. The conventional path planner assumes the obstacle to be static and tries to get around the left side of the obstacle (cycle 60). As the object moves, the passage between the obstacle and the wall gets too narrow and the path has to be planned out of the emerging local minimum and finally surrounds the obstacle on the right.

Figure 7.8: The path planner using the time variant potential field with the Euclidean distance estimator incorporates the velocity of the obstacle and predicts the position over time. Thus, for the same scenario the path is planned around the right side of the obstacle right from the beginning, resulting in a smooth and efficient path. While the conventional path planner is still avoiding the obstacle in cycle 100, the new path planner already reaches the target at the same time.

with $L_{b,k}$ being the length of the path planned backwards using $\widehat{T}_{e,k}^{-}$ as estimation, we compute the a priori estimation for the next iteration by

$$\widehat{T}_{e,k+1}^{-} = \widehat{T}_{e,k}^{-} + \gamma(\widehat{T}_{e,k} - \widehat{T}_{e,k}^{-}), \quad \gamma \in [0,1] \tag{7.20}$$

Thus, in each iteration we add a fraction γ of the estimation error between the a priori estimation and the a posteriori time to the a priori estimation to approach the real value of T. The iterative process stops, if either the estimation error is below a threshold

$$\widehat{T}_{e,k} - \widehat{T}_{e,k}^{-} \leq \xi \tag{7.21}$$

or if a maximum number of iterations $K_{\max}$ is reached. Secondly, a different a priori estimation of the time is generated by planning the path in forward direction and calculating the time needed to follow this path

$$\widehat{T}_{f,k}^{-} = \frac{L_f}{\mathbf{v}_{\max}} \tag{7.22}$$

where L_f is the length of the path planned in forward direction. This estimator is called the *forward planning estimator*. The subsequent iterative process is identical.

The predicted position of the moving obstacles in each time step of the path planner extremely depends on the estimation of T. An obstacle moving at 2 m/s changes its position by up to 40 cm if the time estimation varies by 0.2 s. While the algorithm might be able to plan a smooth curve behind the obstacle in one iteration, the same obstacle can force the planning into a local minimum in the next iteration, now being predicted to a different position. Thus, small variations in the a priori estimation $\widehat{T}^-$ can result in extreme variations of $\widehat{T}$. Therefore, the parameters γ and ξ have a strong influence on the performance of the algorithm which is investigated thoroughly in the following experiments.

Experimental Results

Initially the influence of the factor γ and the threshold ξ on the number of iterations is tested. Then, the paths planned by the method of Weigel *et al.* are compared to those planned with the proposed algorithm for two scenarios with moving obstacles. Finally, the length of the paths planned by these two methods is compared for several random scenarios, as the length of the path is a measure of the efficiency of the planned path. For all experiments the parameters given in Table 7.1 were used.

ρ_{att}	ρ_{obs}	ρ_{wall}	R_{obs}	R	ϵ	M_{obs}	M_{wall}	α	m
$1 \cdot 10^6$	$4 \cdot 10^5$	$2 \cdot 10^5$	25 cm	20 cm	5 cm	50 cm	20 cm	10 cm	5

Table 7.1: The parameter set used for the path planning experiments.

To investigate the influence of the factor γ and the threshold ξ on the number of iterations made in each cycle of the planning algorithm, two different experiments were carried out for different values of γ and ξ. The first experiment was the simple scenario that was used to create the snapshots in Figure 7.8, while the second experiment was a more complex scenario including three moving obstacles on a field of $8 \times 12\,m^2$ size where a path was planned over more than 12 m from the lower right corner of the field to the upper left. Obstacle o_1 starts on the left side of the robot and moves into nearly the same direction crossing the diagonal at the middle of the field, thus extremely interfering with the direct path of the robot. Obstacle o_2 moves at a low speed from near the target point into the direction of the robot, so that the robot has to surround the obstacle at the end of the path. The third obstacle (o_3) moves in the upper half from right to left obstructing the pathway around the second obstacle on the right side (cf. Figure 7.11 on page 152). Four different values for the threshold ξ controlling the difference between a priori estimation and a posteriori time were used ranging from 0.1 s to 0.25 s. The maximum difference in the position estimation of an obstacle for these values ranges from 0.2 m to 0.5 m for obstacles moving at 2 m/s. However, this maximum difference affects only obstacles near the target, as the uncertainty in the predicted time is very low at the beginning of the path. Thus, the direction of movement averaged over the first way points does not contain this difference, and the robot still avoids bumping into the obstacles. For each value of ξ, 10 different values of the factor γ controlling the amount of the estimation error that is added to the estimation for the next iteration were tested ranging from 0.05 to 0.5. In addition,

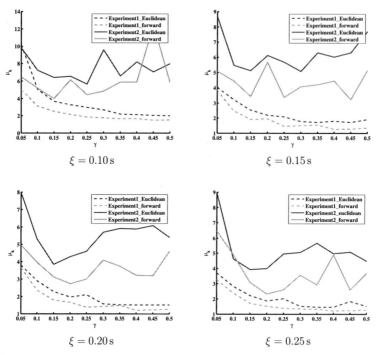

Figure 7.9: These graphs investigate the influence of the factor γ and the threshold ξ on the number of iterations made in each cycle of the planning algorithm. The mean number of iterations $\mu(k)$ over all cycles of the path planning for two different experiments is compared for different values of γ and ξ. The first experiment is the simple scenario that was used to create the snapshots in Figure 7.8, while the second experiment is a complex scenario including three moving obstacles on a field of 8x12 m^2 size where a path is planned over more than 12 m (cf. Figure 7.11).

the maximum number of iterations was set to $K_{\max} = 50$. Finally, all runs were carried out once for the Euclidean distance estimator and for the forward planning estimator.

Figure 7.9 shows the resulting mean number of iterations $\mu(k)$ over all cycles of the path planning for each parameter set and estimator used. Several aspects of the influence of γ and ξ can be gathered from these results. Firstly, it is obvious, that the mean number of iterations for the simple experiment is lower than the mean number of iterations for the more complex experiment in nearly all runs, as the influence of the obstacles on the time estimation is higher for the complex scenario. Also, as only a single obstacle is interfering with the robot in the simple experiment, the a posteriori times are a good estimation and therefore lower values of γ result in a higher number of iterations as only a small fraction of the estimation error is added to the a priori estimation, while raising the factor results in less iterations needed to let the estimation error drop below the threshold ξ. For the complex scenario, the influence of the factor γ is diverse. On the one hand, values above 0.25 change the estimated time from one iteration to the next so much, that the a posteriori time using these different a priori estimations oscillates. Using these values the maximum number of iterations was reached more often, as the iterative process could not converge. On the other hand, values lower than 0.15 converge reliably but too slowly, again needing a higher number of iterations. The total number of iterations needed to push the estimation error below the threshold ξ rises for lower values of the threshold. The few exceptions to this statement concerning the complex experiment come from a different movement in the first cycles due to a higher estimation error, resulting in a less optimal position for the later cycles. Finally, the mean number of iterations needed in each cycle of the Euclidean distance estimator is higher than that of the forward planning estimator. However, the extra computation time needed in the forward planning step has to be considered for the forward planning estimator, as it is comparable to an additional iteration.

Based on these experiments, values of $\gamma = 0.25$ and $\xi = 0.2$ were chosen for the following experiments as these values seemed to be a good compromise for a low number of iterations in all types of scenarios, simple as well as complex. For the chosen values, the two experiments are compared concerning the efficiency on the Pentium-M 2 GHz onboard computer of the new robots. To limit the computation time, the maximum number of iterations was set to $K_{max} = 5$. The mean computation time per cycle $\mu(t_n)$ and the length of the planned path in cycles N is shown in Table 7.2. Graphical visualizations of the planned path are shown in Figure 7.8 for the simple and Figure 7.11 for the complex experiment. Although the computation time is much higher for the complex scenario when using the proposed approach, it is still able to run in the 20 ms cycle of the system.

	Simple experiment		Complex experiment	
	N	$\mu(t_n)$	N	$\mu(t_n)$
Conventional path planner	52	0.64 ms	140	2.61 ms
Euclidean distance estimator	46	1.47 ms	106	9.34 ms
Forward planning estimator	46	1.43 ms	107	8.70 ms

Table 7.2: The results for the simple and the complex experiment.

In order to compare the performance of the path planning algorithm based on time variant potential fields to the conventional path planner of Weigel *et al.* in typical RoboCup scenarios, 100 random scenarios were created. On a field of $8\mathrm{x}12\,\mathrm{m}^2$ size seven obstacles were created at random positions with a random but fixed vector of movement. The number of obstacles was chosen to be seven, as this is the usual number of field players in the RoboCup MSL apart from the own robot. The obstacles keep their movement until they reach the field boundaries, where their movement is reflected back into the field. The

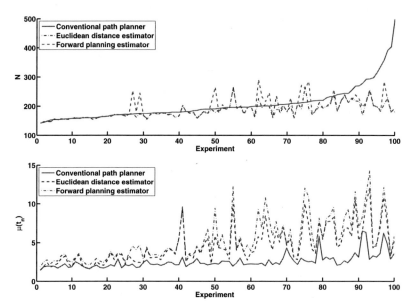

Figure 7.10: The performance of the conventional path planner compared to the presented path planner based on time variant potential fields. 100 random scenarios were created on a field of $8 \times 12\,m^2$ size by randomly choosing the position and velocity of 7 obstacles and start and target point of the path. The graphs show the results concerning the number of cycles N needed to follow the planned path and the mean time per cycle $\mu(t_n)$ needed to compute the path.

start and target points of the robot are chosen randomly, too, such that they do not lie inside an obstacle. Furthermore, the target is only accepted if the Euclidean distance to the start is not less than 6 m to get reasonable scenarios and not more than 8 m, as this is the maximum distance to a target used in the tactical roles. Again, the maximum number of iterations is limited to $K_{\max} = 5$.

Figure 7.10 presents the results of the 100 runs for the conventional method and each estimator. The upper graph displays the number of cycles N it took to follow the planned path, as this is directly linked to the efficiency of the planned path concerning the time needed to follow the path and the length of the path. The lower graph shows the mean time per cycle $\mu(t_n)$ as a measure of the computational load needed to compute the path. For better visibility the random runs are sorted by the number of cycles of the conventional planner. In the first 60 experiments all three path planners are comparable in terms of the path length apart from single outliers for the forward planning estimator. Although not meaningful in its absolute value (these experiments were run on an AMD-Opteron cluster), the mean time per cycle is higher for the proposed path planner, as it takes several iterations per cycle to estimate the time T. Nevertheless, the path planned by the proposed algorithm with the Euclidean distance estimator is more efficient in nearly all experiments. The most impressive difference appears in experiment 100, where the path planned by the conventional planner is 150% longer than the path planned by the proposed algorithm. Although this is an exceptional result, the fact that the new path planner could reach the target 300 cycles before the conventional path planner is impressive, as this means an extra pathway of 12 m or a time gap of 6 s at 2 ᵐ/s maximum speed. Taking all experiments into account, the mean number of cycles per experiment $\mu(N)$ is 184.62 for the Euclidean distance estimator and 191.41 for the forward planning estimator compared to 205.72 for the conventional planner. Thus, the average path length for the Euclidean distance estimator is only 89.74% of the path length planned with the conventional planner and 93.04% for the forward planning estimator. On the other hand, the mean time per cycle needed to compute the path averaged over all experiments $\mu(\mu(t_n))$ is by a factor of 1.77 higher for the Euclidean distance estimator and 2.09 for the forward planning algorithm. See Table 7.3 for the exact values.

	$\mu(N)$	$\sigma(N)$	$\mu(\mu(t_n))$	$\sigma(\mu(t_n))$
Conventional path planner	205.72	58.29	2.56 ms	0.95 ms
Euclidean distance estimator	184.62	26.30	4.53 ms	2.36 ms
Forward planning estimator	191.41	35.09	5.34 ms	2.80 ms

Table 7.3: The results concerning the efficiency of the path planning algorithms.

Finally, the comparison between the two time estimators contains interesting results. Although the forward planning estimator should compute a better estimation of T than the Euclidean distance estimator, the latter performs better on the conducted experiments. Apart from the mean number of cycles, the Euclidean distance estimator is also more efficient in planning its paths as the cycle time shows. In only 3% of the experiments the planned paths are more than 10 cycles longer than those planned by the forward planning estimator, while in 17% of the experiments the paths are more than 10 cycles shorter.

In conclusion, the iterative path planning algorithm using the time variant potential fields is able to improve the paths for many scenarios with dynamic obstacles. However, the additional computation time needed to iteratively estimate T for the prediction of the obstacle positions for the backwards planning uses more computational resources, which might not be available, depending on the given application. From the two presented estimators the Euclidean distance estimator outperforms the forward planning estimator both in efficiency and in computation time of the planned paths. The reason for this might be the underestimation of T of the Euclidean distance estimator and the parameter $\gamma = 0.25$, which is very low, so that the correct estimation of T is approached in small steps. Further experiments with real robots have to be conducted to investigate the influence of opponents reacting to the movements that result from the new path planner. Nevertheless, the first results using the path planner on the new RoboCup robots were promising.

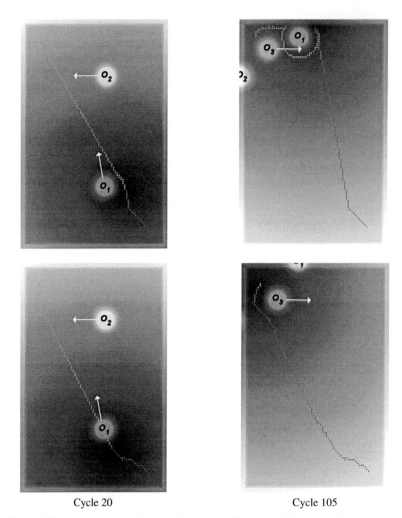

Cycle 20   Cycle 105

Figure 7.11: In this experiment the robot is located in the lower right corner and plans a path towards the target in the upper left corner. A moving obstacle o_1 starts on the left of the robot and moves into nearly the same direction crossing the diagonal at the middle of the field. The conventional path planner (upper images) tries to get around the right side of the obstacle until it finally has to completely surround the obstacle in cycle 105. The path planner using the time variant potential field with the Euclidean distance estimator incorporates the velocity of the obstacle and plans its path to the left of the obstacle directly from the beginning.

Chapter 8

Competition Results

Besides the experimental results given in the respective sections of the last chapters, this chapter contains an overview of the team results at the different national and international RoboCup competitions over the past four years. Since the overall team performance is closely related to the improvements and achievements in hardware and software, these results provide a good way to compare the robot system presented in this thesis with that of the other teams in the RoboCup MSL. Figure 8.1 shows the development of the defensive and offensive behavior of the Attempto Tübingen Robot Soccer Team throughout these competitions as a graph of the mean number of goals received and scored per game.

At the beginning of the development presented in this thesis, the team's offensive accomplishments were at an absolute minimum with no goal scored at all at the German Open 2003. In addition, also the defensive behavior of the team was disastrous with a total of nearly 3.5 received goals per game. This performance was mainly due to the removal of the field boundaries and hence the failure of the laser scanner based self-localization. Although a preliminary self-localization using the white field lines and the ability to play with a black and white colored standard FIFA ball allowed the team to win the Technical Challenge Award at the world championships in Padova 2003, the in-game results were comparable to that of the German Open.

The first significant progress in the defensive behavior, and thus a decrease in the number of received goals per game by nearly 50% could be achieved with the introduction of the omni-directional goalkeeper at the German Open 2004. Although the self-localization still was far away from being perfect, the high amount of line data in the goal area allowed for a reasonable localization of the goalkeeper and hence a good performance of the defense, while the offense still was at the same level scoring hardly one goal per game.

The world championship in Lisbon in 2004 represented an interim maximum of the overall performance with all pioneer robots being functional, the introduction of the new self-localization and a stable software system. Since the new image-based self-localization enabled the field players to play a whole game without losing their position, the offensive

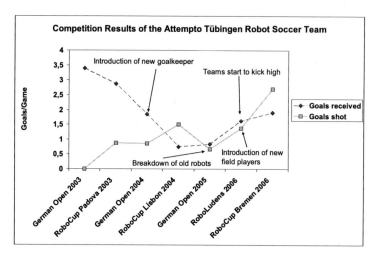

Figure 8.1: The development of received and shot goals per game as a measure for the efficiency of the defensive and the offensive behaviors of the Attempto Tübingen Robot Soccer Team.

results could be raised to 1.5 scored goals per game while the goalkeeper supported by two defenders could lower the goals received per game to an all-time minimum. Nevertheless, this was the maximum that could be achieved with the old platform, as the German Open 2005 showed, where nearly all pioneer robots broke down. Furthermore, the rules concerning the constancy of the lighting conditions over the field were considerably relaxed resulting in new problems with the vision-based self-localization.

The time from 2004 to 2006 could therefore be used to develop the new omni-directional field player platform and the vision algorithms that adapted to different lighting conditions. Accordingly, at the RoboLudens competition in 2006 the team could successfully demonstrate their new hardware and software design with a raise in the offensive score by 100%. Nevertheless, the high-level control of the field players was still in development and basic functionality like intercepting balls and ball handling was not optimal. Furthermore, the defensive score dropped, as many teams started to kick the ball high above the robot were the camera could not track the ball.

Although the high balls were still a problem to the defense at the RoboCup World Cup in Bremen 2006, the performance reached its maximum with fully functional ball handling and ball interception behaviors, in-game passing and stable vision processing even with indirect daylight on the field. The goals scored per game hit an all-time maximum and the goal balance was highly positive. Finally, for good passing behavior and the presentation of the automatic camera calibration and adaptation algorithms the team again ranked first place in the Technical Challenge together with the Tribots team from Osnabrück.

Chapter 9

Conclusions and Future Work

This thesis is concerned with the hardware and software development of a team of fully autonomous soccer playing robots. As a benchmark for robotics and artificial intelligence systems, RoboCup has a large number of participating teams doing research in several areas covered in this thesis. Yet, the concentration of different research areas covered in this thesis is one of the rare attempts to integrate all necessary steps of robot system design in a single self-contained publication. For this, the need to develop a new multi-robot team from scratch was a serendipity, as the co-design of hardware and software allowed for a consequent focusing on the reactiveness of the system. The omni-directional drive with a controller that processes 50 commands per second and the omni-directional camera with a framerate of 50 fps were especially selected and combined with an extremely efficient software system to fulfill the real-time constraints for playing soccer in a highly dynamic environment. Accordingly, one of the main results of this thesis as a whole, is the 20 ms cycle of the complete system. Another result of the system design is the adaptability and reusability of the software. This was primarily achieved through the use of a client/server architecture with the main parts of the software encapsulated in single processes communicating via shared memories and the implementation of a hardware abstraction layer in the low-level processes.

Apart from the contributions of the system as a whole, the major topics of this thesis, image processing, environment modeling, and high-level control contain specific results. A biologically inspired color segmentation algorithm that increases the fault tolerance of the segmentation combined with an efficient clustering algorithm establishes the basis for a fast and accurate image processing approach, that reliably detects objects and landmarks in the RoboCup environment. To cope with a changing camera geometry and different lighting scenarios, this image processing approach was extended with automatic calibration algorithms. On the one hand, the geometric camera calibration enables the vision algorithm to run on different hardware platforms without the need for manual adaptation. On the other hand, the automatic color calibration permits real-time adaptation of the image processing to temporal and spatial variation in lighting. Thus, these algorithms address one of the major research topics for future RoboCup and robotics applications.

The thoroughly probabilistic environment modeling process features a novel self-localization algorithm that efficiently combines a particle filter and a tracking approach. Using a variable number of samples that is tuned to extreme performance, this self-localization algorithm gradually switches from global localization to local pose tracking and outperforms reference Monte-Carlo Localization algorithms both in terms of accuracy and computation time. In addition to the robot's pose, the environment model also includes the position and velocity of other objects on the field. With covariance matrices for all relevant parameters, sensor fusion in this model is done even with the data of other robots. Tracking of the three-dimensional trajectory of a ball kicked high is thus possible as outlined in [74].

With the new high-level control architecture, the performance of the system at recent championships was excellent. The good defensive result is mainly due to the highly reactive architecture of superimposed behaviors used to control the goalkeeper. For the offense, however, a more complex hybrid control system was designed, that combined tactical roles, efficient path planning, and a set of reactive behaviors. This combination resulted in good cooperative game play, performing successful in-game passes and reaching a new peak in the goals scored per game ratio. Finally, the novel path planning algorithm that incorporates the velocity of obstacles showed good performance and is a first attempt for a new way of path planning in highly dynamic environments.

Nevertheless, the presented algorithms are also a good source for future research and improvements. The current version of the automatic calibration is only a small step towards the truly illumination invariant algorithms needed for a robust vision processing of robots working in natural environments. Furthermore, future enhancements to the image processing algorithms could involve an additional camera on the robot dedicated to track the high balls. Finally, with the limited field of view of the current vision system, it will be challenging to collect the relevant environmental data from the gradually enlarged fields.

Therefore, further research has to be conducted to analyze the performance of the self-localization algorithm with a reduced set of landmark information, too. In addition, the ideas for a complete exchange of the environmental data between the robots of the team to build a common model for better cooperative play should be further investigated.

The high-level control is the area with the most potential for further research. On larger fields, passing becomes more feasible even if long passes are more likely to be intercepted by the opponent team. Therefore, the presented strategies for the supporting player to break clear should be further developed. Furthermore, the path planning approach using time variant potential fields should be thoroughly tested in a real competition. Finally, it would be desirable not to plan the path of the robot and compute local deviations for dribbling the ball, but to plan the trajectory of the ball and to compute the corresponding movements of the robot under the constraint not to lose the ball.

Appendix A

List of Symbols

I	Global reference frame
X, Y	Axes of I
$\begin{bmatrix} x & y \end{bmatrix}^T$	Position of the robot or an object in I
θ	Orientation of the robot in I
$\mathbf{l} = \begin{bmatrix} x & y & \theta \end{bmatrix}^T$	Pose of the robot including position and orientation in I
$\mathbf{v} = \begin{bmatrix} v_x & v_y & v_\theta \end{bmatrix}^T$	Velocity of the robot in I
I_r	Robot reference frame
X_r, Y_r	Axes of I_r
$\begin{bmatrix} x_r & y_r \end{bmatrix}^T$	Position of an object in I_r
$\begin{bmatrix} r_r & \varphi_r \end{bmatrix}^T$	Polar coordinates of an object in I_r
$\mathbf{v}_r = \begin{bmatrix} v_{r,x} & v_{r,y} & \omega_r \end{bmatrix}^T$	Velocity of the robot in I_r
$R_{w,i}$	Radius of wheel i
$\omega_{w,i}$	Angular speed of wheel i
$v_{w,i} = \omega_{w,i} R_{w,i}$	Translational velocity of wheel i
I_p	Image reference frame
X_p, Y_p	Axes of I_p
$\begin{bmatrix} x_p & y_p \end{bmatrix}^T$	Coordinates of a pixel in I_p
$\begin{bmatrix} r_p & \varphi_p \end{bmatrix}^T$	Polar coordinates of a pixel in I_p
I_c	Reference frame of a color space (RGB, HSI, YUV)
X_c, Y_c, Z_c	Axes of I_c
$\mathbf{c} = \begin{bmatrix} x_c & y_c & z_c \end{bmatrix}^T$	Coordinates (the color value) of a color in I_c

Appendix B

Self-Localization Results

This appendix contains the figures showing the true and the estimated pose of the test robot for the experiments described in Section 6.3.3. In all runs, the test robot starts near the upper left corner of the penalty area and moves in positive direction of the X-axis. The red line marks the ground truth position from the laser scanner object detection and the dashed blue line shows the estimation results of the specific version of the self-localization algorithm. The numbers indicate the pose estimation of the self-localization algorithm after 1 cycle and after the initial global localization, i. e. the convergence to the initial position.

Test Runs with $v = 1$ m/s, Differential Drive

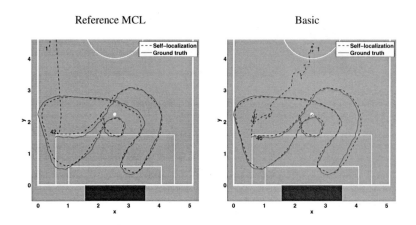

Reference MCL   Basic

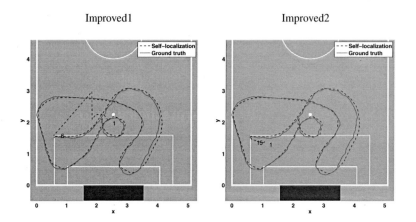

Improved1   Improved2

Improved3

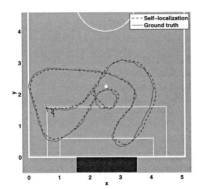

Improved4

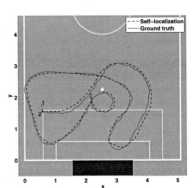

Improved5

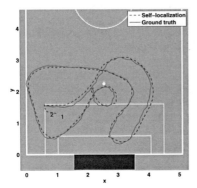

Results

Algorithm	e [cm]	N_{mean}	T_{tot} [ms]
Differential drive 1 m/s			
Basic	12.17	23.84	2.31
Improved1	10.89	6.31	0.77
Improved2	10.87	3.20	0.55
Improved3	9.66	2.02	1.63
Improved4	8.58	1.94	4.70
Improved5	8.77	2.08	4.81
MCL Reference	13.79	200.00	18.06

Test Runs with v = 1 m/s, Omni-Directional Drive

Reference MCL   Basic

Improved1   Improved2

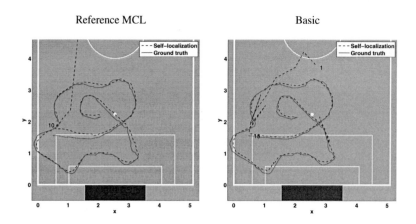

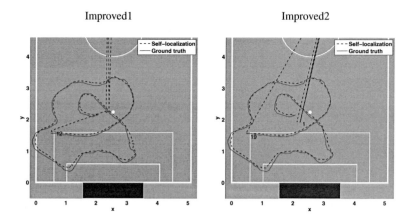

Improved3

Improved4

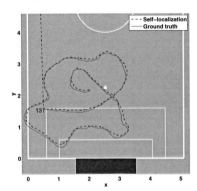

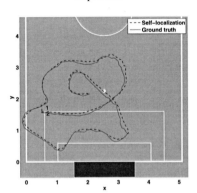

Improved5

Results

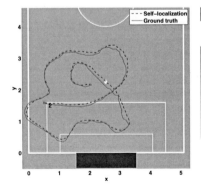

Algorithm	e [cm]	N_{mean}	T_{tot} [ms]
Omni-directional drive 1 m/s			
Basic	13.37	10.16	1.21
Improved1	12.50	9.84	1.10
Improved2	12.85	9.30	0.99
Improved3	11.00	3.79	1.81
Improved4	7.93	1.94	4.80
Improved5	7.88	1.96	4.66
MCL Reference	10.84	200.00	18.19

Test Runs with $v = 2$ m/s, Differential Drive

Reference MCL

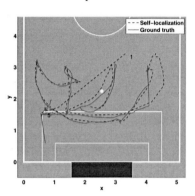

Improved4

Improved5

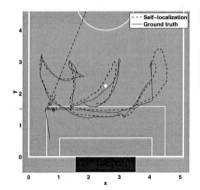

Results

Algorithm	e [cm]	N_{mean}	T_{tot} [ms]
Differential drive 2 m/s			
Improved4	13.02	2.76	4.90
Improved5	13.29	2.61	4.80
MCL Reference	25.62	200.00	18.14

Test Runs with v $= 2$ ᵐ/s , Omni-Directional Drive

Reference MCL

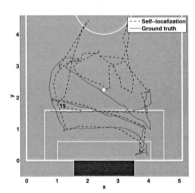

Improved4

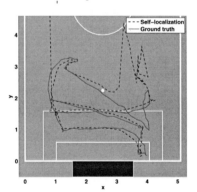

Improved5

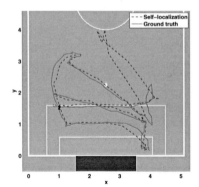

Results

Algorithm	e [cm]	N_{mean}	T_{tot} [ms]
Omni-directional drive 2 ᵐ/s			
Improved4	22.91	10.30	5.37
Improved5	15.66	5.61	5.15
MCL Reference	33.16	200.00	18.03

Appendix C

High-Level Control Results

This appendix shows several in-game scenarios of the Attempto Tübingen Robot Soccer Team as series of still images taken from video material recorded at the RoboCup World Cup 2006 in Bremen. These scenarios feature some of the basic skills of the team, like passing in standard situations (goal kick, throw-in, free kick), intercepting the ball, and dribbling with the ball. Furthermore, two of the best in-game passes played by the team at the championship are shown in the last two scenes. The still images in the following figures are chronologically sorted line by line, from left to right and from top to bottom.

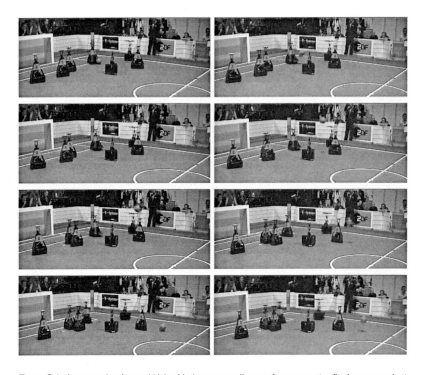

Figure C.1: An example of a goal kick with the new goalkeeper from a quarter final game against the CoPs at the RoboCup World Cup 2006 in Bremen. With the new kicker, the goal keeper is able to kick the ball over an attacking robot into the opponent field half.

Figure C.2: An example of a throw-in from a quarter final game against the FU-Fighters at the RoboCup World Cup 2006 in Bremen. It is clearly visible how the `InterceptBall` behavior of the pass receiver anticipates the velocity of the ball by driving backwards to get the ball under control.

Figure C.3: An example of a free kick from a round robin game against AIS/BIT at the RoboCup World Cup 2006 in Bremen. As soon as the Supporter is in control of the ball and becomes the Attacker it moves towards the fixpoint on its own side of the field. The former Attacker which is now the new Supporter instead moves towards the fixpoint on the other side of the field. Thus, a crossing behavior emerges by changing the sides, which is considered as good offensive play in real soccer, but which was not explicitly programmed.

Figure C.4: An example of the `StealBall` behavior from a round robin game against ISePorto at the RoboCup World Cup 2006 in Bremen. The attacking robot effectively removes the ball from the opponent, wins the tackling, and finally scores.

Figure C.5: An example of the `BallHandling` behavior from a round robin game against AIS/BIT at the RoboCup World Cup 2006 in Bremen. The attacking robot moves into the tight situation between the two opponents, takes the ball, dribbles out of the situation avoiding a third approaching opponent, and finally shoots towards the goal.

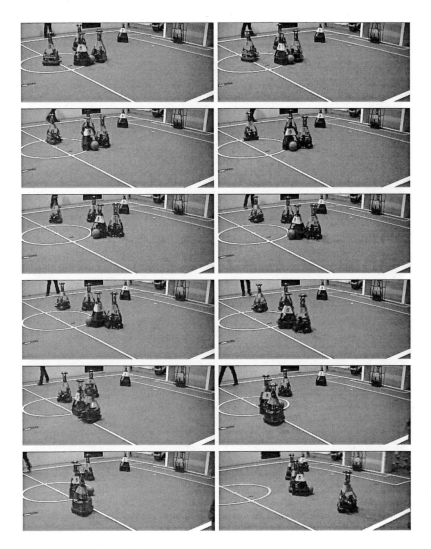

Figure C.6: Another example of the `BallHandling` behavior from a round robin game against the Brainstormers Tribots at the RoboCup World Cup 2006 in Bremen. Here, the attacking robot makes a full rotation around the ball, thus shielding it from the attacking opponent, and is finally able to approach the goal.

Figure C.7: An example of in-game passing from a round robin game against the Brainstormers Tribots at the RoboCup World Cup 2006 in Bremen. This is one of the best in-game passes played at the RoboCup in Bremen. The `Attacker` is surrounded by three opponent robots and play a clearing pass to the `Supporter` which awaits the pass at the fixpoint on the other side of the field.

Figure C.8: An example of in-game passing from a quarter final game against the FU-Fighters at the RoboCup World Cup 2006 in Bremen. This pass was played into the movement of the Supporter, who tries to break clear at the other fixpoint.

Bibliography

[1] G. Adorni, S. Cagnoni, S. Enderle, G. K. Kraetzschmar, M. Mordonini, M. Plagge, M. Ritter, S. Sablatnög, and A. Zell. Vision-based localization for mobile robots. *Robotics and Autonomous Systems*, 36(2-3):103–119, 2001.

[2] G. Adorni, S. Cagnoni, M. Mordonini, and M. Piaggio. Team/Goal-Keeper Coordination in the RoboCup Mid-Size League. In Stone et al. [186], pages 279–284.

[3] G. Adorni, M. Mordonini, S. Cagnoni, and A. Sgorbissa. Omnidirectional stereo systems for robot navigation. In *2003 Conference on Computer Vision and Pattern Recognition Workshop*, volume 7, pages 79–89, 2003.

[4] J. Albus. Outline for a Theory of Intelligence. *IEEE Transactions on Systems, Man and Cybernetics*, 21(3):473–509, 1991.

[5] Allied Vision Technologies GmbH. The Marlin F-046C VGA Camera IEEE 1394. http://www.alliedvisiontec.de/produktinfos.html?t=produktinfos&o=29&a=selectid, August 2006.

[6] F. Anzani, D. Bosisio, M. Matteucci, and D. G. Sorrenti. On-Line Color Calibration in Non-stationary Environments. In Bredenfeld et al. [24], pages 396–407.

[7] M. Arbatzat, S. Freitag, M. Fricke, R. Hafner, C. Heermann, K. Hegelich, A. Krause, J. Krüger, M. Lauer, M. Lewandowski, A. Merke, H. Müller, M. Riedmiller, J. Schanko, M. Schulte-Hobein, M. Theile, S. Welker, and D. Withopf. Creating a Robot Soccer Team from Scratch: the Brainstormers Tribots. In Polani et al. [159]. CD-Supplement.

[8] R. C. Arkin. *Behavior-Based Robotics*. The MIT Press, 1998.

[9] M. Asada and H. Kitano, editors. *RoboCup-98: RobotSoccer World Cup II*, volume 1604 of *Lecture Notes in Artificial Intelligence*. Springer, 1999.

[10] M. Asada, Y. Kuniyoshi, A. Drogoul, H. Asama, M. Mataric, D. Duhaut, P. Stone, and H. Kitano. The RoboCup Physical Agent Challenge: Phase-I. *Applied Artificial Intelligence*, 12:251–263, 1998.

[11] L. Asplund. The Middle-Size League Homepage for 2006. http://www.idt.mdh.se/
     rc/Mid-Size/, August 2006.

[12] D. Bahadir. Effektive Ballannahme mit einem omnidirektionalen RoboCup-
     Roboter. Studienarbeit, Universität Tübingen, 2006.

[13] J. Baltes and N. Hildreth. Adaptive Path Planner for Highly Dynamic Environ-
     ments. In Stone et al. [186], pages 76–85.

[14] T. Bandlow, M. Klupsch, R. Hanek, and T. Schmitt. Fast Image Segmentation,
     Object Recognition and Localization in a RoboCup Scenario. In Veloso et al. [200],
     pages 174–185.

[15] T. Bäck, D. Fogel, and Z. Michalewicz. *Handbook on Evolutionary Computation*.
     Oxford University Press, 1997.

[16] H. Becker. Anbindung der RoboCup-Software an den Simulator SimSrv. Studien-
     arbeit, Universität Tübingen, 2006.

[17] S. Behnke and R. Rojas. A hierarchy of Reactive Behaviors Handles Complexity.
     In Hannebauer et al. [77], pages 125–136.

[18] A. Birk, S. Coradeschi, and S. Tadokoro, editors. *RoboCup 2001: Robot Soccer
     World Cup V*, volume 2377 of *Lecture Notes in Artificial Intelligence*. Springer,
     2002.

[19] P. E. Black, editor. *Dictionary of Algorithms and Data Structures [online]*. U.S.
     National Institute of Standards and Technology, 2005. http://www.nist.gov/dads/.

[20] S. Blackman and R. Popoli. *Design and analysis of modern tracking systems*.
     Artech House radar library. Artech House, 1999.

[21] H. A. P. Blom. An efficient filter for abruptly changing systems. In *Proceedings of
     the 23rd IEEE Conference on Decision and Control*, pages 656–658, 1984.

[22] A. Bonarini, P. Aliverti, and M. Lucioni. An omnidirectional vision sensor for fast
     tracking for mobile robots. In *Proceedings of the IEEE IMTC99*, pages 151–155.
     IEEE Computer Press, 1999.

[23] J. Borenstein, H. R. Everett, and L. Feng. *Navigating Mobile Robots: Systems and
     Techniques*. A. K. Peters, 1996.

[24] A. Bredenfeld, A. Jacoff, I. Noda, and Y. Takahashi, editors. *RoboCup 2005:
     Robot Soccer World Cup IX*, volume 4020 of *Lecture Notes in Artificial Intelli-
     gence*. Springer, 2006.

[25] J. Bresenham. Algorithm for computer control of a digital plotter. *IBM Systems Journal*, 4(1):25–30, 1965.

[26] R. Brooks. A Robust Layered Control System for a Mobile Robot. *IEEE Journal of Robotics and Automation*, RA-2(1):14–23, 1986.

[27] J. Bruce, T. Balch, and M. Veloso. Fast and inexpensive color image segmentation for interactive robots. In *Proceedings of the 2000 IEEE/RSJ International Conference on Intelligent Robots and Systems (IROS '00)*, volume 3, pages 2061–2066, 2000.

[28] J. Brusey, A. Jennings, M. Makies, C. Keen, A. Kendall, L. Padgham, and D. Singh. RMIT Raiders. In Veloso et al. [200], pages 741–744.

[29] T. Buchheim, G. Kindermann, R. Lafrenz, H. Rajaie, M. Schanz, F. Schreiber, O. Zweigle, and P. Levi. Team Description Paper 2004 CoPS Stuttgart. In Nardi et al. [149]. CD-Supplement.

[30] S. Buck, T. Schmitt, and M. Beetz. Reliable Multi-robot Coordination Using Minimal Communication and Neural Prediction. In *Advances in Plan-Based Control of Robotic Agents : International Seminar Dagstuhl Castle, Germany, October 21-26, 2001. Revised Papers*, volume 2466 of *Lecture Notes in Artificial Intelligence*, pages 36–51. Springer, 2002.

[31] W. Burgard, A. Derr, D. Fox, and A. Cremers. Integrating global position estimation and position tracking for mobile robots: the Dynamic Markov Localization approach. In *Proceedings of the 1998 IEEE/RSJ International Conference on Intelligent Robots and Systems (IROS '98)*, pages 730–735, 1998.

[32] W. Burgard, D. Fox, D. Hennig, and T. Schmidt. Estimating the Absolute Position of a Mobile Robot Using Position Probability Grids. In *Proceedings of the 13th National Conference on Artificial Intelligence (AAAI '96)*, volume 2, pages 896–901, 1996.

[33] H.-D. Burkhard, J. Bach, R. Berger, B. Brunswieck, and M. Gollin. Mental Models for Robot Control. In *Advances in Plan-Based Control of Robotic Agents : International Seminar Dagstuhl Castle, Germany, October 21-26, 2001. Revised Papers*, volume 2466 of *Lecture Notes in Artificial Intelligence*, pages 71–88. Springer, 2002.

[34] A. de Cabrol, P. Bonnin, T. Costis, V. Hugel, P. Blazevic, and K. Bouchefra. A New Video Rate Region Color Segmentation and Classification for Sony Legged RoboCup Application. In Bredenfeld et al. [24], pages 436–443.

[35] D. Cameron and N. Barnes. Knowledge-Based Autonomous Dynamic Colour Calibration. In Polani et al. [159], pages 226–237.

[36] Y. U. Cao, A. S. Fukunaga, and A. B. Kahng. Cooperative Mobile Robotics: Antecedents and Directions. *Autonomous Robots*, 4:7–27, 1997.

[37] C. Castelpietra, A. Guidotti, L. Iocchi, D. Nardi, and R. Rosati. Design and Implementation of Cognitive Soccer Robots. In Birk et al. [18], pages 312–318.

[38] A. Cisternino and M. Simi. Layered Reactive Planning in the IALP Team. In Veloso et al. [200], pages 263–273.

[39] A. Colombo, M. Matteucci, and D. G. Sorrenti. Calibration of General Non Single Viewpoint Catadioptric Sensors. In Lakemeyer et al. [119].

[40] B. Damas, P. Lima, and L. Custódio. A Modified Potential Fields Method for Robot Navigation Applied to Dribbling in Robotic Soccer. In Kaminka et al. [108], pages 65–77.

[41] F. Dellaert, W. Burgard, D. Fox, and S. Thrun. Using the Condensation Algorithm for Robust, Vision-based Mobile Robot Localization. In *Proceedings of the IEEE Computer Society Conference on Computer Vision and Pattern Recognition (CVPR'99)*, pages 588–594, June 1999.

[42] M. Dietl, J.-S. Gutmann, and B. Nebel. CS Freiburg: Global View by Cooperative Sensing. In Birk et al. [18], pages 133–143.

[43] A. Doucet, N. de Freitas, and N. Gordon, editors. *Sequential Monte Carlo Methods in Practice*. Information Science and Statistics. Springer, 2001.

[44] D. Douxchamps, D. Dennedy, and G. Peters. SourceForge.net: 1394-based DC Control Library. http://sourceforge.net/projects/libdc1394, August 2006.

[45] R. O. Duda and P. E. Hart. Use of the Hough transformation to detect lines and curves in pictures. *Communications of the ACM*, 15(1):11–15, 1972.

[46] G. Dudek and M. Jenkin. *Computational Principles of Mobile Robotics*. Cabridge University Press, 2000.

[47] G. Dudek, M. R. M. Jenkin, E. Milios, and D. Wilkes. A Taxonomy for Multi-Agent Robotics. *Autonomous Robots*, 3(4):375–397, December 1996.

[48] A. Egorova, M. Simon, F. Wiesel, A. Gloye, and R. Rojas. Plug and Play: Fast Automatic Geometry and Color Calibration for Cameras Tracking Robots. In Nardi et al. [149], pages 394–401.

[49] J. van Eijck and G. Corrente. Sourceforge.net: The RoboCup MSL refbox. http://sourceforge.net/projects/msl-refbox, August 2006.

[50] J. Encarnacao, W. Strasser, and R. Klein. *Graphische Datenverarbeitung 2: Modellierung komplexer Objekte und photorealistische Bilderzeugung.* Oldenbourg, 4. edition, 1997.

[51] S. Enderle, M. Ritter, D. Fox, S. Sablatnög, G. Kraetzschmar, and G. Palm. Soccer-Robot Localization Using Sporadic Visual Features. In E. Pagello, F. Groen, T. Arai, R. Dillmann, and A. Stentz, editors, *Proccedings of the Intelligent Autonomous Systems 6 (IAS-6)*, pages 959–966, Amsterdam, The Netherlands, 2000. IOS Press.

[52] S. Enderle, M. Ritter, D. Fox, S. Sablatnög, G. Kraetzschmar, and G. Palm. Vision-based Localization in RoboCup Environments. In Stone et al. [186], pages 291–296.

[53] S. Engelson and D. McDermott. Error correction in mobile robot map learning. In *Proceedings of the 1992 IEEE International Conference on Robotics and Automation (ICRA '92)*, pages 2555–2560, 1992.

[54] J. M. Evans. HelpMate: an autonomous mobile robot courier for hospitals. In *Proceedings of the IEEE/RSJ/GI International Conference on Intelligent Robots and Systems (IROS '94)*, volume 3, pages 1695–1700, 1994.

[55] Federation of International Robot-soccer Association (FIRA). The FIRA Official Site. http://www.fira.net, August 2006.

[56] J. D. Foley. *Computer graphics: principles and practice.* The systems programming series. Addison-Wesley, 2. edition, 1990.

[57] D. Fox. *Markov Localization: A Probabilistic Framework for Mobile Robot Localization and Navigation.* PhD thesis, University of Bonn, Germany, 1998.

[58] D. Fox. Adapting the sample size in particle filters through KLD-sampling. *International Journal of Robotics Research (IJRR)*, 22(12):985–1004, 2003.

[59] D. Fox, W. Burgard, F. Dellaert, and S. Thrun. Monte Carlo Localization: Efficient Position Estimation for Mobile Robots. In *Proceedings of the National Conference on Artificial Intelligence*, pages 343–349, 1999.

[60] D. Fox, W. Burgard, H. Kruppa, and S. Thrun. Efficient multi-robot localization based on monte carlo approximation. In *In Proceedings of the 9th International Symposium of Robotics Research*, pages 113–120, 1999.

[61] D. Fox, W. Burgard, and S. Thrun. Markov Localization for Mobile Robots in Dynamic Environments. *Journal of Artificial Intelligence Research*, 11:391–427, 1999.

[62] D. Fox, J. Hightower, H. Kauz, L. Liao, and D. Patterson. Bayesian Techniques for Location Estimation. In *Proceedings of Workshop on Location-aware Computing, part of UBICOMP Conference, Seattle*, pages 16–18, 2003.

[63] D. Fox, J. Hightower, L. Liao, D. Schulz, and G. Borriello. Bayesian Filtering for Location Estimation. *IEEE Pervasive Computing*, 2(3):24–33, 2003.

[64] U. Franke, D. Gavrila, S. Görzig, F. Lindner, F. Paetzold, and C. Wöhler. Autonomous Driving Goes Downtown. *IEEE Intelligent Systems*, 13(6):40–48, 1998.

[65] G. Fraser and F. Wotawa. Cooperative Planning and Plan Execution in Partially Observable Dynamic Domains. In Nardi et al. [149], pages 524–531.

[66] B. P. Gerkey and M. M. Mataric. On Role Allocation in RoboCup. In Polani et al. [159], pages 43–53.

[67] C. Geyer and K. Daniilidis. Catadioptric Camera Calibration. In *Proceedings of the International Conference on Computer Vision 1999*, pages 398–404, 1999.

[68] W. K. Giloi. *Rechnerarchitektur*. Springer, 2nd edition, 1993.

[69] C. Gönner, M. Rous, and K.-F. Kraiss. Real-Time Adaptive Colour Segmentation for the RoboCup Middle Size League. In Nardi et al. [149], pages 402–409.

[70] E. Grillo, M. Matteucci, and D. G. Sorrenti. Getting the Most from Your Color Camera in a Color-Coded World. In Nardi et al. [149], pages 221–235.

[71] K. Gunnarsson, F. Wiesel, and R. Rojas. The Color and the Shape: Automatic On-Line Color Calibration for Autonomous Robots. In Bredenfeld et al. [24], pages 347–358.

[72] J.-S. Gutmann, W. Hatzack, I. Herrmann, B. Nebel, F. Rittinger, A. Topor, T. Weigel, and B. Welsch. The CS Freiburg Robotic Soccer Team: Reliable Self-localization, Multirobot Sensor Integration, and Basic Soccer Skills. In Asada and Kitano [9], pages 93–108.

[73] J.-S. Gutmann, T. Weigel, and B. Nebel. Fast, Accurate, and Robust Self-Localization in Polygonal Environments. In *Proceedings of the IEEE/RSJ International Conference on Intelligent Robots and Systems (IROS '99)*, pages 304–317, 1999.

[74] J. Haase. Multi-Sensor-Fusion der Daten mobiler Roboter auf statistischer Basis. Diplomarbeit, Universität Tübingen, 2006.

[75] R. Hanek, T. Schmitt, S. Buck, and M. Beetz. Fast Image-based Object Localization in Natural Scenes. In *Proceedings of the 2002 IEEE/RSJ International Conference on Intelligent Robots and Systems (IROS '02)*, pages 116–122, 2002.

[76] R. Hanek, T. Schmitt, S. Buck, and M. Beetz. Towards RoboCup without Color Labeling. In Kaminka et al. [108], pages 426–434.

[77] M. Hannebauer, J. Wendler, and E. Pagello, editors. *Balancing Reactivity and Social Deliberation in Multi-Agent Systems*, volume 2103 of *Lecture Notes in Artificial Intelligence*. Springer, 2001.

[78] P. Heinemann, H. Becker, J. Haase, and A. Zell. The Attempto Tübingen Robot Soccer Team 2006. In Lakemeyer et al. [119]. CD-Supplement.

[79] P. Heinemann, H. Becker, and A. Zell. Improved Path Planning in Highly Dynamic Environments based on Time Variant Potential Fields. In *Proceedings of the International Symposium on Robotics (ISR 2006)*, volume 1956 of *VDI-Berichte*, 2006. CD-Supplement.

[80] P. Heinemann, J. Haase, and A. Zell. Verbesserte Effizienz der Monte-Carlo-Lokalisierung im RoboCup. In P. Levi, M.Schanz, R. Lafrenz, and V. Avrutin, editors, *AMS 2005*, Informatik aktuell, pages 19–24. Springer, 2005.

[81] P. Heinemann, J. Haase, and A. Zell. A Combined Monte-Carlo Localization and Tracking Algorithm for RoboCup. In *Proceedings of the 2006 IEEE/RSJ International Conference on Intelligent Robots and Systems (IROS '06)*, pages 1535–1540, 2006.

[82] P. Heinemann, J. Haase, and A. Zell. A Novel Approach to Efficient Monte-Carlo Localization in RoboCup. In Lakemeyer et al. [119], pages 321–328.

[83] P. Heinemann, M. Plagge, A. Treptow, and A. Zell. Tracking Dynamic Objects in a RoboCup Environment - The Attempto Tübingen Robot Soccer Team. In Polani et al. [159]. CD-Supplement.

[84] P. Heinemann, T. Rückstieß, and A. Zell. Fast and Accurate Environment Modelling using Omnidirectional Vision. In U. Ilg, H. Bülthoff, and H. Mallot, editors, *Dynamic Perception 2004*, pages 9–14. Infix Verlag, 2004.

[85] P. Heinemann, F. Sehnke, F. Streichert, and A. Zell. An Automatic Approach to Online Color Training in RoboCup Environments. In *Proceedings of the 2006 IEEE/RSJ International Conference on Intelligent Robots and Systems (IROS '06)*, pages 4480–4485, 2006.

[86] P. Heinemann, F. Sehnke, F. Streichert, and A. Zell. Automatic Calibration of Camera to World Mapping in RoboCup uing Evolutionary Algorithms. In *Proceedings of the IEEE Congress on Evolutionary Computation (CEC 2006)*, pages 4459–4466, 2006.

[87] P. Heinemann, F. Sehnke, and A. Zell. Towards a Calibration-Free Robot: The ACT Algorithm for Automatic Online Color Training. In Lakemeyer et al. [119], pages 362–369.

[88] P. Heinemann, A. Treptow, and A. Zell. The Attempto Tübingen Robot Soccer Team. In Nardi et al. [149]. CD-Supplement.

[89] R. Hicks and R. Bajcsy. Reflective Surfaces as Computational Sensors. *Image and Vision Computing*, 19(11):773–777, 2001.

[90] F. von Hundelshausen and R. Rojas. Localizing a robot by the marking lines on a soccer field. In O. Drbohlav, editor, *Proceedings of the Computer Vision Winter Workshop, CVWW03*, pages 135–140, 2003.

[91] F. von Hundelshausen and R. Rojas. Tracking Regions. In Polani et al. [159], pages 250–261.

[92] F. von Hundelshausen, M. Schreiber, F. Wiesel, A. Liers, and R. Rojas. MATRIX: A force field pattern matching method for mobile robots. Technical Report B-08-03, Free University of Berlin, 2003.

[93] IEEE Standards Association. The IEEE 802.11 LAN/MAN Wireless LAN Standard. http://standards.ieee.org/getieee802/802.11.html, August 2006.

[94] H. Igarashi, S. Kosue, and M. Miyahara. Individual Tactical Play and Pass with Communication between Players. In Asada and Kitano [9], pages 364–370.

[95] L. Iocchi. Robust Color Segmentation through Adaptive Color Space Transformation. In Lakemeyer et al. [119].

[96] L. Iocchi and D. Nardi. Self-Localization in the RoboCup Environment. In Asada and Kitano [9], pages 318–330.

[97] L. Iocchi, D. Nardi, and M. Salerno. Reactivity and Deliberation: A Survey on Multi-Robot Systems. In M. Hannebauer, J. Wendler, and E. Pagello, editors, *Balancing Reactivity and Social Deliberation in Multi-Agent Systems*, volume 2103 of *Lecture Notes in Artificial Intelligence*, pages 9–32. Springer, 2001.

[98] H. Jaeger and T. Christaller. Dual Dynamics: Designing behavior systems for autonomous robots. *Journal on Artificial Life and Robotics*, 2:108–112, 1998.

[99] M. Jamzad and A. K. Lamjiri. An Efficient Need-Based Vision System in Variable Illumination Environment of Middle Size RoboCup. In Polani et al. [159], pages 654–661.

[100] M. Jamzad, B. Sadjad, V. Mirrokni, M. Kazemi, H. Chitsaz, A. Heydarnoori, M. Hajiaghai, and E. Chiniforooshan. A Fast Vision System for Middle Size Robots in RoboCup. In Birk et al. [18], pages 71–80.

[101] M. Jäger. *Kooperierende Roboter: Gemeinsame Erledigung einer Reinigungsaufgabe.* PhD thesis, University of Freiburg, Germany, 2002.

[102] M. Jüngel. Using Layered Color Precision for a Self-Calibrating Vision System. In Nardi et al. [149], pages 209–220.

[103] M. Jüngel, J. Hoffmann, and M. Lötzsch. A Real-Time Auto-Adjusting Vision System for Robotic Soccer. In Polani et al. [159], pages 214–225.

[104] F. de Jong, J. Caarls, R. Bartelds, and P. P. Jonker. A Two-Tiered Approach to Self-Localization. In Birk et al. [18], pages 405–410.

[105] P. Jonker, J. Caarls, and W. Bokhove. Fast and Accurate Robot Vision for Vision based Motion. In Stone et al. [186], pages 149–158.

[106] S. J. Julier and J. K. Uhlmann. New extension of the Kalman filter to nonlinear systems. In I. Kadar, editor, *Proceedings of SPIE, Signal Processing, Sensor Fusion, and Target Recognition VI*, volume 3068, pages 182–193, 1997.

[107] R. E. Kalman. A New Approach to Linear Filtering and Prediction Problems. *Transactions of the ASME–Journal of Basic Engineering*, 82(Series D):35–45, 1960.

[108] G. A. Kaminka, P. U. Lima, and R. Rojas, editors. *RoboCup 2002: Robot Soccer World Cup VI*, volume 2752 of *Lecture Notes in Artificial Intelligence*. Springer, 2003.

[109] K. Kaplan, B. Celik, T. Mericli, C. Mericli, and H. L. Akin. Practical Extensions to Vision-Based Monte Carlo Localization Methods for Robot Soccer Domain. In Bredenfeld et al. [24], pages 624–631.

[110] A. Karol and M.-A. Williams. Distributed Sensor Fusion for Object Tracking. In Bredenfeld et al. [24], pages 504–511.

[111] O. Khatib. Real-Time Obstacle Avoidance for Manipulators and Mobile Robots. In *Proceedings of the 1985 IEEE International Conference on Robotics and Automation (ICRA '85)*, pages 500–505, 1985.

[112] T. Kikuchi, K. Umeda, R. Ueda, Y. Jitsukawa, H. Osumi, and T. Arai. Improvement of Color Recognition Using Colored Objects. In Bredenfeld et al. [24], pages 537–544.

[113] H. Kitano, M. Asada, Y. Kuniyoshi, I. Noda, and E. Osawa. RoboCup: The Robot World Cup Initiative. In *Proceedings of the First International Conference on Autonomous Agents (Agents'97)*, pages 340–347. ACM Press, 1997.

[114] H. Kitano, M. Asada, Y. Kuniyoshi, I. Noda, E. Osawa, and H. Matsubara. Robo-Cup: A challenge problem of AI. *AI Magazine*, 18:73–85, 1997.

[115] Kontron AG, formerly JUMPtec AG. The coolMONSTER/P3 PISA Slot CPU. http://www.kontron.de/index.php?id=226&cat=52&productid=232, August 2006.

[116] S. Kubina. Fraunhofer Institute for Autonomous Intelligent Systems: The TMC200 Triple Motor Controller for DC Motors - Calibration and User Guide. http://www.ais.fraunhofer.de/BE/volksbot/tmc-download/Firmware/ver1.16/doc/v1_17_TMC200HandbuchEnglish_.pdf, August 2006.

[117] S. Kubina. Fraunhofer Institute for Autonomous Intelligent Systems: The TMC200 Triple Motor Controller for DC Motors - Overview. www.ais.fraunhofer.de/BE/volksbot/TMC200-eng.pdf, August 2006.

[118] N. Kurihara, R. Hayashi, H. Fujii, D. Sakai, and K. Yoshida. Intelligent Control of Autonomous Mobile Soccer Robot Adapting to Dynamical Environment. In Polani et al. [159], pages 568–575.

[119] G. Lakemeyer, E. Sklar, D. G. Sorrenti, and T. Takahashi, editors. *RoboCup 2006: Robot Soccer World Cup X*, volume 4434 of *Lecture Notes in Artificial Intelligence*. Springer, 2007.

[120] J.-C. Latombe. *Robot motion planning*, volume 124 of *The Kluwer international series in engineering and computer science (SECS)*. Kluwer, 1996.

[121] M. Lauer, S. Lange, and M. Riedmiller. Modeling Moving Objects in a Dynam-ically Changing Robot Application. In U. Furbach, editor, *KI 2005: Advances in Artificial Intelligence*, volume 3698 of *Lecture Notes in Artificial Intelligence*, pages 291–303. Springer, 2005.

[122] M. Lauer, S. Lange, and M. Riedmiller. Calculating the Perfect Match: An Efficient and Accurate Approach for Robot Self-localization. In Bredenfeld et al. [24], pages 142–153.

[123] H. Lausen, J. Nielsen, M. Nielsen, and P. Lima. Model and Behavior-Based Robotic Goalkeeper. In Polani et al. [159], pages 169–180.

[124] S. Lenser, J. Bruce, and M. Veloso. A Modular Hierarchical Behavior-Based Ar-chitecture. In Birk et al. [18], pages 423–428.

[125] A. Lilienthal and T. Duckett. An Absolute Positioning System for 100 Euros. In *Proceedings of the IEEE International Workshop on Robotic Sensing (ROSE 2003)*, Örebro, Sweden, 2003.

[126] P. Lima, A. Bonarini, C. Machado, F. Marchese, F. Ribeiro, and D. Sorrenti. Omni-directional catadioptric vision for soccer robots. *Robotics and Autonomous Systems*, 36(2-3):87–102, 2001.

[127] P. Lima, R. Ventura, P. Aparicio, and L. Custodio. A Functional Architecture for a Team of Fully Autonomous Cooperative Robots. In Veloso et al. [200], pages 378–389.

[128] Lippert Automationstechnik GmbH. The Thunderbird Mini-ITX Motherboard. http://www.lippert-at.com/index.php?id=95, August 2006.

[129] N. Lovell. Illumination Independent Object Recognition. In Bredenfeld et al. [24], pages 384–395.

[130] A. K. Mackworth. On Seeing Robots. In A. Basu and X. Li, editors, *Computer Vision: Systems, Theory, and Applications*, pages 1–13. World Scientific Press, 1993.

[131] J. B. MacQueen. Some Methods for classification and Analysis of Multivariate Observations. In *Proceedings of 5-th Berkeley Symposium on Mathematical Statistics and Probability*, volume 1, pages 281–297. University of California Press, 1967.

[132] F. M. Marchese and D. G. Sorrenti. Omni-directional Vision with a Multi-part Mirror. In Stone et al. [186], pages 179–188.

[133] C. Marques and P. Lima. Vision-Based Self-Localization for Soccer Robots. In *Proceedings IEEE/RSJ International Conference on Intelligent Robots and Systems (IROS 2000)*, volume 2, pages 1193–1198, 2000.

[134] C. F. Marques and P. U. Lima. A Localization Method for a Soccer Robot Using a Vision-Based Omni-Directional Sensor. In Stone et al. [186], pages 96–107.

[135] M. J. Mataric. Behavior-based robotics. In R. A. Wilson and F. C. Keil, editors, *MIT Encyclopedia of Cognitive Sciences*, pages 74–77. MIT Press, 1999.

[136] N. Matthew and R. Stones. *Linux Programmierung*. MITP Verlag, 2000.

[137] Maxon Motor AG. DC Motors Online Catalogue. http://www.maxonmotor.com/ch/en/dc_motor.asp, August 2006.

[138] P. S. Maybeck. *Stochastic models, estimation, and control*, volume 1 of *Mathematics in Science and Engineering*. Academic Press, 1979.

[139] G. Mayer, H. Utz, and G. Kraetzschmar. Towards autonomous vision self-calibration for soccer robots. In *Proceedings of the 2002 IEEE/RSJ Intl. Conference on Intelligent Robots and Systems (IROS '02)*, volume 1, pages 214–219, 2002.

[140] G. Mayer, H. Utz, and G. Kraetzschmar. Playing Robot Soccer under Natural Light: A Case Study. In Polani et al. [159], pages 238–249.

[141] E. Menegatti, F. Nori, E. Pagello, C. Pellizzari, and D. Spagnoli. Designing an Omnidirectional Vision System for a Goalkeeper Robot. In Birk et al. [18], pages 81–91.

[142] E. Menegatti, A. Pretto, and E. Pagello. Testing omnidirectional vision-based Monte Carlo localization under occlusion. In *Proceedings of the 2004 IEEE/RSJ International Conference on Intelligent Robots and Systems (IROS '04)*, volume 3, pages 2487–2493, 2004.

[143] E. Menegatti, A. Pretto, and E. Pagello. A New Omnidirectional Vision Sensor for Monte-Carlo Localization. In Nardi et al. [149], pages 97–109.

[144] E. Menegatti, A. Pretto, A. Scarpa, and E. Pagello. Omnidirectional vision scan matching for robot localization in dynamic environments. *IEEE Transactions on Robotics*, 22(3):523–535, 2006.

[145] A. Merke, S. Welker, and M. Riedmiller. Line base robot localisation under natural light conditions. In *ECAI Workshop on Agents in Dynamic and Real-Time Environments*, 2004.

[146] MobileRobots Inc., formerly ActivMedia Robotics. The Pioneer AT Platform. http://www.activrobots.com/ROBOTS/p3at.html, August 2006.

[147] MobileRobots Inc., formerly ActivMedia Robotics. The Pioneer DX Platform. http://www.activrobots.com/ROBOTS/p3dx.html, August 2006.

[148] Y. Nakagawa, H. G. Okuno, and H. Kitano. Bridging Gap between the Simulation and Robotics with a Global Vision System. In Stone et al. [186], pages 209–218.

[149] D. Nardi, M. Riedmiller, S. C., and J. Santos-Victor, editors. *RoboCup 2004: Robot Soccer World Cup VIII*, volume 3276 of *Lecture Notes in Artificial Intelligence*. Springer, 2005.

[150] G. Neto, H. Costelha, and P. Lima. Topological navigation in configuration space applied to soccer robots. In Polani et al. [159], pages 551–558.

[151] W. Nisticò, M. Hebbel, T. Kerkhof, and C. Zarges. Cooperative Visual Tracking in a Team of Autonomous Mobile Robots. In Lakemeyer et al. [119].

[152] I. Noda, H. Matsubara, and K. Hiraki. Learning Cooperative Behavior in Multi-Agent Environment - A Case Study of Choice of Play-Plans in Soccer. In N. Y. Foo and R. Goebel, editors, *PRICAI'96: Topics in Artificial Intelligence, 4th Pacific Rim International Conference on Artificial Intelligence, 1996, Proceedings*, volume 1114 of *Lecture Notes in Artificial Intelligence*, pages 570–579. Springer, 1996.

[153] E. Pagello, A. D'Angelo, F. Montsello, F. Garelli, and C. Ferrari. Cooperative Behaviors in Multi-Robot Systems Through Implicit Communication. *Journal on Robotics and Autonomous Systems*, 29(1):65–77, 1999.

[154] D. A. Patterson and J. L. Hennessy. *Computer Architecture A Quantitative Approach*. Morgan Kaufmann, third edition edition, 2003.

[155] D. Pelleg and A. Moore. X-means: Extending K-means with Efficient Estimation of the Number of Clusters. In *Proceedings of the Seventeenth International Conference on Machine Learning*, pages 727–734. Morgan Kaufmann, 2000.

[156] M. Plagge, B. Diebold, R. Günther, J. Ihlenburg, D. Jung, K. Zahedi, and A. Zell. Design and Evaluation of the T-Team of the University of Tübingen for Robo-Cup'98. In Asada and Kitano [9], pages 464–472.

[157] M. Plagge, R. Günther, J. Ihlenburg, D. Jung, and A. Zell. The Attempto RoboCup Robot Team. In Veloso et al. [200], pages 424–433.

[158] M. Plagge and A. Zell. Bildverarbeitungsbasierte Selbstlokalisation in einer RoboCup-Umgebung. In P. Levi and M. Schanz, editors, *Autonome Mobile Systeme 2001*, Informatik aktuell, pages 50–56. Springer, 2001.

[159] D. Polani, B. Browning, A. Bonarini, and K. Yoshida, editors. *RoboCup 2003: Robot Soccer World Cup VII*, volume 3020 of *Lecture Notes in Artificial Intelligence*. Springer, 2004.

[160] M. E. Pollack, L. Brown, D. Colbry, C. Orosz, B. Peintner, S. Ramakrishnan, S. Engberg, J. T. Matthews, J. Dunbar-Jacob, and C. E. McCarthy. Pearl: A mobile robotic assistant for the elderly. In *Proceedings for the AAAI Workshop on Automation as Caregiver*, 2002.

[161] L. Priese, V. Rehrmann, R. Schian, and R. Lakmann. Traffic Sign Recognition Based on Color Image Evaluation. In *Proceedings of the IEEE Intelligent Vehicles Symposium '93*, pages 95–100, 1993.

[162] T. Rückstieß. Echtzeit-Objekterkennung mit Omnidirektionaler Kamera. Studienarbeit, Universität Tübingen, 2005.

[163] T. Röfer and M. Jüngel. Vision-Based Fast and Reactive Monte-Carlo Localization. In *Proceedings of the 2003 IEEE International Conference on Robotics & Automation*, pages 856–861, 2003.

[164] T. Röfer and M. Jüngel. Fast and Robust Edge-Based Localization in the Sony Four-Legged Robot League. In Polani et al. [159], pages 262–273.

[165] M. Riedmiller and H. Braun. A Direct Adaptive Method for Faster Backpropagation Learning: The RPROP Algorithm. In *Proceedings of the IEEE International Conference on Neural Networks*, pages 586–591, 1993.

[166] RoboCup Federation. The RoboCup Official Site. http://www.robocup.org, August 2006.

[167] RoboCup MSL Technical Committee 1997-2006. Middle Size Robot League Rules and Regulations for 2006. http://www.ais.fraunhofer.de/ paul/msl2006final.pdf, August 2006.

[168] T. Schmitt, R. Hanek, M. Beetz, and S. Buck. Watch their Moves: Applying Probabilistic Multiple Object Tracking to Autonomous Robot Soccer. In *AAAI National Conference on Artificial Intelligence*, pages 599–604, 2002.

[169] T. Schmitt, R. Hanek, S. Buck, and M. Beetz. Cooperative Probabilistic State Estimation for Vision-Based Autonomous Soccer Robots. In Birk et al. [18], pages 192–203.

[170] T. Schmitt, R. Hanek, S. Buck, and M. Beetz. Probabilistic Vision-Based Opponent Tracking in Robot Soccer. In Kaminka et al. [108], pages 426–434.

[171] R. D. Schraft and G. Schmierer. *Serviceroboter - Produkte, Szenarien, Visionen.* Springer, 1998.

[172] F. Sehnke. Modellunterstützte Online-Optimierung zur Selbstadaption eines omnidirektionalen Vision-Systems im RoboCup. Diplomarbeit, Universität Tübingen, 2005.

[173] D. Sekimori, T. Usui, Y. Masutani, and F. Miyazaki. High Speed Obstacle Avoidance and Self-Localization for Mobile Robots Based on Omni-directional Imaging of Floor Region. In Birk et al. [18], pages 204–213.

[174] W.-M. Shen, R. Adobatti, J. Modi, and B. Salemi. Purposeful Behavior in Robot Soccer Team Play. In Veloso et al. [200], pages 460–468.

[175] SICK AG. Laser Measurement Sensors. http://www.mysick.com/partnerPortal/ ProductCatalog/DataSheet.aspx?ProductID=9168, August 2006.

[176] R. Siegwart and I. Nourbakhsh. *Introduction to Autonomous Mobile Robots*. MIT Press, 2004.

[177] T. F. Smith and M. S. Waterman. Identification of Common Molecular Subsequences. *Journal of Molecular Biology*, 147(1):195–197, 1981.

[178] J. R. del Solar and P. A. Vallejos. Motion Detection and Tracking for an AIBO Robot Using Camera Motion Compensation and Kalman Filtering. In Nardi et al. [149], pages 619–627.

[179] Sony Corporation. Sony AIBO Website. http://www.sony.net/Products/aibo/, 2006.

[180] H. W. Sorenson. Least-squares estimation: from Gauss to Kalman. *IEEE Spectrum*, 7:63–68, July 1970.

[181] D. Sorrenti and H. Fujii. The Homepage of the RoboCup Middle-Size League for 2005: Summary of Team Questionnaires. http://old.disco.unimib.it/robocup05msl/TQv4.html, November 2006.

[182] M. Sridharan and P. Stone. Towards Illumination Invariance in the Legged League. In Nardi et al. [149], pages 196–208.

[183] M. Sridharan and P. Stone. Towards Eliminating Manual Color Calibration at RoboCup. In Bredenfeld et al. [24], pages 673–681.

[184] C. Stanton and M.-A. Williams. A Novel and Practical Approach Towards Color Constancy for Mobile Robots Using Overlapping Color Space Signatures. In Bredenfeld et al. [24], pages 444–451.

[185] G. Steinbauer and H. Bischof. Illumination Insensitive Robot Self-Localization Using Panoramic Eigenspaces. In Nardi et al. [149], pages 84–96.

[186] P. Stone, T. Balch, and G. Kraetzschmar, editors. *RoboCup 2000: Robot Soccer World Cup IV*, volume 2019 of *Lecture Notes in Artificial Intelligence*. Springer, 2001.

[187] A. Strack, A. Ferrein, and G. Lakemeyer. Laser-Based Localization with Sparse Landmarks. In Bredenfeld et al. [24], pages 569–576.

[188] Y. Takahashi, T. Tamura, and M. Asada. Strategy Learning for a Team in Adversary Environments. In Birk et al. [18], pages 224–233.

[189] A. S. Tanenbaum. *Structured Computer Organization*. Prentice-Hall, fourth edition edition, 1999.

[190] F. Torterolo and C. Garbay. A Hybrid Agent Model, Mixing Short Term and Long Term Memory Abilities - An Application to RoboCup Competition. In Asada and Kitano [9], pages 246–260.

[191] A. Treptow, A. Masselli, and A. Zell. Real-Time Object Tracking for Soccer-Robots without Color Information. In *European Conference on Mobile Robotics (ECMR 2003)*, pages 33–38, 2003.

[192] A. Treptow and A. Zell. Real-Time Object Tracking for Soccer-Robots without Color Information. *Robotics and Autonomous Systems*, 48(1):41–48, 2004.

[193] R. Tsai. A versatile camera calibration technique for high-accuracy 3D machine vision metrology using off-the-shelf TV cameras and lenses. *Robotics and Automation*, 3(4):323–344, August 1987.

[194] E. Uchibe, M. Nakamura, and M. Asada. Cooperative Behavior Acquisition in a Multiple Mobile Robot Environment by Co-evolution. In Asada and Kitano [9], pages 273–285.

[195] E. Uchibe, M. Yanase, and M. Asada. Evolutionary Behavior Selection with Activation/Termination Constraints. In Birk et al. [18], pages 234–243.

[196] University of Osnabrück. The Homepage of the Brainstormers Tribots MSL Team. http://www.ni.uos.de/index.php?id=2, August 2006.

[197] H. Utz, A. Neubeck, G. Mayer, and G. Kraetzschmar. Improving Vision-Based Self-localization. In Kaminka et al. [108], pages 25–40.

[198] L. T. Vaughn. *Client/Server System Design & Implementation*. Series on Computer Communications. McGraw-Hill, 1994.

[199] B. van der Vecht and P. Lima. Formulation and Implementation of Relational Behaviours for Multi-robot Cooperative Systems. In Nardi et al. [149], pages 516–523.

[200] M. Veloso, E. Pagello, and H. Kitano, editors. *RoboCup-99: Robot Soccer World Cup III*, volume 1856 of *Lecture Notes in Artificial Intelligence*. Springer, 2000.

[201] P. Viola and M. Jones. Rapid Object Detection Using a Boosted Cascade of Simple Features. In *CVPR*, volume I, pages 511–518, 2001.

[202] E. Wan and R. van der Merwe. The Unscented Kalman Filter for Nonlinear Estimation. In *Proceedings of the IEEE Symposium on Adaptive Systems for Signal Processing, Communications, and Control 2000 (AS-SPCC)*, pages 153–158, 2000.

[203] T. Weigel, W. Auerbach, M. Dietl, B. Dümler, J.-S. Gutmann, K. Marko, K. Müller, B. Nebel, B. Szerbakowski, and M. Thiel. CS Freiburg: Doing the Right Thing in a Group. In Stone et al. [186], pages 52–63.

[204] T. Weigel, A. Kleiner, F. Diesch, M. Dietl, J. Gutmann, B. Nebel, P. Stiegeler, and B. Szerbakowski. CS Freiburg 2001. In Birk et al. [18], pages 26–38.

[205] G. Welch and G. Bishop. An Introduction to the Kalman Filter. Technical Report TR 95-041, University of North Carolina at Chapel Hill, 1995.

[206] T. Wisspeintner. Fraunhofer Institute for Autonomous Intelligent Systems: The AISVision Omnidirectional Camera System. http://www.ais.fraunhofer.de/BE/volksbot/AISVision-eng.pdf, August 2006.

[207] J. Wolf and A. Pinz. Particle Filter for Self Localization using Panoramic Vision. *ÖGAI Journal*, 22(4):8–15, 2003.

[208] K. Yokota, K. Ozaki, N. Watanabe, A. Matsumoto, D. Koyama, T. Ishikawa, K. Kawabata, H. Kaetsu, and H. Asama. UTTORI United: Cooperative Team Play Based on Communication. In Asada and Kitano [9], pages 479–484.

[209] W. Zhang and G. Zelinsky. Current Advances in Computer-based Object Detection and Target Acquisition. Technical Report EYECOG-04-01, Cognitive - Experimental Psychology Group State University of New York at Stony Brook, May 2004.

[210] S. W. Zucker. Region growing: Childhood and adolescence. *Computer Graphics and Image Processing*, 5:382–399, 1976.